Looking at

A Reader in Cornish Literature
900–1900

Alan M. Kent was born in St Austell and grew up in the china clay mining region of mid-Cornwall. In addition to being a poet, novelist and dramatist, he was awarded a doctorate for his research into Cornish and Anglo-Cornish literature. He is the editor of *Voices from West Barbary: An anthology of Anglo-Cornish poetry 1549–1928* also published by Francis Boutle Publishers and is currently completing a new verse adaptation of the *Ordinalia*.

Tim Saunders, poet and linguist, was born in Northumberland and brought up in Cornwall. His poems have appeared in the anthology *Writing the Wind: A Celtic Resurgence* and in *The High Tide: Collected poems in Cornish 1974–1999*. He is the editor of *The Wheel: An Anthology of Modern Cornish Poetry 1850–1980* published by Francis Boutle Publishers. He is a bard of the Cornish Gorseth.

Benjamin Luxon was born in Camborne and has an international reputation as a singer. He has sung at most of the major opera houses in the world as well as with the great symphony orchestras. His career has been one of great versatility, embracing not only the sung, but the spoken word. He is a bard of the Cornish Gorseth.

Alan M. Kent
and Tim Saunders

Looking at the Mermaid

A Reader in Cornish Literature 900–1900

edited and translated by Alan M. Kent
and Tim Saunders

with a preface by Benjamin Luxon CBE

Francis
Boutle
Publishers

First published by Francis Boutle Publishers
23 Arlington Way
London EC1R 1UY
(020) 7278 4497
email: mermaid@francisboutle.demon.co.uk
www.francisboutle.demon.co.uk

Introduction, translation and selection copyright © Alan M. Kent
and Tim Saunders 2000

All rights reserved.
No part of this book may be reproduced, stored
in a retrieval system, or transmitted, in any form
or by any means, electronic, mechanical photocopying
or otherwise without the prior permission of the publishers.

ISBN 1 903427 01 0

Printed in Great Britain by Redwood Books

Acknowledgements

We would like to thank the following people for their help assembling this Reader: Brian Murdoch, Charles Thomas, Amy Hale, Philip Payton, Evelyn S. Newlyn, Richard Gendall, Jan Gendall, Neil Kennedy, Matthew Spriggs, Oliver Padel, Ken George, Julyan Holmes, Melissa Hardie, Andrew Symons, Audrey Pool, G.S. Symondson, Bernard Deacon, Kenneth MacKinnon, Craig Weatherhill, Graham Sandercock, Garry Tregidga, Richard Jenkin, Charles Causley, James Whetter, Angela Broome, Roger Penhallurick and the staff of the Royal Institution of Cornwall Library in Truro, Terry Knight, Kim Cooper and staff at the Cornish Studies Library in Redruth, the Morrab Library in Penzance, the Salisbury Library, University of Wales College, Cardiff, the National Library of Wales, Aberystwyth, the Bodleian Library, Oxford, Cambridge University Library, Les and Gill Goldman and Rachel Cardew. The editors would also like to express their sincere thanks to Clive Boutle and David Russell at Francis Boutle Publishers for their tactful editing and to Benjamin Luxon for his insightful preface.

Alan M. Kent and Tim Saunders

For Amy and Ceridwen
'Mermaids both'

Contents

- 15 Preface
- 17 Introduction
- 21 A guide to pronunciation
- 25 A note on the texts

Texts in Cornish
- 28 **1** *From* Vocabularium Cornicum/The Old Cornish Vocabulary
- 30 **2** 'Golsoug ty cowez'/The Charter Endorsement
- 32 **3** 'In Polsethow'/War Meane Merlyn/Two Cornish Prophecies

Selections from the Ordinalia:
Origo Mundi – The Beginning of the World
- 34 **4** 'En tas a nef y'm gylwyr'/The Creation
- 38 **5** 'Yt'hanwaf bugh ha tarow'/The Naming of the Animals
- 40 **6** 'Seth pan-dra yv the nygys'/The Errand of Seth
- 46 **7** 'Damsel er the gentylys'/David and Bathsheba
- 54 **8** 'Dun the leuerel yn scon'/Solomon and the Temple builders

Passio Christi – Christ's Passion
- 56 **9** 'Mara ieves yl dybbry'/The Temptation of Jesus
- 64 **10** 'Newethow mere clewes'/Palm Sunday
- 66 **11** 'Arluth henna yv gurys da'/Mary Magdalene
- 70 **12** 'Sevyn yn ban'/The Arrest of Jesus
- 76 **13** 'Mar a pythe dylyfrys'/Prosecution and defence
- 82 **14** 'Ellas a cryst'/The Lament of Mary

Resurrexio Domini – The Resurrection of Our Lord
- 86 **15** 'Why pryncys a'n dewolow'/The Harrowing of Hell
- 86 **16** 'Lowene thy's syr pilat'/Pilate and the Sepulchre Guards
- 92 **17** 'Nep a wruk nef'/Mary Magdalene and Jesus
- 98 **18** 'Ow dewolow duegh gynef'/Pilate taken to Hell

Selections from Pascon agan Arluth – The Passion of Our Lord

- 102 **19** 'Tays ha mab han speris sans'/Father and Son and Holy Ghost
- 104 **20** 'Dew zen crist a zanvonas'/The Last Supper
- 108 **21** 'Han zewna pan vons squyth'/The Scourging of Christ
- 112 **22** 'Rag porrys rys o zozo'/The Death of Christ
- 114 **23** 'Mam Ihesus Marya wyn'/The Price of Sin

Selections from Beunans Meriasek – The Life of St Meriasek

- 118 **24** 'A das ha mam ov megyans'/The Education of Meriasek
- 124 **25** 'Marners dorsona dywy'/Meriasek comes to Cornwall
- 126 **26** 'A vreten sur then povma'/Meriasek and Teudar
- 142 **27** 'Mayl at eua'/The Emperor's Doctors
- 148 **28** 'Me yv outlayer'/Outlaws
- 152 **29** 'Me yv duk'/The Duke of Cornwall challenges Teudar
- 156 **30** 'Ser duk me a wel tevdar'/The Great Battle
- 166 **31** 'Ellas ow holen yv trogh'/The Two Mothers
- 178 **32** 'Dugh why thym'/The Death of Meriasek

- 182 **33** *From* Homelyes XIII in Cornish/The Tregear Homilies by John Tregear

Selections from the Creacion of the World by William Jordan

- 186 **34** Death and Lamech
- 202 **35** The Flood

- 212 **36** One Parson's Certificate to Another, to Marry a Couple, whose Banns had been called, from Mr. Drake, Vic. of St. Just, to Mr. Trythal, Cur. of Sennen by William Drake
- 212 **37** John of Chyanhor by Nicholas Boson as transcribed by Edward Lhuyd
- 218 **38** Nebbaz Gerriau Dro Tho Carnoack/A Few Words about Cornish by Nicholas Boson
- 224 **39** 'Menja Tiz Kernuack buz gasowas'/'If Cornish people would but listen' by John Tonkin

226	40	'Ni Venja pea a munna seer'/A Cornish Song, to the Tune of the Modest Maid of Kent by John Tonkin
228	41	'Ha mî ow môs en gûn lâs'/'As I went on a green plain' by Noel Cater
228	42	'Pela era why moaz, moz, fettow teag?'/'Where are you going pretty fair maid?' by Edward Chirgwin
230	43	Two Poems of Advice by James Jenkins
232	44	In Obitum Regis Wilhelmi 3tii Carmen Britannicum, Dialectu Cornubiensis; Ad Normam Poetarum Seculi Sexti / On the Death of King William III, a British Song in the Cornish Dialect; according to the pattern of the poets of the sixth century by Edward Lhuyd
236	45	A Cornish Proverb by William Allen
236	46	'Ma Canow vee wor Hern gen Cock ha Rooz'/The Pilchard Curing Rhyme by John Boson
238	47	'An [Why] poble hui, en pow America'/'You people in the Land of America' by William Gwavas
238	48	Letters in Cornish by William Gwavas and Oliver Pender
240	49	'En Lavra coth pa vo Tour Babel gwres'/An Elegy on the Death of James Jenkins by John Boson
240	50	'Padn an mean, ma Deskes broaz Dean'/Epitaph for the Death of James Jenkins by William Gwavas
240	51	Advice to a Friend by John Boson
240	52	On the Death of Mr. John Keigwin by John Boson
242	53	On a Lazy Weaver by William Gwavas
242	54	Verses on the Marazion Bowling-Green and Club by William Gwavas
242	55	Advice to Drunkards by William Gwavas
242	56	A Cornish Riddle by William Gwavas
242	57	'Chee dên krêv'/Advice to all Men by William Gwavas
242	58	'Hithow gwrâ gen skîanz da'/'Today act with good knowledge' by William Gwavas
244	59	'Cara, Gorthya, ha ouna Dêw'/'Love, worship and fear God' by William Gwavas
244	60	War an Lavar gwir a'n Dewthack Tiz pêg a'n Pow Middlesex; ha an Brêz a'n padgwar Braneriow enna/On the verdict of the twelve honest men of the

	County of Middlesex; and the judgment of the four Barons therein – Gwavas versus Kelynack
244	**61** 'Contrevack Nicholas Pentreath'/To Neighbour Nicholas Pentreath by William Gwavas
244	**62** William Bodinar's Letter
246	**63** 'Coth Doll Pentreath'/Epitaph for Dolly Pentreath by Thomson
248	**64** Cornish proverbs and sayings from Archæalogia Cornu-Britannica by William Pryce
248	**65** Padar a'n Arluth/The Lord's Prayer from Archæologia Cornu-Britannica by William Pryce
248	**66** Cornish Family Mottoes
248	**67** Two Poems by Georg Sauerwein
252	**68** 'A Grankan, a grankan'/The Crankan Rhyme by John Davey

Complementary texts

256	**69** *From* The Bodmin Manumissions
256	**70** *From* The History of the Kings of Britain by Geoffrey of Monmouth
257	**71** The Prophecy of Merlin by John of Cornwall
260	**72** *From* The Cornish Glosses of the Prophecy of Merlin by John of Cornwall
261	**73** *From* The Romance of Tristan by Béroul
263	**74** *From* A Letter to certain Cardinals by John de Grandisson, Bishop of Exeter
263	**75** *From* The Translation of Ranulf Higden's Polychronicon by John Trevisa
263	**76** Some Accounts for Cornish Drama
263	**77** *From* Utopia by Thomas More
264	**78** *From* Itinerary by John Leland
265	**79** *From* The Fyrst Book of the Introduction of Knowledge: The Apendix in the Fyrst Chapter, Treatinge of Cornewall, and Cornyshe Men by Andrew Boorde
267	**80** *From* The Articles of the Rebels
267	**81** *From* The Reply to the Rebels by Edward Seymour, Duke of Somerset
268	**82** *From* The Image of Idleness by Oliver Oldwanton
268	**83** *From* The Bishops' Consistory Court Depositions at Exeter
269	**84** St Ives Accounts for Cornish drama

- 269 **85** *From* A Topographical and Historical Description of Cornwall by John Norden
- 270 **86** *From* The Green Book of St Columb Major
- 270 **87** *From* Relation of the visit of the Catholic Kings by Don Antonio Ortes
- 270 **88** *From* The Survey of Cornwall by Richard Carew
- 273 **89** *From* The Lives of the Saints by Nicholas Roscarrock
- 275 **90** *From* The Probate Documents of Francis John Trevallacke of Wendron by His Testator
- 275 **91** *From* The Northern Lasse by Richard Brome
- 276 **92** *From* Diary of the Marches of the Royal Army during the Civil War by Richard Symonds
- 276 **93** *From* Itinerary by John Ray
- 276 **94** *From* The Dutchesse of Cornwall's progresse to see the Land's End & to visit the mount by Nicholas Boson
- 281 **95** Antiquities Cornuotanic: The Causes of Cornish Speech's Decay by William Scawen
- 293 **96** *From* The First English Translation of William Camden's Britannia by Edmund Gibson
- 293 **97** *From* Letters written to Thomas Tonkin by Edward Lluyd
- 303 **98** *From* The Exmoor Scolding by Andrew Brice
- 303 **99** *From* The Compleat History of Cornwall by William Hals
- 304 **100** *From* Archæologia Cornu-Britannica by Thomas Tonkin
- 304 **101** *From* Antiquities Historical and Monumental of the County of Cornwall by William Borlase
- 305 **102** *From* The Natural History of Cornwall by William Borlase
- 306 **103** On the Expiration of the Cornish Language by Daines Barrington
- 308 **104** *From* An Explanation of Cornu-Technical Terms and Idioms of Tinners in Mineralogia Cornubiensis by William Pryce
- 309 **105** *From* Universal Magazine by Peter Pindar
- 309 **106** *From* Archæologia Cornu-Britannica by William Pryce
- 309 **107** *From* To the Courteous and Noble Inhabitants of Cornwall .... by Edward Lhuyd as found in Archæologia Cornu-Britannica by William Pryce
- 310 **108** *From* Ancient Cathedral of Cornwall and

	Supplement to Polwhele's First and Second Books of the History of Cornwall by John Whitaker
311	**109** *From* The History of Cornwall by Richard Polwhele
311	**110** *From* Magna Britannia: Cornwall by Daniel Lysons and Samuel Lysons
312	**111** Two Cornish Poems by Robert Stephen Hawker
313	**112** *From* Mount Calvary, edited by Davies Gilbert
315	**113** Cornish Cantata by Edward Collins Giddy
316	**114** *From* Rambles Beyond Railways by Wilkie Collins
317	**115** *From* Netherton's Cornish Almanac
317	**116** Two Notes about Cornish Speakers by John Bodinar and Matthias Wallis
318	**117** The Memorial to Dolly Pentreath at Paul
318	**118** *From* On the Cornish Language by John Bellow
319	**119** *From* The Gentleman's Magazine by J. H. Nancekivell
319	**120** *From* Popular Romances of the West of England: The Drolls, Traditions, and Superstitions of Old Cornwall by Robert Hunt
321	**121** *From* Stories and Folk-Lore of West Cornwall by William Bottrell
322	**122** A Letter to Henry Jenner by W. S. Lach-Szyrma
322	**123** A Letter to Henry Jenner by William Copeland Borlase
323	**124** *From* Last Relics of the Cornish Language by W. S. Lach-Szyrma
326	**125** *From* Stories and Folk-Lore of West Cornwall by William Bottrell
329	**126** *From* Bibliotheca Cornubiensis by G. C. Boase and W. P. Courtney
329	**127** *From* The Introduction to An English-Cornish Dictionary by Frederick W. P. Jago
330	**128** *From* Guavas the Tinner by Sabine Baring-Gould
330	**129** *From* Cornish Whiddles for Teenin' Time by Mrs Frank Morris
333	**130** *From* Mystère de St-Gwénolé – The Celtic Drama Revived by R. A. H. Bickford Smith

337 **131** *From* A Book of the West by Sabine Baring-Gould
338 **132** *From* The Literature of the Celts by Magnus Maclean
338 **133** *From* From a Cornish Window by Arthur Quiller Couch

339 Glossary
341 Commentaries
361 Sources
365 Further reading

Preface

En termen ez passiez.... (In the time that is past...)

It is with this phrase that the writer Nicholas Boson opens his classic Cornish narrative *John of Chyanhor* – a story which has for one of its settings St Hilary Downs, which I can see from the window of my house. It was written around 1665 and now some three hundred years later we are at the dawn of a new millennium. We are approaching a time when more information than ever before is being made accessible to a large percentage of the human race. We are experiencing a veritable explosion of facts and data on every aspect of human life and achievement on this planet. Now we can also savour the achievement of Cornish and share it with the rest of the world. The editors of this anthology, Alan M. Kent and Tim Saunders have compiled a lively, immensely varied and ground-breaking selection of works written in Cornish along with other complementary texts illuminating the tradition of Cornish literature.

The volume here covers an unbelievable number of topics: religion, history, morality, myth, fishing, mining, legal wranglings and practical advice on a great number of subjects – both serious and comic – ranging between practical advice to a Cornishman on a visit to London in the eighteenth century, techniques in 'chatting up a maid', to the best way to cure that great Cornish fish, the pilchard. The topics covered also show the beauty and poetry of the language as expressed, for instance in the extraordinary work, the *Ordinalia*, ranging from the vivid and dynamic drama of The Beginning of the World to the philosophical observations of the Passion and the Resurrection plays.

This is an essential book for anyone who wants to know what the Cornish had to say about themselves and the world around them during the last thousand years. It is amazing and inspiring to me that so much writing in Cornish still exists. This erudite and scholarly book in one scoop, so to speak, brings so many important texts together and pays homage to all the exceptional workers in the Cornish language who have through their dedication and love of the language managed to keep it alive for future generations.

Much time has passed since Cornish was first spoken and written and I feel sure that this Reader will help guarantee that it continues to flourish.

Benjamin Luxon CBE, St Hilary, Kernow/Cornwall

Introduction

This Reader brings to light the substance of literature in Cornish from the post-Roman period to the turn of the twentieth century. It is the first such collection and texts in Cornish are presented in the original with a facing English translation. There are selections from the major works of Cornish literature, including the *Ordinalia*, *Beunans Meriasek* and *The Creacion of the World*, as well as from a range of significant later texts such as *The Tregear Homilies*, *John of Chyanhor* and the multitude of surviving poems, songs and proverbs.

Although many of these texts have been published before, a number are difficult to find. They appeared in relatively inaccessible publications, or circulated only among Cornish language activists. Such texts, however, form a central strand of European literary culture and demonstrate the flourishing literary energy of Cornwall and its contribution from the post-Roman period onwards. It is fair to say that many of them deserve a much wider readership. The later texts which form the bulk of Cornish literature from 1550 onwards are even more difficult for readers to obtain, so our purpose here has been to situate them chronologically, and to celebrate their survival. Rather than being epic dramas they are windows into Cornish society in a period of modernisation and change. Not only do they offer profound insights into the concerns of Cornish people, their temperament, values and history, but into their tenacity, humour and passions as well.

The second section of the Reader presents Anglo-Saxon, Latin, French and English texts to illumine the continuum of writing *about* Cornwall. A selection has been made ranging from such authors as the historian and chronicler Geoffrey of Monmouth, the Anglo-Cornish poet and topographical writer Richard Carew and the Celtic scholar Edward Lhuyd to the folklorists William Bottrell and Sabine Baring-Gould, all of them observing Cornish culture and revealing much about Cornish language and literature. Some comment upon the state of the language or join debate over the direction of Cornish literature. Others are of interest in showing socio-linguistic shift in Cornwall as it moved over time from an agrarian to a post-industrial society. In some of the material from the nineteenth century we begin to see a 'gathering of the fragments' of Cornish culture in preparation for the revival of the twentieth century. We hope to show how these complementary texts slot into the overall picture of Cornish writing.

The texts range from the *Bodmin Manumissions* (a manuscript containing a number of glosses in Cornish) and *The Prophecy of Merlin* (a text perhaps originally written in Cornish) to the observations of Robert Hunt (on the greater land area of 'Old Cornwall') and Arthur Quiller Couch (commenting on the practicalities of reviving medieval Cornish drama in the twentieth century).

The Celtic languages of these islands may be divided into two groups: Goidelic (Gaelic or Q-Celtic) and Brythonic (British or P-Celtic). The former is spoken in Ireland, Scotland and the Isle of Man, while the latter is to be heard in Wales, Brittany and Cornwall. Cornish is closest to Breton and can be divided into three distinctive periods of development. Old Cornish denotes the phase of the language between about 800–1250, when Cornish was first emerging from its parent Brythonic. From this phase the glosses of the *Bodmin Manumissions* and the *Old Cornish Vocabulary* survive. Middle Cornish refers to that phase of the language between 1250–1550 and its texts include *Pascon agan Arluth* and the *Ordinalia*. Late Cornish is the label most usually given to that phase of the language from around 1550 to its decline in the nineteenth century. Its literature includes more secular writings such as folk songs, narratives, poems as well as translations from the Bible. Two texts straddle the Middle and Late Cornish periods – *Beunans Meriasek* and *The Tregear Homilies*. Though they resemble Middle Cornish, these texts have many of the qualities of Late Cornish. Revived Cornish applies to that phase of the language from the end of the nineteenth century to the present, and though nothing from that period is anthologised here, we make reference to the revival of the language in our commentaries. By the term Cornish literature we mean literature written in Cornish. By the term Anglo-Cornish literature we refer to literature written in English about or relating to Cornwall. We use the term Cornu-English to denote those writings often labelled as 'dialect', but which often have a significant relationship to Cornish. Cornu-English is as important a marker of identity as the Cornish language itself.

Cornish literature has often been dismissed by scholars in the field of Celtic Studies as 'not Celtic enough'. This view is misguided and has done much disservice to writing of the past and present in Cornwall. While Cornish literature lacks the mythical or heroic elements of Irish and Welsh literature, the development of Cornwall's literary tradition appears to have been linked to drama, very much part of community, festival and entertainment. Often the narratives had Biblical or hagiographic origins, yet into these Cornish folklore, superstition and identity were carefully woven. If Cornwall's literature is more closely connected with the English literary continuum, then we need to make sense of that connection, and in particular the fact that Cornwall was the first Celtic territory to be 'accommodated'.

In anthologising writing from Cornwall over a millennium our principal aim has been to offer a selection in chronological order. Within the scope of this volume it has not been possible to include the longer extant texts; *Ordinalia, Pascon Agan Arluth, Beunans Meriasek* and *The Creacion of the World,* in their entirety. However, we have tried to demonstrate their considerable range and vitality and have selected both the most well-known sequences from these plays and the sections which are most dramatically exciting and vibrant. Despite the importance of a text such as *The Tregear Homilies* in helping us to understand the development of Cornish, we also felt space might be better devoted to some of the later texts which show a wider range of secular subject-matter. The complementary texts section of the volume hopefully provides illumination on the Cornish continuum as well as the Cornu-English and Anglo-Cornish traditions.

The editors of this collection have wondered why a volume like this has not been published before. As the language develops beyond the confines of the revival, there is an extraordinary demand for Cornish-related material, yet significant examples of the literature remain in obscurity. The aim here is to put before both the academic and the general reader those texts which in our view have something meaningful to say at the start of a new millennium of writing in Cornish. Our short-term aim is to help many more people gain access into the rich Cornish literary tradition. Our long-term hope is that one day all the texts in Cornish will be more widely available and that those pieces (such as some by John Keigwin and William Rowe) we have had to omit because of lack of space will also be anthologised and celebrated.

Scholars of Cornish have already done much work on establishing chronology of composition and charting linguistic variation, but that is not our purpose here. Though at points in our commentaries and notes we give a flavour of linguistic shift and change, our principal concern has been to present the texts as literature. Like any history, the development of Cornish is much contested and debated. In the suggestions for further reading we list books that will fill in the background of its development. Where titles in Cornish of the texts are disputed we have used the opening lines of the Cornish text as the title. The commentaries provide historical and material context, together with observations on language and style.

The title of this Reader is derived from a sequence in the Passion play of the *Ordinalia*. Two learned men debate whether Jesus Christ can be both God and man. To demonstrate his point, one of them asks us to look at the mermaid, who is both fish and woman. In this way, Jesus Christ is compared to the mermaid, a central mythical figure within Cornwall's literary continuum and symbolic of the sea that is so much part of its history. In the nineteenth century, the Cornish folklorist William Bottrell collected the story of the Mermaid of Zennor, and a version of it is found in his *Traditions and Hearthside Stories of West Cornwall* (1873). Padstow and Cury have their own mermaid narratives too, but it is the story of Mathey Trewella at Zennor which has captured people's imagination. Zennor itself holds much interest for the enthusiast of Cornish. A plaque on the church commemorates the life of John Davey, a reputed Cornish speaker and writer who died in 1891. Zennor churchyard is also where Robert Morton Nance and Peter Pool are buried, two twentieth-century champions of Cornish literature. In the church is the famous carved wooden Mermaid bench-end which forms the cover of this collection.

Compared to many cultures of the world the amount of extant Cornish literature is not large, but as this volume hopes to show, there is a great deal to interest scholars and general readers. Considering Cornwall's history and its early 'accommodation' within these islands, we should not be amazed nor saddened at how little literature there is, but encouraged by how much wonderful writing has survived.

Alan M. Kent
Tim Saunders

A guide to pronunciation

This is a basic guide, intended to give the reader a working approximation of the sounds of the Cornish language before our time. We have tried to avoid technical terms as far as possible. For convenience, the charts below will give the letters used nowadays by most modern Cornish speakers to represent the sounds, and then show how they were represented in different phases of Cornish. You will also hear local and other variations, naturally enough, from modern Cornish speakers. A number of books listed in the bibliography will provide further guidance.

Vowels

Usually, a vowel will be long followed by a single consonant, or no consonant at all. Otherwise it will be short. Cornish vowels are generally clearer and purer than in English. The symbol *x* represents a consonant followed by a silent **e**, as in the word **cane**, which is pronounced with one syllable.

Letter	Long	Short
a	Like the 'a' in 'father'	Like the 'a' in 'bat'
Old Cornish	a	a
Middle Cornish	a, ay	a
Late Cornish	a, â, a, ae ,ah, axe	a, e
e	Like the 'a' in 'make'	Like the 'e' in 'bet'
Old Cornish	e	e
Middle Cornish	e, ey	e
Late Cornish	e, ê, ea, ee, exe	e
eu	Like the 'e' in 'server'	Like the 'e' in 'the'
Old Cornish	o	o
Middle Cornish	e, ue	e, ue
Late Cornish	e, ue	e, ue
i	Like the 'ee' in 'seen'	Like the 'i' in 'pin'
Old Cornish	i	i
Middle Cornish	y	y
Late Cornish	ee, î, y, yxe	i, y
o	Like the 'au' in 'taught'	Like the 'o' in 'cot'
Old Cornish	o	o
Middle Cornish	o, oe, oy	o
Late Cornish	o, ô, oa, oe, oh, oxe	o
u	Like French 'u' in 'vu'	Like German 'ü' in 'grün'
Old Cornish	u	u
Middle Cornish	u, ue	u, ue
Late Cornish	ee, î, ue, y, yxe	e, i, y
w	Like the 'oo' in 'tool'	Like the 'oo' in 'book'
Old Cornish	u	u
Middle Cornish	ou, u	ou, u
Late Cornish	ew, ow, u, û, uxe, w	ou, u, w
y	A sound between	A sound between
	e and i	e and i
Old Cornish	i	i
Middle Cornish	y,e	y, e
Late Cornish	e, ê, ea, ee, exe, î, y, yxe	e, i, y

In Late Cornish, unaccented **e** can sound like **a**, **eu** shifts towards **e**, and so does **y**.

21

Diphthongs
Colloquially they often sound like simple long vowels.

Letters		Pronunciation
ae		Like the 'i' in 'fire'
Old Cornish	ae	Like the 'i' in 'fire'.
Middle Cornish	ae, ay, e, ey	Like the 'i' in 'fire'
Late Cornish	ae ,ê, ea,exe	Like the 'ea' in 'great'
ai		Like the 'ay' in 'day'
Old Cornish	ai	Like the 'ay' in 'day'
Middle Cornish	ay	Like the 'ay' in 'day', or the 'ea' in 'great'
Late Cornish	ae, ey, eye	Like the 'ea' in 'great'
ei		Like the 'ai' in 'complain'
Old Cornish	ei	Like the 'ai' in 'complain'
Middle Cornish	e, ey, y	Like long 'ai' in 'complain', or the 'ee' in seen
Late Cornish	ê, ea, ei, exe, y	Like the 'ea' in 'great', or the 'ee' in 'seen'
ew		Like the 'e' in 'get' followed by the 'oo' in 'too'
Old Cornish	eu	Like the 'e' in 'get' followed by the 'oo' in 'too'
Middle Cornish	eu, ew	Like the 'e' in 'get' followed by the 'oo' in 'too'
Late Cornish	eu, ewe, u, ue	Like the 'ue' in 'due'
ey		Like the 'e' in 'get' followed by the 'i' in 'bin'
Old Cornish	ei	Like the 'e' in 'get' followed by the 'i' in 'bin'
Middle Cornish	e, ey, y	Like the 'ai in 'complain', or the 'ee' in seen
Late Cornish	ê,ea,ei,exe,y	Like the 'ea' in 'great', or the 'ee' in 'seen'
iw		Like the 'i' in 'bit' followed by the 'oo' in 'too'
Old Cornish	iw	Like the 'i' in 'bit' followed by the 'oo' in 'too'
Middle Cornish	ew, yw	Like the 'i' in 'bit' followed by the 'oo' in 'too'
Late Cornish	eu, ewe, u, ue	Like the 'ue' in 'due'
oe		Like the 'o' in 'bore followed by the 'ay in 'say'
Old Cornish	oe, oi	Like the 'o' in 'bore followed by the 'ay in 'say'
Middle Cornish	o, oa, oe, oy	Like the 'oi' in 'coin', or the 'oo' in school'
Late Cornish	o, oa, oe, oy	Like the 'oi' in 'coin', or the 'oo' in school'
ow		Like the 'o' in 'bone'.
Old Cornish	ou	Like the 'oi' in 'coin', or the 'oo' in school'
Middle Cornish	ou,ow	Like the 'oi' in 'coin', or the 'oo' in school'
Late Cornish	oh, ou, ow	Like the 'oi' in 'coin', or the 'oo' in school'
yw		Like the 'i' in 'fit' followed by the 'oo' in 'too'
Old Cornish	iw	Like the 'i' in 'fit' followed by the 'oo' in 'too'
Middle Cornish	ew, yw	Like the 'i' in 'fit' followed by the 'oo' in 'too'
Late Cornish	eu, ewe, u, ue	Like the 'ue' in 'due'

Consonants

They usually have three values. The primary value is the basic, normal sound of the consonant, the intervocalic value is how it sounds between vowels and the final value is how it sounds when nothing follows it. In formal pronunciation there is not always much difference, but there can be considerable variation colloquially. Where the consonant is doubled it is pronounced in full, so that *pell* 'far' is almost *pel–l*, whereas *pel* will sound almost like 'pale'. The pronunciation of some of the double consonants varies a little more, and this is indicated.

Letter	Pronunciation
b	Like the 'b' in 'beat'
Old Cornish	**b** always at the beginning of word, elsewhere, often **p**
Middle Cornish	**b** usually; sometimes **p** at the end of a word
Late Cornish	**b**
ch	Like the 'ch' in 'chip'
Old Cornish	
Middle Cornish	**ch**
Late Cornish	**ch, tsh**
d	Like the 'd' in 'deal'. Final **d** like **t**
Old Cornish	d always at the beginning of a word, elsewhere often **t**
Middle Cornish	**d** usually; sometimes **t** at the end of a word
Late Cornish	**th, dhc'h**
dh	Like the 'th' in 'this'. Final **dh** can disappear
Old Cornish	**d** often in middle of words, often **th**
Middle Cornish	**th** usually; sometimes **z**
Late Cornish	**th, dh**
f	Like the 'f' in 'fear'
Old Cornish	**f**
Middle Cornish	**f**
Late Cornish	**f, ph**
g	Like the 'g' in 'get'. Final **g** like **k**
Old Cornish	**g** always at the beginning of a word, elsewhere often **c**
Middle Cornish	**g** usually; sometimes **gu**
Late Cornish	**g, gu**
gh	Like a strong **h**. Intervocalic or final **gh** can disappear
Old Cornish	**gh, h**
Middle Cornish	**gh, h**
Late Cornish	**gh,**x. Like the 'h' in 'horrible'
h	Like the 'h' in 'horrible'.
Old Cornish	**h**
Middle Cornish	**h**
Late Cornish	**h**
j	Like the 'j' in judge'. Final **j** like **ch**
Old Cornish	
Middle Cornish	**j, g**
Late Cornish	**j, g, dzhk.** Like the 'c' in 'comb'
k	Like the 'c' in 'comb'
Old Cornish	**c, k**
Middle Cornish	**c, k**
Late Cornish	**c, k**
l	Like the 'l' in 'let'.
Old Cornish	**l**
Middle Cornish	**l**
Late Cornish	**l**
m	Like the 'm' in 'mother'. **mm** like **bm**
Old Cornish	**m**
Middle Cornish	**m**
Late Cornish	**m**
n	Like the 'n' in 'not'. **nn** like **dn**
Old Cornish	**n**
Middle Cornish	**n**
Late Cornish	**n**
p	Like the 'p' in 'perhaps'

Old Cornish	p
Middle Cornish	p
Late Cornish	p
r	Like the 'r' in 'race', but trilled
Old Cornish	r
Middle Cornish	r
Late Cornish	r
s	Like the 's' in 'see'. Intervocalic **s** can be like the 's' in 'those'.
Old Cornish	s
Middle Cornish	s
Late Cornish	s, z
t	Like the 't' in 'tell'
Old Cornish	t
Middle Cornish	**t**, usually
Early Modern	t
th	Like the 'th' in 'thin'. Final **th** can disappear
Old Cornish	th
Middle Cornish	**th**, sometimes **z**
Late Cornish	th
v	Like the 'v' in 'very'. Final **v** can disappear
Old Cornish	**b** between vowells, **v**
Middle Cornish	**v, f** at ends of words.
Late Cornish	v, f
w	Like the 'w' in 'want'.
Old Cornish	u
Middle Cornish	w, u
Late Cornish	w
y	Like the 'y' in 'yet'.
Old Cornish	i, y
Middle Cornish	y
Late Cornish	i, y

A note on the texts

In the translations to the following texts we have have tried strike a balance between accurate renderings of the originals and readability for the modern audience. All the texts have been newly translated by the editors. Our aim has been to obtain the earliest sources with original spellings. In a few cases minor changes have been made to make the text clearer. Where no title exists for the texts we have given the first line as the title. Often the English versions have commonly recognised titles, in which case we have given them, otherwise we have used titles that reflect the subject matter. In the complementary texts the sources are mostly English. Where they are in translation, this has been noted in the commentaries. Where we have made editorial decisions on the chronology of the texts we have indicated in the commentaries if there is some debate about the dating. There is a glossary of terms and proper names at the back of the book, followed by commentaries on each text, containing biographical, textual and historical information.

Texts in Cornish

1   *From* **Vocabularium Cornicum (c.1000)**

    ancredwur mor
    bahet
    baneu
    barth hirgorn
    bat
    benen rid
    caid prinid
    caur march
    chefuidoc
    chelioc redan
    chereor
    chetua
    guenoin
    guiden
    guinfellet
    gulat
    hichhewoil
    hihsommet
    huchot
    huhelwur
    leid
    leu
    manteilu
    nenbren
    oleubren
    saithor
    scolheic
    tiogou
    tolcorn
    wedresif

1   *From* **The Old Cornish Vocabulary (c.1000)**

viking [lit. 'sea-unbeliever']
boar
sow
trumpeter [lit. 'long horn bard']
coin
womankind
bought slave
camel [lit. 'giant horse']
almighty
grasshopper [lit. 'cock of the bracken']
shoemaker
assembly
poison
tree
vinegar [lit. 'spoiled wine']
country
vigilant [lit. 'highly watching']
bat [lit. 'high flitter']
upwards
noble [lit. 'high man']
tribe
lion
matriarch [lit. 'mother of household']
roofbeam [lit. 'ceiling tree']
olive tree [lit. 'oil tree']
archer
scholar
farmers
clarion [lit. 'hole horn']
newt

2 'Golsoug ty cowez' (c.1380)

golsoug ty cowez
byz na borz mez
dyyskyn ha powes
ha zymo dus nes
mar cozes ze les
ha zys y rof mowes
ha fest unan dek
genes mar a plek
ha tanha y
kymmerr y zoz wrek
sconye zys ny vek
ha ty a vyz hy

Hy a vyz gwreg ty da
zys ze synsy
pur wyr a lauara
ha govyn worty

Lemen yz torn my as re
ha war an greyz my an te
nag usy par
an barz ma ze pons tamar
my ad pes worty byz da
ag ol ze voz hy a wra
rag flog yw ha gensy doz
ha gaffy ze gafus hy boz
kenes mes zymmo ymmyug
eug alema ha fystynyug

dallaz a var infrez dar war
oun na porzo
ef emsettye worzesy
kam ma vezo
mar az herg zys gul nep tra
lauar zesy byz ny venna
lauar zozo gwra mar mennyz
a wos a gallo na wra tra vyz
in vrna yz sens ze vez meystres
hedyr vywy hag harluzes
ras o ganso ren offeren
curtes yw ha deboner
zys dregyn ny wra
mar an kefyth in danger
sense fast in della

2   The Charter Endorsement (c.1380)

Listen, friend,
never be ashamed;
come down and rest,
come closer to me
if you know what's good for you,
to you I shall give a girl
and a very beautiful one
if she pleases you.
O take her,
take her to be your wife;
she will not refuse you,
and you shall possess her.

She will be a good wife
for you to have,
I'm telling you,
O ask her!

Now I shall deliver her into your hands
and by my faith I swear
that there is not her like
this side of the Tamar bridge
I'm telling you: be good to her,
and she will do your bidding
for she is a child and it is wise
to get her consent and mine.
Although it is a shame for me, kiss,
get out of here and be quick about it.

Start out early, be quick, and be wary
of the fearless man
so that he will not dare
to attack you.
If he orders you to do something
say to yourself, 'I never will.'
But say to him, 'I shall if you wish.'
In spite of what he could do, he will do nothing
and he will consider you a mistress and a lady
as long as you live.
He was gracious, by the Mass,
he is courteous and well-mannered.
He will do no harm to you
if you keep him in your power:
Make sure you keep a hold on him.

3 'In Polsethow'/War Meane Merlyn (c.1265 and no date)

In Polsethow ywhylyr anethow

Ewra teyre a war meane Merlyn
Ara lesky Pawle Pensanz ha Newlyn

3 Two Cornish Prophecies (c.1265 and no date)

In Polsethow shall be seen marvels [or dwellings].

They shall land on the Rock of Merlin
Who shall burn Paul, Penzance and Newlyn.

Selections from the Ordinalia (c.1380)

4   'En tas a nef y'm gylwyr' (Origo Mundi)

Deus Pater
En tas a nef y'm gylwyr
   formyer pub tra a vyt gvrys
Onan ha try on yn gvyr
   en tas ha'n map ha'n spyrys
ha hethyv me a thesyr
   dre ov grath dalleth an beys
y lauaraf nef ha tyr
   bethens formyys orth both ov brys

lemmen pan yv nef thy'n gwrys
   ha lenwys a eleth splan
ny a vyn formye an bys
   par del on try hag onan
an tas ha'n mab ha'n spyrys
   pur ryel yn sur certan
an re-ma yv oberys
   del vynsyn agan honan

yn secund dyth y fynna
   gruthyl ebron nef hynwys
rag ythevel thym bos da
   yn kynsa dyth myns vs gvrys
bethens ebron dreys pup tra
   rak kvthe myns vs formyys
rak synsy glaw a wartha
   the'n nor veys may fe dyllys

yn tresse dyth dybarth gvraf
   yntre an mor ha'n tyryow
hag yn tyr gorhenmennaf
   may tefo gveyth ha losow
pub gvethen tefyns a'y saf
   ov ton hy frvt ha'y delyow
ha'n losowys erbyn haf
   degyns has yn erberow

yn peswere gvres perfyth
   the'n beys ol golowys glan
h'aga hynwyn y a vyth
   an houl ha'n lor ha'n stergan
my a set ahugh a'n gveyth
   yn creys a'n ebron avan

Selections from the Ordinalia (c.1380)

4   The Creation (The Beginning of the World)

God the Father
I am called the Father of Heaven,
  the Creator of everything :
One and Three are we,
  Father, Son and Holy Spirit.
And today I intend
  by my grace to begin the world:
I say: let Heaven and Earth
  be created according to my will.

When Heaven is made
  and filled with bright angels,
then we will create the world,
  for we are Three and One,
Father, Son and Holy Spirit,
  most royal, steadfast and enduring:
these things are made
  as we ordain.

On the second day, I will
  make a vault, called Heaven,
for all that was made on the first day
  seems good to me.
Let there be sky over everything
  to cover all that is created,
to hold rain above
  so that it may be released onto the Earth.

On the third day I shall separate
  the sea from land,
and on the land I shall command
  that trees and plants grow.
Let every tree grow upright
  bearing fruit and leaves,
and let the plants in summer
  bear seed in gardens.

On the fourth day, let there be made
  perfect bright lights for all the world,
and their names shall be
  sun and moon and starlight.
I shall place above the trees,
  in the middle of the sky

An Ior yn nos houl yn geyth
   may rollons y golow splan

yn pympes dyth me a vyn
   may fo formyes dre ov nel
bestes puskes hag ethyn
   tyr ha mor the goullenwel
rag y whyrvyth an tyrmyn
   drethe may fether the wel
thethe me a worhemmyn
   encressyens ha bewens pel

[*Hic descendit Deus de pulpito et dicit Deus*
   Hic Iudit Lucifer de celo]

hethyw yw an whefes dyth
   aban dallethys gonys
may rug nef mor tyr ha gveyth
   bestes puskes golowys
gosteyth thy'mo y a vyth
   kekemys vs ynne gvreys
map den a bry yn perfyth
   me a vyn y vos formyys

[*Hic faciat Adam et dicit Deus*]
Del ony onen ha try
   tas ha map yn trynyte
ny a'd wra ty then a bry
   haval d'agan face whare
ny a whyth in thy vody
   sperys [may] hylly bewe
ha'n bewnans pan y'n kylly
   the'n dor ty a dreyl arte

Adam saf yn ban yn clor
   ha treyl the gyk ha the woys
preder my the'th whul a dor
   haval they'm a'n pen the'n troys
myns vs yn tyr hag yn mor
   warnethe kemer galloys
yn bys-ma rak dry ascor
   ty a vew bys may fy loys

Adam del of dev a ras
   bos gvythyas a wrontyaf thy's
War paradys my a'th as
   saw gvra vn dra a'n govys
War bup frut losow ha has

the moon at night, sun in the day,
   that they shall give brightness.

On the fifth day, I command
   that there be created by my power
beasts, fish and birds,
   to fill up land and sea,
for the time shall come to pass
   when things will improve because of them:
I command them
   to increase and live long.

[*Here God comes down from the platform and God shall say: Here Lucifer appears from Heaven*]

Today is the sixth day
   since I began work
making Heaven, sea, land and trees,
   beasts, fish, light:
they shall obey me
   in their own fashion.
I ordain that man be made
   perfectly from clay.

[*Here let him make Adam, and God says:*]
As we are One and Three,
   Father, Son in Trinity,
We shall make thee, Man, of clay,
   directly in our own image:
we shall blow into thy body
   spirit so that thou mayst live,
and when you shall lose your life
   to the earth you shall return.

Adam, stand up calmly,
   and turn into flesh and to blood:
remember that I made you of earth
   in my image from head to foot.
Take power over all that is
   in the land and sea,
you shall live until you are grey
   to bring offspring into the world.

Adam, as I am a God of grace,
   I shall let you stay in Paradise
to be its steward
   (do that one thing on our behalf)
over all fruit, plants and seed

a vo ynny hy tevys
saw a'n frut ny fyth kymmyas
  yw pren a skeyanz hynwys
Mar a tybbryth a henna
  yw hynwys pren a skyens
yn mes alemma ty a
  hag a fyth marow vernens

Adam
A das map ha spyrys sans
  gorthyans the'th corf wek pup prys
ow formye tek ha dyblans
  ty ru'm gruk pur havel thy's
rag governye ow bewnans
  yma loer orth both ow brys
pur luen yma ty'm ow whans
  a'n ven cowethes ordnys

5   'Yt'hanwaf bugh ha tarow' (Origo Mundi)

Adam
yt'hanwaf bugh ha tarow
ha margh yw best hep parow
  the vap den rag ymweres
gaver yweges karow
daves war ve lavarow
  hy hanow da kemeres

lemyn hanwaf goyth ha yar
a sensaf ethyn hep par
  the vegyans den war an beys
hos payon colom grvgyer
swan bargos bryny ha'n er
  moy drethof a vyth hynwys

y rof hynwyn the'n puskes
porpus sowmens syllyes
  oll thy'm gustyth y a vyth
lenesow ha barfusy
pysk ragof ny wra skvsy
  mar corthyaf dev yn perfyth

    which may be growing there,
except one forbidden fruit
    named the Tree of Knowledge.
If you eat from that
    which is named Tree of Knowledge,
you will be cast out
    and will die a death.

Adam
O Father, Son and Holy Spirit,
    praise to your sweet body always:
you have made me beautiful and well-wrought
    in your very image.
To live my life
    there is enough to satisfy my mind:
But I strongly desire
    the ordained female companion.

5   The Naming of the Animals (The Beginning of the World)

Adam
I shall name cow and bull,
and horse, a beast without equal
    to give help to mankind;
goat, hind, deer,
sheep, to take a name
    from my words.

Now I shall name goose and hen,
that I hold to be birds without equal
    to feed man in the world;
duck, peacock, pigeon, partridge,
swan, kite, crow and eagle,
    more will be named by me.

I shall give names to the fishes,
porpoise, salmon, eel,
    all of them will be subject to me,
ling and cod,
not a fish shall escape me
    if I worship God perfectly.

6 'Seth pan-dra yv the nygys' (Origo Mundi)

Cherubin
seth pan-dra yv the nygys
mar hyr forth dones may fynsys
   lauar d'ymmo vy whare

Seth
A el me a leuer thy's
ov thas ev coth ha squytheys
   ny garse pelle bewe

ha genef ef a'd pygys
   a leuerel guyroneth
a'n oyl dotho dythywys
   a versy yn deyth dyweth

Cherubin
Agy the'n yet gor the ben
Ha y syl vyth ol na gen
   pe-penag-ol a wylly
ha myr a pup tenewen
aspy yn-ta pup eghen
   whythyr pup tra ol bysy

Seth
fest yn lowen me a wra
   guyn ow bys kafus cummyas
the wothfos pyth vo ena
   rag y leuerel thu'm tas

[*et respicit et vertit se dicens*]
dev tek a wel yw homma
   goef a gollas an wlas
sav an wethen thy'm yma
   hy bos syghys marthys vras
Saw my a greys hy bos segh
ha gurys noth ol rag an pegh
   a pehas ov thas ha'm mam
avel olow aga threys
sygh yns ol kepar ha leys
   ellas pan thybrys an tam

Cherubin
A Seth osa dynythys
agy the yet paradys
   lauar thy'm pan-dra wylsta

6 The Errand of Seth (The Beginning of the World)

Cherub
Seth, what is your errand
that you have come so far?
   Tell me now.

Seth
O Angel, I shall tell you:
my father is old and weary,
   and no longer wants to live.

And he asked me to ask you,
   to tell the truth,
about the Oil promised him,
   for Mercy's sake on the last day.

Cherub
Put your head through the gate
and you will see everything
   there is to see:
Look about on every side,
take notice of everything,
   examine everything diligently.

Seth
Very happily I shall:
   I am glad to be allowed
to find out what is in there,
   so that I can tell my father.

[*And he looks, and turns round, saying:*]
God! what a wonderful sight –
   woe to him who lost this country!
But the tree, I am greatly surprised
   to see it withered.
But I know it is dried up
and leafless for the sin
   my father and mother committed.
Like their footprints
in mud, they are all dry:
Alas, for that bite!

Cherub
O Seth, you are come
to the gate of Paradise:
   tell me what you saw.

Seth
ol an tekter a wylys
ny yl taves den yn bys
   y leuerel bynytha
A frut da ha floures tek
menestrouthy ha can whek
   fenten bryght Avel arhans
ha pedyr streth vras defry
ov resek a-dyworty
   worte myres may tho whans

warnethy yma gvethen
vhel gans lues scoren
   saw noth ol yns hep dylyow
hag adro thethy rusken
nynsese a'n blyn the'n ben
   noth yv ol hy scorennow

ha war woles pan vyrys
   my a welas hy gurythyow
bys yn yffarn dywenys
   yn mysk mur a tewolgow
ha'y branchys yn van tyvys
   bys yn nef vhel golow
ha hy warbarth dyruskys
   kefrys ben ha barennow

Cherubin
wheth myr arte aberveth
hag ol ken ty a welfeyth
   kyns ys dones a le-na

Seth
bos cummyas thy'm guyn ov bys
my a the'n yet desempys
   may callaf gueles ken ta

[*vadit et respiciet et revertit*]

Cherubin
A wylsta ken yn tor-ma
   ys del ege agensow

Seth
vn sarf in guethen yma
   best vthek hep falladow

Seth
All the beauty I saw
no tongue of man in the world
   can ever tell,
of good fruit and fair flowers,
minstrelsy and sweet song,
   a stream as bright as silver,
and four great springs, indeed,
running from it,
   that transfixed your gaze.

There is a tree in it,
high, with many branches,
   but they are all naked and leafless,
and there is no bark about it
from the top to the trunk,
   all its boughs are bare.

And at the bottom when I looked
   I saw its roots
plunged into Hell
   amongst much darkness,
and its branches grew up
   into the high light of Heaven,
but it is peeled of bark,
   both trunk and boughs.

Cherub
Look inside once more,
and you will see everything
   before you leave this place.

Seth
Blessed am I that I might
go to the gate straightaway
   to see the other good things.

[*He goes and looks and turns back*]

Cherub
Do you see anything this time
   other than what was there before?

Seth
There is a serpent in the tree,
   a fearful beast undoubtedly.

Cherubin
ke weth tresse treveth th'y
  ha myr gvel orth an wethen
myr pan-dra wylly ynny
  kefrys gwrythyow ha scoren

[*iterum vadit in superum*]

Seth
Cherubyn el dew a ras
yn wethen me a welas
  yn ban vhel worth scoren
flogh byen nowyth gynys
hag ef yn quethow maylys
  ha kylmys fast gans lysten

Cherubin
Mab dev o neb a wylsys
avel flogh byhan maylys
  ef a bren adam the das
gans y gyk ha wos kefrys
pan vo termyn denythys
  ha'th vam hag ol an dus vas

ef yv an oyl a versy
  a fue the'th tas dythywys
dre y vernans yredy
  ol an bys a fyth sylwys

Seth
Benygys nefre re by
  a dev lemyn guyn ov bys
gothfos guyr ol yredy
  my a vyn mos thyworthy's

Cherubin
kemer tyyr spus a'n aval
  a dybrys adam the das
pan varwo gorr'y hep fal
  yntre y thyns ha'y davas
Anethe ty a wylfyth
  tyr gvethen tevys whare
rag ny vew moy es tryddyth
  war lergh the vones the dre

Seth
bynyges re by pup tyth
  my a'd worth pur wyr nefre

Cherub
Go a third time
 and look a bit closer at the tree.
See what there is to see,
 in the roots and branches.

[*Again he shall go up*]

Seth
Cherub, angel of the God of grace,
in the tree I saw,
 high above on a branch,
a little new-born child,
wrapped in cloth,
 and bound tightly in swaddling.

Cherub
It is the Son of God you saw
wrapped like a little child:
 He will redeem Adam your father
with his flesh and blood
when the time is come,
 and your mother too and all good people.

He is the Oil of Mercy
 that was promised to your father:
through his death, clearly,
 the whole world will be saved.

Seth
May he be forever blessed,
 O God, I am happy
to know the truth, indeed:
 I will leave you.

Cherub
Take three pips from the apple
 that your father Adam ate.
When he dies, put them without fail
 between his teeth and tongue.
Soon you shall see
 three trees growing,
for he will live no more than three days
 after you get home.

Seth
Blessed may you be every day!
 Truly, I shall honour you forever.

ov das fest lowenek vyth
  mar scon a'n bys tremene

7 'Damsel er the gentylys' (Origo Mundi)

[*Et dicit rex David ad bersabe
  abluendo vestem in rivilo*]

Rex DD
Damsel er the gentylys
  dysque thy'm a'd kerense
rag bytqueth my ny welys
  benen thy'm a wel plekye
    wheth yn nep le

    rof thy's ov thour
    hel ha chammbour
    vethaf the wour
    warbarth ny a dryg nefre

Bersabe
ov arluth ker caradow
  myghtern os war ol an bys
assevye plygadow
  genef gruthyl both the vrys
a callen hep kelladow
  ha dout ov vos hellyrghys
mar cothfo an casadow
  dystough y fyen lethys

[*bersabe tranceat domum cum rege dd*]

Rex DD
Bersabe flour ol an byss
  certus rag the gerense
syr vrry a vyth lethys
  my a'n te thy's ru'm leute
rag ol ov yeues pup prys
  ty a vyth pur wyr nefre
growet yn guely a hys
  may hyllyf genes coske

Bersabe
my ny allaf the nahe
lemyn pup tra ol gronntye
  theworthyf a wovynny
ov arluth whek ol lathe

My father will be very happy
   to pass so quickly from the world.

7   David and Bathsheba (The Beginning of the World)

[*And King David shall say to Bathsheba,
  washing a dress in a stream*]

King David
Damsel, for your gentility,
   show me how to love you,
for never did I see
   in any place
     a woman who pleased me better.

   I shall give you my tower,
   my hall and my chamber,
   I shall be your husband,
   and we shall live together forever.

Bathsheba
My dear beloved lord,
   you are king of all the world.
How pleasant it would be
   to do with you what is on your mind,
if only I could openly
   and without fear of retribution.
If the hateful one knew
   I should be killed at once.

[*Let Bathsheba go over to the house with King David*]

King David
Bathsheba, flower of all the world,
   certainly, for your love
Sir Uriah will be killed,
   I promise by my troth,
for you shall have forever
   my undying love.
Lie down on the bed
   that I might sleep with you.

Bathsheba
I shall not deny you,
but rather grant you
   all that you ask of me.
My sweet lord, kill him

ken ef a wra ov shyndye
   mar clew vyth agan guary

Rex DD
ov holon ger caradow
   dew rvth ros flour hy hynse
syr urry a fyth lethys
   my a'n te thy's ru'm leute
ef a vyth hep falladow
   marow rag the gerense

Rex DD
vrry ov marrek guella
   my a vynsa the pysy
gor ost genes yrvys da
   the omlath del y'm kerry
vn eskar bras thy'm yma
   war ov thyr ov gul mestry
marogeth my ny alla
   yma cleves y'm body

Hurias
Syr arluth ker del vynny
my a wra prest hep ynny
   ol thu'm gallus vynytha
ha del oma marrek len
venythe ny thof a'n plen
   er na'n prenne an guas-na.

Rex DD
A vrry assos os gentyl
my a'd car mur ru'm peryl
   rag the worthebow ev tek
gueyt bos a rag yn voward
ma na vy synysys coward
   nag awos den vyth ovnek

Hurias
ov arluth my a'n te thy's
re'n ordyr a recevys
   ny'm pref den war gowardy
rag my a vyth an kynso
bom yn vyag a rollo
   hag a perfo ov meystry

farwel ov arluth guella
ny vynna streche pella
   son vy kyns mos my a'd pys

or he will hurt me
  if he hears a word of our sport.

King David
My dear beloved heart,
  God has made you the flower of womankind.
Sir Uriah will be killed,
  I swear by my troth:
Without fail he shall be killed
  for love of you.

King David
Uriah, my finest knight,
  as you love me,
I would ask you
  to take a well-armed host,
to fight a great enemy
  who is violating my land:
I cannot ride myself,
  as I am sick in my body.

Uriah
My dear sir lord, I shall do your bidding
with all my power
  always without urging,
and as I am a faithful knight
I shall not leave the battlefield
  until the fellow pays for it.

King David
O Uriah, how noble you are!
On my peril, I love you greatly,
  for your responses are fair.
Take care to be in the vanguard
so that you may not be held a coward,
  nor fearful of any man.

Uriah
My lord, I swear it to you,
by my order of knighthood,
  that no man shall convict me of cowardice,
for I shall be the first
to give a blow in the contest
  and that shall show my mastery.

Farewell, my best lord,
I will delay no longer:
  bless me before I go, I pray you.

Rex DD
ov banneth thy's vynytha
ov messyger genes a
   ha'm botler kefrys yrvys

Hurias
rys ev thy'm kevsel defry
   orth ow gwrek kyns mos a dre
marsellen hep cous orty
   hy holon hy a torse
[*dicit ad bersabe*]
bersabe ov whek e vy
   rys yv dy'mmo lafurye
the vn vatel yredy
   sav dystough hy a vyth due

[*hic paratur et armatur hurias*]

Bersabe
Na wreugh why war ov ene
   theworthef vy vynythe
ma ov wolon ov ranne
   pan glewaf cous an par-ne
ov arluth by my leute
   my a der crak ov conne
marsevgh lemyn mes a dre
   nefre ny thebraf vare

Hurias
bersabe ov fryes lel
rys yv gruthyl dyogel
   voth agan arluth sefryn
ny allaf pella trega
my a vyn dy'so amma
   ha pys genef fest yn tyn

[*ascendit ea et vadit*]
   [*hic descendit uryas*]

Bersabe
ogh govy pan vef genys
gans moreth ythof lynwys
   war the lergh ov arluth whek
sav vynerre thewhylly
genes my a wra pysy
   ha henna a vye tek

[*hic descendit gabriel*]

King David
My blessing to you always:
my messenger will go with you,
   and my manservant, also armed.

Uriah
Indeed I must speak
   to my wife before I leave.
If I went without speaking to her
   her heart would break.
[*He says to Bathsheba:*]
Bathsheba, my sweet,
   I must go away
indeed, to do battle,
   but it will soon be over.

[*Here Uriah is prepared and armed*]

Bathsheba
On my soul, do not ever
   go away from me:
my heart will rend
   to hear such talk.
My lord, by my troth,
   I shall break my neck with a crack:
if you go away,
   I shall never eat bread again.

Uriah
Bathsheba, my faithful wife,
it is necessary immediately to do
   the bidding of our sovereign lord.
I can no longer stay,
I will kiss you,
   pray for me sincerely.

[*She goes up, and leaves*]
   [*Here Uriah comes down*]

Bathsheba
Woe is me that I was born!
I am filled with grief
   for my sweet lord.
May you always return:
I shall pray for you,
   and that would be pleasing to me.

[*Here Gabriel comes down*]

Hurias
My a'd pys now messyger
dog manerlich ov baner
   del vynny bos rewardyys
ha ty in weth botteler
my a'd pys may fe asper
   avel marrek fyn yrvys

[*hic ascendit super equum*]

II Nuncius
my a leuer thy's vrry
na borth dout ahanaf vy
   certan nefre
rag ny fyth ken the perth y
my a leuer theughwhy why
   war ov ene

[*Et tunc equitabunt extra ludum*]

[*et postea venit nuncius et dicit ad
   Dd regem*]

ov arluth lowene thy's
ov ote vy devethys
   arte the dre
sav syve vrry ev lethys
ha the votteler kekyfrys
   govy ragthe

Rex DD
dar marow yv syr vrry
lauar thy'm del y'm kerry
   pan vernans a'n geve ef
ha fetel vefe lethys
rag ef o stout ha gothys
   hag a ym-sensy den cref

II Nuncius
marow yv by godys day
ef a vynse gul deray
   hag a ros strokosow tyn
saw vn marrek a'n lathas
ha the'n dor scon a'n goras
   hag a'n hakyas the dymmyn

Uriah
I pray you now, messenger,
carry my flag valiantly
   if you want to be rewarded.
And you too, manservant,
I pray you be bold,
   like a well-armed knight.

[*Here he goes up on a horse*]

2nd Messenger
I tell you, Uriah,
certainly do not
   doubt me ever.
For there is no cause for it,
I tell you
   upon my soul.

[*And then they shall ride out of the arena*]

[*And afterwards the messenger comes and says to King David*]

My lord, hail to you!
I am come
   home again,
but Sir Uriah is killed,
and your manservant also,
   woe upon them!

King David
Alas! Is Sir Uriah dead?
Tell me, as you love me,
   when death found him
and how he was killed,
for he was steadfast and proud,
   and held himself a strong man.

2nd Messenger
He is dead, by God's day!
He made havoc
   and gave grievous blows,
but a certain knight killed him
and quickly put him on the ground,
   and hacked him to pieces.

[*Tunc veniet angelus ad regem dauid et querat questionem et dicit*]

Gabriel
gortheb thy'm ty myghtern bras
den an geffe cans dauas
   ha'y kentrevek saw onan
mar a's ladtre theworto
pan pyn a gotho thotho
   lauar en guyr thy'm certan

Rex DD
my a wortheb thy's whare
   yn certan na vy lettyys
dre guyr vrus sur y cothe
   dotho gothaf bod lethys
     yn pur defry
     nep a rella
     yn ketella
mernans yv gvyw th'y vody

Gabriel
yn ketella ty re wruk
ha theworth vrry re thuk
   y vn wrek dauid certan
ha thy'so gy ythese
benenes lour ha plente
   gothaf the vrus the honan

Rex DD
arluth gevyans thu'm ene
govy pan wruge pehe
   gans corf a'n debel venen
deus mei miserere
herweth the grath ha'th pyte
   na'm byma peyn yn gorfen

[*Et tunc sub arbore scientiae incipit psalterium, viz. Beatus vir*]

8 'Dun the leuerel yn scon' (Origo Mundi)

IIs Carpenter
dun the leuerel yn scon
d'agan arluth salamon
   bones an temple coul wrys
[*ad regem salamon*]

[*Then the angel Gabriel shall come and ask him a
question, and he says:*]

Gabriel
Answer me, great king:
a man had a hundred sheep
   and his neighbour had only one:
if he stole it from him,
what penalty would be due to him?
   Tell me the truth, certainly.

King David
I shall answer you directly,
   and not cross you:
true judgement certainly would dictate
   that he be killed:
     quite definitely,
     whoever did
     such a thing
deserves death for his body.

Gabriel
It was just the same when you
took from Uriah
   his one wife, David, for sure,
and you had
plenty enough wives:
   suffer your own judgement!

King David
Lord, have mercy on my soul !
Woe is me, for I did sin
   with the body of the wicked woman.
God have mercy on me
according to your grace and pity,
   may I not be punished at the end.

[*And then under the Tree of Knowledge he begins
the Psalter, viz., Blessed is the man*]

8   Solomon and the Temple Builders (The Beginning of the World)

2nd Carpenter
Let us quickly go to tell
our lord Solomon
   that the Temple is completed.
[*To King Solomon:*]

heyl ov arluth yn the thron
gurys yv the temple hep son
   agan gobyr ny a'th pys

Rex Sal
banneth a'n tas re ges bo
why as-byth by godys fo
   agas gobyr yredy
warbarth ol gueel behethlen
ha coys penryn yn tyen
   ma a's re lemyn theugh why
     hag ol guer-thour
an enys hag arwennek
tregenver ha kegyllek
   annethe gureugh theugh chartour

Is Carpenter
gromersy arloth hep par
   ny a yl lour bones prout
ny's teve tus vyth hep mar
   roow mar tha by myn hout

9 'Mara ieves yl dybbry' (Passio Christi)

Sathanas
Mara ieves yl dybbry
me a wor guyr yredy
   yn certan nag ywe dew
my a vyn mos th'y temptye
mar a callaf y tenne
   the wuel glotny war nep tw

sur awos ol ow gallos
byth ny allaf yn ow ros
   the wul pegh vyth y cachye
den yw the pup the weles
saw y ober ha'y thyskes
   pup ol a wra tremene

[*hic descendit satnas et dicit ad jhm*]
thy'so gy y leuara
mar sos map dev awartha
   dysempys argh ha lavar
the'n cals meyn-ma bos bara
me a worthvyth yn vr-na
   pyth yw the gallos hep mar

Hail, my lord on your throne!
The Temple is made noiselessly:
   we ask for our wages.

King Solomon
The Father's blessing upon you!
You shall indeed have, by God's faith,
   your reward:
all the fields of Bohelland together
and all of the wood of Penryn
   I shall now give to you
     and all of Gwerthour.
The Island and Arwennack,
Tregenver and Kegyllack,
   make yourselves a charter for them.

1st Carpenter
Thank you, incomparable Lord!
   We can now be proud:
No people ever, without doubt, had
   such good gifts, by my head.

9   The Temptation of Jesus (Christ's Passion)

Satan
If he has the urge to eat
I shall know for sure
   that he is not God.
I will go to tempt him,
that I might entice him
   into some kind of gluttony.

But in spite of all my power
I can never trap him in my net
   to commit any sin.
He is a man for all to see,
but without his work and teaching
   everyone will die.

[*Here Satan goes down and he says to Jesus:*]
To you I say:
if you are the Son of God on high,
   straightway command and say
to this pile of stones be bread.
Then I shall know
   the extent of your power without doubt.

IHS
map den hep ken ys bara
 byth nyn ieves ol bewues
leman yn leuarow da
 a thue thyworth an drenses
[*ad discipulos*]
ow dyscyblyon dre henna
 leman why a yl gueles
laver dev maga del wra
 neb a yl y kemeres

Johannes
a mester ker caradow
 del leueryth my a grys
y fyth agan enefow
 dre leuarow dev mygys
ha fethys an dywolow
 yn lyfryow del yw scryfys
ny kerghys the'n nef golow
 yn ioy vynytha a pys

Sathanas
mar sos dev a nef golow
dysqua lemman marthusow
 may allyv vy y weles
ke war pynakl a'n temple
hagh ena gura ysethe
 nynsyw thy's tyller pur es

IHS
my a vyn mos ow honan
war an pynakl yn ban
 the ysethe
yma thy'mmo yn certan
the wruthyl vn pols byhan
 takclow pryve

[*tunc diabolus temptet cum dicens*]
Sathanas
huhel ythos ysethys
 ha dyantel ro'm laute
yn lyvyr yma scryfys
 bos eleth worth the wythe
ragh ovn the vos desesys
the tros worth men pystige
mar sos map dev a mur prys
 dyyskyn ha the'n dor ke

Jesus
Mankind cannot live
  by bread alone,
but by the good words
  that come from the Trinity.
[*To the disciples:*]
My disciples, by this
  you can see now
how the word of God feeds
  whosoever will take it.

John
O dearly beloved Master!
  Even as you say, I believe,
that our souls will be
  fed by the word of God,
and the devils defeated
  as is written in books,
and we will be taken to bright heaven
  in joy that will last forever.

Satan
If you are the God of the bright heaven,
perform some miracle
  that I might see it.
Go to the pinnacle of the temple
and sit there:
  It is not a very easy place for you.

Jesus
I will go myself
up to the pinnacle
    to sit:
I have indeed
a few private matters
    that will take a moment.

[*Then the devil tempts him, saying:*]
Satan
You are seated on high,
  and not very safely, by my troth.
It is written in the Book
  that angels guard you
for fear you will hurt
  your foot against a stone.
If you are truly the precious Son of God,
  come down to the ground.

IHS
yma scryfys yn lyfryow
ny goth thy's temptie the thew
    yn nep maner
saw the arluth dev a'n nef
y coth thy's y worthye ef
    yn pup tyller

[*descendit jhs*]

dvn alemma cowythe
war menythyow the wandre
    ha the pigy
ow thas ker a thy-lawe
dre y voth th'gas gwythe
    ragh terrygy

Andreas
ol del vynny arluth ker
my a wra yn pup tyller
    hedre veyn bev yn bys-ma
gans penys ha gologhas
my a pys dev mer y ras
    danvon gras thy'nny omma

Bartholomeus
mester ker re by gorthys
del goth gans tus ol a'n bys
    rag the thescas yv pur da
guyn y vys a vo trigys
yn the seruys ragh tristys
    nyn d'y gemmer vynytha

[*iterum diabolus temptet eum dicens*]
  [*hic descendit Gabriell*]

Sathanas
ot omma meneth huhel
ha me a thysque thy's guel
    a veur a pow
ol an bys-ma ty a fyth
cole worthyf mar mynnyth
    yn sur hep gow

myr lowene ol an bys
cytes rych trevow a brys
    castilly bras hagh huhel

Jesus
It is written in books:
you should not tempt your God
    in any way,
but you should worship
the Lord your God
    in every place.

[*Jesus descends*]

Let us come away from here, my friends,
to wander on the mountains
    and pray
to my dear Father and sing his praises,
that His will may keep you
    from disasters.

Andrew
All that you wish, dear Lord,
I shall do in every place,
    while I live in this world,
with penance and praise.
I shall pray that the God of grace
    sends grace to us here.

Bartholomew
Dear Master, may you be praised
by all the people of the world as is fitting,
    for your teaching is very good.
Blessed is he who remains
in your service, for he shall
    never know sadness.

[*Again the devil tempts him, saying:*]
[*Here Gabriel descends*]

Satan
Here is a high mountain,
and I shall show you a view
    of many countries.
Without a word of a lie,
the whole world will be yours
    if you will believe in me.

Look at the joy of the whole world,
rich cities and towns of price,
    great and high castles.

ol an re-ma ty a fyth
ow gorthye mara mennyth
   war pen the thew glyn ysel

IHS
ty sathnas deawl mylygys
   yma scryfys yn lyfryow
yn pup maner y coth thy's
   gorthye the dev ha'y hanow
ke the ves ymskemenys
   yn defyth yn tewlogow
the vestry a vyth leyhys
   neffre war an enevow

Sathanas
go vy vyth pan yth thotho
pan of fythys thyworto
   ter-gwyth hythew
ha'n maystri bras ol a'm bo
my re'n collas quyt dretho
   may canaf trew
[*recedit satanas*]

———————

Deus Pater
ow eleth seveugh yn ban
eugh alemma ahanan
   the seruye ow map kerra
re fethas an fals ievan
hythyw ter-gwyth yn certan
   gvyn vys nep a'n gorth yn ta

Michael
a tas dev gallosek fest
the gorhemynnadow prest
   sur ny a wra
ihesus crist the vn vap ker
   my a'n serf gans onor mer
     ha maria

[*hic descendant angeli*]

All these you will have
if you will only worship me
   low on your knees.

Jesus
Satan, you accursed devil,
   it is written in books
that in every way you should
   worship your God and His name.
Go hence, banished
   into the desert in darkness:
Your power over souls
   is destroyed for ever.

Satan
Woe is me that I ever went to him,
as I am cast from him
      three times today,
and all the great power I had
I have completely lost because of him,
   so I shall sing, alas!
[*Satan leaves*]

God the Father
My angels, rise up,
and go from us
   to serve my dearest son
who has conquered the false demon
three times today for sure.
   Blessed is he who honestly worships Him.

Michael
O Father, most almighty God,
we shall always follow
      your commandments.
Jesus Christ, your beloved only son
   I shall serve with great honour,
      and Mary.

[*Here let the angels come down*]

10 'Newethow mere clewes' (Passio Christi)

[*Tunc veniunt pueri ebreorum et deferant
palmas et flores contra ihesum
et dicit primus puer*]

Is Puer
newethow mere clewes
bones ihesus bynyges
   ow tos omms the'n cite
er y byn mennaf mone
me a garse y weles
   ef yw dev luen a pite

IIs Puer
   ol ny a vyn
   mos er y byn
   rak y worthe
   dev a mercy
   the pup huny
   sur ythywe

IIIs Puer
   fleghes ebbrow
   dvn yn vn rew
   scon hep lettye
   er byn ihesu
   neb yv guyr dev
   ow tos the'n dre

IVs Puer
yn kettella ny a vyn
branchys olyf pan kyffyn
   me a seta thyragtho
hagh a'n gorth guel hagh yllyn
peb ol war penn y dev glyn
   a gan yn gorthyans dotho

Vs Puer
ma ny gaffaf branchys vas
me a thystryp ow dyllas
   hag a's set y dan y treys
hagh a gan th'agan sylwyas
bynyges yv map a ras
   yn hanow dev devethys

VIs Puer
me a vyn sur yn della
dysky ow dyllas guella

10 Palm Sunday (Christ's Passion)

> [*Then the children of the Hebrews come, and let the
> carry palms and flowers to meet Jesus,
> and the first boy says:*]

1st Boy
I heard great news,
that the blessed Jesus
  is coming to the city.
I will go to meet Him:
I would love to see Him,
  for he is God, full of pity

2nd Boy
> All of us will
> go to meet Him
> so that we may worship Him.
> He surely is
> the God of mercy
> to one and all.

3rd Boy
> Hebrew children,
> quickly, let us go in a row
> without hesitation
> to meet Jesus
> the true God
> who is coming to town.

4th Boy
We will do this:
I will get olive branches
  to place before Him,
and we shall worship him as best we can,
everyone on his knees
  to sing His praises.

5th Boy
If I can find no suitable branches
I shall take off my clothes
  to place under His feet,
and I shall sing to our blessed Saviour
who is a Son of Grace
  come in the name of God.

6th Boy
I will certainly
take off my best clothes

ha tywlel a thyragtho
yma gynef flowrys tek
yn onor thu'm arluth whek
　aga skulye yn danno

VIIs Puer
　palm ha bayys
　byxyn erbys
　gynef yma
　arluth a nef
　guyth ow enef
　rak pup drok tra

11 'Arluth henna yv gurys da' (Passio Christi)

[*hic veniet maria magdalena ad jhesu
　cum domino symon lepros*]

Juda
arluth henna yv gurys da
why wor pyth yw gwella
　theugh the wruthyl
guel ys ol tus a'n bys-ma
del os dalleth a pup tra
　y reyth kusyl

Mar. Magd
me a vyn mos the vre
ow arluth treys ha devle
　gans onement
ha war y pen y scullye
a pup squythens y sawye
　hagh ylye y vrewyan

mester whek thy's lowene
me a vyn the'th treys amme
　dre the voth ken nag of gvyw
yma daggrow ow klybye
the dreys rak evn kerenge
　saw me a's segh gans ow blew

ow box mennaf the terry
　a dal mur a vone da
war the pen y thenewy
　ha war the treys magata

and cast them before Him.
I have beautiful flowers
in honour of my sweet Lord
   to scatter beneath Him.

7th Boy
   Palm and bay,
   box and herbs
   I have:
   Lord of Heaven,
   keep my soul
   from every evil thing.

11 Mary Magdalene (Christ's Passion)

[*Here Mary Magdalene comes to Jesus;
   and Simon the Leper with the Lord*]

Judas
Lord, that is well done:
you know how best
   to act,
better than all the men in this world.
As you are the beginning of everything
   you will give counsel.

Mary Magdelene
I will go to anoint
my Lord's feet and hands,
   with precious oil
and pour it on his head,
to cure him of every weariness
   and salve his bruises.

Sweet Master, joy unto you!
If you will allow me
   I will kiss your feet, though I am unworthy.
Though tears wet
your feet for true love's sake,
   I shall dry them with my hair.

I will break open my box
   that is worth much money,
and pour it on your head,
   and on your feet too.

Symon Leprosus
a pe profus bynyges
   yn sur ef a wothfye
y bos hy peghadures
   ny's gasse th'y ylye

IHS
symon del of yrvyrys
   yma thy'mmo ru'm laute
nebes the leuerel
   gosleuw orthyf vy wharre

Symon Leprosus
mester lauar dysempys
   yn scon dy'mmo hep lettye
an dra vs sur war the vreys
   er-the-byn ny wraf sconye

IHS
kyns yn vn teller yn beys
   dev kendoner yth ege
the vn dettor me a grys
   an nyl thotho a delle
pymp cans dyner monyys
   ha hanter cans y gyle
y's gavas thethe keffrys
   rak ny's teve man th'y pe

lauar thy'mmo a ver spys
py nyl o mogha sengys
   an keth den-ma the care

Symon Leprosus
me a re scon gorthyp thy's
neb may fe moghya geffys
   a gar moghye yn pup le

IHS
certan guyr vres yv honna
ty a wel an venen-ma
   whet aban thuthe y'th chy
golhy ow treys ny hyrsys
homma gans daggrow keffrys
   re's holhas yn surredy

gans y blew y fons syhys
bythqueth bay thy'm ny ryssys
   ha homma vyth ny sestyas
aban duthe yn chy thy's

Simon the Leper
If he were indeed a blessed prophet
   surely he would know
that she is but a sinner:
   he would not let her anoint him.

Jesus
Simon, as I am a guest,
   I have something to say,
by my troth:
   listen to me now.

Simon the Leper
Master, say right away,
   quickly without delay,
what is on your mind:
   I shall not refuse you.

Jesus
Once, in a certain place,
   there were two debtors
to a certain creditor, and I believe,
   one owed
five hundred pence in cash,
   and the other fifty.
He forgave them both
   for there was nothing to pay him with.

Tell me directly
which of them was more obliged
   to love this man.

Simon the Leper
I shall answer you straight away:
whoever is forgiven the most
   will love the most every time.

Jesus
Certainly, that is a sound judgement.
You see this woman:
   since I came to this house
you have not ordered my feet to be washed –
yet she has certainly washed them
   even with her tears.

And with her hair they were dried:
never a kiss did you give me,
   yet this woman never ceased
kissing my feet

    pup vr ol amme thu'm treys
      ha'm pen ol hy ru'm vras

    ha rak henna yn certan
    warbarth ol y feghas gvlan
      dethy hy y feyth gyfys
    ragh kemmys hy tho'm care
    the fay re wruk the sawye
      ke yn cres lauaraf thy's

Judas Iscariot
pyth yv an ethom vye
an onyment ker y skullye
    ef a galse bos guyrthys
a try cans dyner ha moy
ha re-na galser the rey
    the voghesegyon yn beys

[*hic surgant omnes et ambulant*]

IHS
na thegovgh sor yn colon
    worth neb a wra ow vre
rak ow thorment a the scon
    genogh na'm byve tryge
why a gyf bohosugyon
    pup vr warnogh ow karme
pan vynnogh agas honon
    why a gyl gul da thethe

en keth oynement scollyas
warnaf rak ow anclythyas
    hy a'n gruk dre kerense
puppenak ma fo redys
an awayl-ma taveth lys
    hy a vyth pur wyr neffre

12 'Sevyn yn ban' (Passio Christi)

    [*tunc abient retrorsum et cecident in terra
      et iterum interrogabit eos ihs dicens*]
    whythrough hetheu
    worthyf wharre
    me yw ihesu
    lyureugh whet
    pan theugh mar freth
    pyu a whyleugh

since I came to your house
  and she has anointed my head.

And therefore certainly
all her sins have been completely
  forgiven her
because she loved me so much.
Your faith has made you whole:
  I say to you, go in peace.

Judas Iscariot
What is the need
to waste the precious ointment?
  It could have been sold
for three hundred pence or more:
that money could have been given
  to the poor of the world.

[*Here let all rise, and they walk*]

Jesus
Do not bear anger in your heart
  against she who annoints me,
for my ordeal will come soon:
  I may not stay with you.
You will find the poor
  forever crying out to you:
you can do good to them
  whenever you like.

The same oil she poured
on me for my burial,
  she did for love.
Wherever this is read
certainly she will always
  be spoken of.

12 The Arrest of Jesus (Christ's Passion)

[*Then they shall go back and fall on the earth
  and again Jesus will ask them, saying:*]
  Today, look
  at me now:
  I am Jesus.
  But tell me,
  since you come so hastily,
  whom you seek.

Princeps Annas
    ihesu ru'm feyth
    a nazareth
    ny'n geuyth meugh

IHS
my a leuerys thywhy
ow bosa henna deffry
   ytho mar qureugh ov wylas
gesough ov thus vs gene
the ves quyt the tremene
   yn della yv both ow thas

Princeps Annas
a lorels re's bo drok lam
syttyough dalhennow yn cam
   a leuer y vos map dev
ha dun ny ganso toth bras
bys yn epscop syr cayfas
   yn gueth a prys er y gv

IIIs Tortor
me a'n dalhen fest yn tyn
ha gans ow dornow a'n guryn
   na sowenno

[*et tunc apprehendent eum*]

bys yn epscop fystynyn
warfor streche na wryllyn
   dun scon ganso

[*tunc petrus abscidit auriculum tortoris nomine malcus
   et dicit*]
  [*hic petrus scidit auriculum Malci*]

Petrus
arluth lauar dyssempys
thy'nny mar syv both the vreys
   ha bolenegoth a'n tas
my the wyskel gans clethe
nep vs worth the dalhenne
   scherews drok aga gnas

IIIIs Tortor Malcus
out cowethe gueresough
ow scoforn treghys myrough
   quyt the ves thyworth ow pen

Prince Annas
    Jesus of Nazareth,
    by my faith:
    he will get no bail.

Jesus
I have told you
that I was certainly him.
  Well, if you seek me,
let the people who are with me
leave here freely:
  that is the will of my Father.

Prince Annas
Louts, may misfortune befall you!
Take hold of the criminal
  who says he is the son of God,
and let us take him speedily
to the Bishop, Sir Caiaphas,
  to his disadvantage and his woe.

3rd Torturer
I shall take a tight hold of him,
and twist him with my fists
    so that he may not prosper.

[*And then they seize him*]

Let us hurry to the Bishop,
and not dawdle on the way:
    let us go quickly with him.

[*Then Peter cuts off the ear of the torturer called Malcus
    and says:*]
  [*Here Peter cuts off Malcus' ear*]

Peter
Lord, tell us straight away
if it is the will of your judgement
  and the will of the Father
that I strike with my sword
the man who is seizing you,
  the evil-minded scoundrel.

Fourth Torturer Malcus
Arrgh, friends, help!
Look at my ear, cut
  clean away from my head

gans onan a'y thyskyblon
ma an glovs dre ow colon
   rag gallarow hag anken

[*hic jhs accipiet auriculam malchi et sanabit eum*]

IHS
Gorteugh lymmyn gockyes
the'th scoforn wharre yehes
   sur my a re
abarth ow thas bynyges
th'y thyller arte glenes
   kepar del ve

a peder treyl the clethe
gorre yn y won arte
  yn levyr yma scrifys
dre clethe nep a vewo
ef a vyru yn sur dretho
  ha'n scryptor yw guyr yn wys

dar deseuos a wreugh why
na allaf ow thas pygy
  hag ef a thanfon a'n nef
dev-thek legyon yn vn ro
a eleth wharre thy'mmo
  ny'm nagh mar a'n pesaf ef
yn ketella ythyv reys
  del redyer yn lyes le
the vap den gothof yn beys
  hag entre th'y lowene

[*dicit ad Judeos*]
why re thueth thy'm gans arvow
gans fustow ha clythythyow
  kepar ha pan veue vy
an pure lader yn pow
pan dyskys yn eglusyow
  ny wrug den fyth ow sensy

[*tunc omnes discipuli eius fugient excepte iohanne
  cindone cooperto et petrus]
    [sequebatur eum a longe*]

Is Tortor
a traytor bras sur map gal
the gafus gynen yv mal
  kelmeugh warbarth y thyw-vreg

by one of his disciples.
The agony goes through my heart
   in sorrow and distress.

[*Here Jesus takes the ear of Malcus and will heal him*]

Jesus
Wait, fools!
I shall assuredly heal
   your ear,
for the sake of my blessed Father,
and to its place restore it
   as it was.

O Peter, turn your sword,
and put it in its sheath again.
   In the book it is written,
whoever shall live by the sword
shall certainly perish by it,
   and the Scripture is true indeed.

Do you not believe
that I could pray to my Father
   that He should send from Heaven
twelve legions of angels
all in a host to me directly.
   He would not deny me if I asked Him.
As it is written in many places,
   it is needful that in this way
the Son of Man should suffer in the world,
   and come into his joy.

[*He says to the Jews:*]
You have come to me with weapons,
with clubs and swords,
   as if I were
the worst thief in the land.
When I preached in the temples
   no one arrested me.

[*Then all his disciples flee apart from John,
   with his robe loosened, and Peter*]
     [*He will follow at a distance*]

1st Executioner
O great traitor, son of affliction,
we are eager to get hold of you.
   Bind his arms together

na allo dyank drewal
ef a'n geuyth war an chal
   den vythol na thovtyans peg

[*tunc IIs tortor accipiet iohannem apostolum
   et ipse relicto syndone nudus fugiet*]

IIIs Tortor
kyn fe the thyv-vregh mar bras
my a's kylm re sattenas
   warbarth auel lader pur
hag a'th wor bys yn cayphas
yn dyspyt the'th dev-lagas
   rag na fues kyns lymmyn fur

IIIIs Tortor
hembrynkeugh an harlot guas
ha gans ow wyp me a'n cheas
   ma kertho garwo y cam
ke yn rak wyth yffle gras
me a greys by god ys fas
   an harlot re thellos bram

13 'Mar a pythe dylyfrys' (Passio Christi)

Pilatus
mar a pythe dylyfrys
the ihesu pendra vyth gurys
   leuerough thy'mmo yn scon

Cayphas
yn pren crous bethens gorrys
ha treys ha dyulef kelmys
   ha guenys dre an golon

Pilatus
mara mennough yn della
leuerough dre py laha
   y coth thotho bos lethys

IIs Doctor
henna yn scon ny a wra
dre'n laha a'n pref yn ta
   dalleth cowyth me a'th pys

Is Doctor
by ny heuel dre lagha
   y coth thotho bos dampnys

so that he cannot escape:
He shall catch it on the jaw
   let no man doubt at all.

[*Then the second torturer seizes John
   and having left his robe behind he flees naked*]

3rd Executioner
However great be his arms
I shall bind them, by Satan,
   together like a thief
and shall send you to Caiaphas
in spite of your eyes
   for you were not wise before now.

4th Executioner
Bring this whoreson fellow,
I shall chase him with my whip
   so that he walks with crooked legs.
Go forward with evil grace.
I believe, by God's faith,
   the fellow has farted.

13 Prosecution and defence (Christ's Passion)

Pilate
If he is delivered,
what will be done to Jesus?
   Tell me quickly!

Caiaphas
He will be put on a wooden cross,
his feet and hands bound,
   and pierced through the heart.

Pilate
If that is what you wish
say by what law
   he should be killed.

2nd Doctor
That we shall do straight away,
to prove it in a trial.
   Begin, friend, I pray you.

1st Doctor
It doesn't seem that he should
   be condemned by the law.

tewel auel vn bobba
   a wruk pan fue acussys
nep a tawo yn pow-ma
   thyrag iug ny fyth iuggys
ytho dre pup reson da
   ny goth thotho bos crousys

IIs Doctor
er-the-pyn cousaf cowal
   marth a'm bues a'th lauarow
doctor the geusel mar dal
   gans an bobba casadow
yth ymwruk pur wyr hep fal
   dev ha den gans whethlow gow
thotho y coth by my chal
   kyn nagonse bos marow

Is Doctor
doctor nynsv henna man
   na ny il bos yn della
den the uerwel yn certan
   awos cous lauarow da
myreugh worth an vorvoran
   hanter pysk ha hanter den
y vos dev ha den yn wlan
   the'n keth tra-na crygyans ren

IIs Doctor
syr doctor lauaraf thy's
   ef a goth thotho merwel
an fer a fue dallethys
   dre tus vas berth yn tempel
ena rewlys o an beys
   ha lyes onan the wel
dretho y fue dystrewys
   yn mes y wrugh y teulel

Is Doctor
yma marth thy'm ahanas
   ty a aswon an scryptor
ty the vennas sowthanas
   lemmyn yn mes a pup for
yn chy dev ny goth marghas
   termyn vyth ol war nep cor
saw y worthye ef ha'y ras
   nep yv arluth tyr ha mor

He stayed silent like an idiot
   when he was accused.
And whoever stays silent before a judge
   in this country may not be tried.
So for good reason
   then he should not be crucified.

2nd Doctor
I shall speak against you in every case:
   I marvel at your remarks,
Doctor, to speak so blindly,
   about the dirty idiot.
He made himself out, unmistakably,
   with lying tales to be God and man.
By my jawbone, he should
   be killed, even though he remains silent.

1st Doctor
Doctor, that is not right at all,
   nor can it be so,
that a man should die
   for saying good things.
Look at the mermaid,
   half fish and half man.
Let us believe the same thing of him,
   That he is clearly God and man.

2nd Doctor
Sir Doctor, I'm telling you
   he should die.
The market was started
   by good men in the temple,
there the world was orderly
   and many a one better off for it;
it was destroyed by him,
   and he threw it out.

1st Doctor
I marvel at you
   who know the Scriptures,
that you should want to let Satan
   into every place.
It is not right to set up stall in God's house
   at any time at all,
rather worship him and his grace,
   who is lord of land and sea.

IIs Doctor
pur wyr certan an den-ma
   lyes den re wruk treyle
agan laha ef yma
   pup ur ow contradye
may coth thotho yn tor-ma
   bones marow hep lettye
ol an doctors yn bys-ma
   byth ny yllons y sawye

Is Doctor
thotho ef nyn sos cothman
   del heuel thy'mmo yn wys
conciens da na syv certan
   lathe den nag yw cablys
ny glowys drok nag onan
   ef the wul bythqueth yn beys
trueth vye den yw gulan
   falslych y vones dyswrys

IIs Doctor
lyes guyth y wruk bostye
   thy'so gy del lauara
terry the'n dor an temple
   yn try geth y wul arta
maga ta bythqueth del fue
   ha henna neffre ny wra
y vevnens nynsus guythe
   na vo marow yn tor-ma

Is Doctor
guryoneth a reys bos dreys
   aberueth yn mater-ma
ha lendury kekeffrys
   rag ymsywye y a wra
yn certan mar a pyth gurys
   sur warlergh an keth dev-ma
ny fyth ef neffre dyswrys
   dre pur reson vynytha

ty a fyn y gafos ef
   del heuel thy'mmo lethys
nep a'n latho dev goef
   the den vyth ny wruk trespys
myschef a goth tyn ha cref
   rak y wos a vyth scollys
rag ef yv map dev a nef
   del leuaraf an guyr thy's

2nd Doctor
Indeed, this man certainly
   has turned many to him.
He constantly
   flouts our laws,
and this time he should
   be killed and no doubt about it.
And all the doctors in the world
   cannot save him.

1st Doctor
You are not a friend to him,
   it seems to me, in truth:
it is not honourable, indeed,
   to kill an innocent man.
Nobody heard that he ever did
   any evil in the world.
It is a pity that a man so pure
   should be falsely destroyed.

2nd Doctor
Many a time he boasted
   to you, as I say,
that he would raze the Temple to the ground,
   and in three days would rebuild it
as good as ever,
   and that he could not do.
There is no saving him
   from being killed now.

1st Doctor
Truth must be brought
   to bear in this matter,
and honesty too,
   for they follow one another.
Certainly, if it is to be done,
   according to these two,
he will never be destroyed
   on grounds of pure reason.

It seems to me
   you want to have him killed:
whoever kills him, God have mercy on him!
   He has done harm to no man:
but harm will come sharp and strong
   of his blood that is shed,
for he is the Son of the God of Heaven,
   and I tell you the truth.

IIs Doctor
me a leuer an guyr thy's
   guel yv y vos ef marow
ys bos an popel kellys
   ha dampnys the tewolgow
argye na moy thy'n ny reys
   na keusel na moy gerryow
a'n rewlens ef an iustis
   hag ol an comners a'n pow

syr pylat nans yv hy prys
whar ihesu cryst a rey brueys
   rak y iugge
ny a vyn the requyrye
ha warbarth ol sur crye
   crucifige

[*et dicunt omnes iudei crucifige*]

14 'Ellas a cryst'(Passio Christi)

ellas a cryst ow map ker
   yn myr payn pan y'th welaf
ellas dre kueth yn klamder
   the'n dor prag na ymwhelaf
dre ov map pyth yv ow cher
   pup vr ol y'n bynygaf
ellas ny won py le y trygaf
    eghan
   rag y fynner
   mara kyller
   gans paynys mer
    ow dyswul glan

[*hic maria dabit obviam Jhu in porta civitatis*]

ogh govy ellas ellas
guelas ov map mar dyflas
   gans tebel wesion dyghtys
a vap the gueth ru'm lathas
na allaf gueles yn fas
   kymmys daggrow re olys
govy ny won pendra wraf
gallas ow colon pur claf
   dre pryderow
ny allaf seuel yn fas
war ow treys ellas ellas
   rak galarow

2nd Doctor
And I shall tell you the truth:
   it is better for him to die
than the people should be lost
   and condemned to darkness.
It is fruitless to argue more
   or speak further.
Let the magistrate make a ruling,
   and all the common people of the country.

Sir Pilate, it is now time
to pass judgement on Jesus Christ,
   to sentence him.
We want you,
certainly to cry out all together
   'Crucify him!'

[*And all the Jews say 'Crucify him!'*]

14 The Lament of Mary (Christ's Passion)

Alas, O Christ, my dear son,
   that I should see you in such pain!
Alas, fainting with grief
   why do I not cast myself upon the ground?
What state has my son brought me to?
   Every hour I shall bless Him.
Alas, I do not know where I shall live!
     Woe,
   for they wish
   to destroy me entirely,
   if possible
     in great agony.

[*Here Mary shall meet Jesus in the gate of the city*]

O woe is me, alas, alas!
To see my son so foully
   treated by evil men!
O son, your sorrows have killed me:
I cannot see,
   for I have wept so many tears.
Woe is me, I do not know what I shall do!
My heart is very sick
   with care:
I cannot stand well, in faith
on my feet, alas, alas,
   for pain.

arlythy caradowyon
dreugh thy'm ow map cuf colon
   ha gesough vy th'y handle

[*Maria accipiet Jhm*]

ellas rak y gallarow
yensen ov bones marow
   yn della y voth a pe
ellas a vap myghtern y'th tron
ellas gueles tol y'th colon
     marow na vef
ellas bones the treys squerdys
ol the yscarn dyscavylsys
    tel y'th dyvluef

sav bytegyns pan y'th welaf
bos hep hyreth my ny allav
   ha nyn syv marth
myres y gorf del yv squerdys
yscarn map dev dygavelsys
    ha dev warbarth

a ihesu ow map ellas
yssyw hemma trueth
  bos the corf ker golyys
gans tebel popel ogh ogh
namnag yv ow colon trogh
   rak galarow ha peynys

my a yl bos morethek
guelas ow map mar anwhek
    dyghtys del yv
nep yv arluth luen a ras
gouy vyth ellas ellas
    ragos ihesu
a thu guyn ov bys neffre
the gorf ker galles handle
   rag map dev os me a grys

Dear Lords,
bring me my dearly-beloved son
   and let me touch Him.

[*Mary will take Jesus*]

Alas, for His pains!
I would wish myself dead
   if that was what He wanted.
Alas, O son, King on your throne!
Alas, to see the hole in your heart!
   I wish I were dead!
Alas, that your feet are torn,
and your bones dislocated,
   and holes in your hands!

Nevertheless when I see you,
I cannot stop yearning,
   and no wonder,
to see your torn body,
the bones of the Son of God dislocated,
   and of God too.

O Jesus, my son, alas!
What great sorrow
   that your dear body is wounded
by an evil people, oh! oh!
My heart is almost broken
   for your pain and agony.

I can mourn
to see my son so unkindly
   treated,
who is Lord, full of grace.
Woe is me forever, alas, alas!
   For you, Jesus!
O blessed Lord, I am honoured for ever
to be able to touch your dear body,
   for I know you are the Son of God.

15 'Why pryncys a'n dewolow' (Resurrexio Domini)

[*hic spiritus uenit ad portas inferni*]

Spiritus Christi
why pryncys a'n dewolow
scon egereugh an porthow
py mar ny wreugh y fyth guow
   yn certan kyns tremene
rak an porthow hep dyweth
a vyth ygerys yn weth
sur may thello aberueth
   an myghtern a lowene

Lucifer
ny dal thy's scornye gyne
pyv myghtern a lowene
   a thesempys thy'm lauar

Spiritus
arluth cref ha galosek
hag yn bateyl barthesek
   rak henna ygor hep mar
     why pryncis

Lucifer
ny dal thy's scornye gyne
pyv myghtern a lowene
   thy'mmo lauar
byth ny thueth agy the'n yet
ke yn kergh dywhans
   na strech hep mar

Spiritus
arluth gallosek ha cref
worto an porthow ny sef
   yn certan kyns tremene

16 'Lowene thy's syr pilat' (Resurrexio Domini)

[*et tunc eant ad pilatum
et dicit IIIIs miles*]
IVs Miles
lowene thy's syr pilat
awos bos ny peswar smat
   guythe an beth ny ylsyn
desefsen dotho ry what

15 The Harrowing of Hell (The Resurrection of Our Lord)

[*Here the Spirit comes to the gates of Hell*]

The Spirit of Christ
You, princes of devils,
open the gates quickly,
for if you do not there will surely
   be trouble before long,
for the eternal gates
will also be opened
so that the King of Joy
   will certainly enter.

Lucifer
It is no good trifling with me.
Who is the King of Joy?
   Quickly, tell me.

Spirit
A strong and powerful lord,
and wondrous in battle:
   therefore, you princes, open up
     without delay.

Lucifer
It is no good trifling with me.
Who is the King of Joy?
   Tell me!
You will never pass through my gate:
Go away quickly, straight away.
   And do not delay.

Spirit
The gates will not withstand
a powerful and strong lord:
   certainly before long.

16 Pilate and the Sepulchre Guards (The Resurrection of Our Lord)

[*And then let them go to Pilate
   and the Fourth Soldier says:*]
4th Soldier
Joy to you, Lord Pilate!
Though we are four lads,
   we could not guard the grave.
We wanted to strike him,

thy'nny ef a wruk an prat
   hag a fyes thyworthy'n

Pilatus
out warnough fals marregion
pyth yw an whethlow ha'n son
   a glewaf aberth yn pow
re vahun y tof yn weth
mar sywe lyddrys a'n beth
   why a's byth ages ancow

Is Miles
pilat the gous nynsyw vas
nep na'n synso y sylwyas
   a thu goef
me a'n guelas dre mur ras
a'n beth gans ov dev lagas
   ow mos the'n nef

Pilatus
tau harlot out of my sygth
rag mar ny'n kefough a plygth
   sur why a'n pren
the'n beth pan y ges gorrys
thy'mmo why a thethywys
   na'n laddro den

IIs Miles
me a leuer thy's rak clem
dyswe thy'nny nychodem
   ha ioseph baramathya
ha ny a thyswe yn weth
an corf a sytseugh yn beth
   yw ihesu map maria

Pilatus
ty was geyler kesadow
ygor scon an darasow
   ha heth an prysners yn mes
otte omma alwhethow
ha mar ny wreth the ancow
   me a vyth by god ys pes

Carcerator
drew hy thy'mmo hep lettye
ha me a's ygor wharre
   an darasow agan naw
na greseugh bos treyson gures

but he tricked us,
   and fled from us.

Pilate
Out with you, false knights!
What are the tales and rumours
   I hear about the country?
By Mahomet, I swear,
that if he is stolen from the grave,
   you will die.

1st Soldier
Pilate, your talk is pointless:
whoever does not count him Saviour,
    will be sorrowful, for he is God!
I saw him, through great grace,
with my own two eyes, ascending to Heaven
    from the grave.

Pilate
Be silent, villain, get out of my sight,
for if you do not, I swear
   you will pay for it.
When you put him in the grave,
you promised me
    that no man would take him.

2nd Soldier
I say to you in defence,
show us Nicodemus
   and Joseph of Arimathea,
and we will show you
the body that you put in the grave,
   of Jesus, the Son of Mary.

Pilate
You fellow, filthy gaoler,
open the doors quickly
   and fetch the prisoners.
Here are the keys,
and if you do not I shall be your death,
   by God's peace!

Gaoler
Bring them to me straight away
and I shall open them soon
   our nine doors.
If you think that we have betrayed you,

guel yv thywhy why mones
   ages honan the'n thev vaw

[*et tunc ipse eat ad carcerem et non inueniet eos
   et dicit pilatus*]

Pilatus
ny geusyth mes a reson
ple thesos ioseph caugyon
   ha'th cowyth nychodemus
a out ple ma an prysnes
mar ny's cafaf scon thu'm dues
   ty a fyth drok oremus

Garcon
a syre na blamyowg ny
   a nyngese alwheow
warbarth yn ages guyth why
   ha dyen an darasow

Pilatus
guyr a geusyth ievody
   hem yv marth hep falladow
rak an darasow deffry
   dyen ol yns ha'n fosow

marregyon theugh ny won blam
rak thy'mmo y fue scham
   gul drok thywhy
an prysners galsons yn weth
ese yn dan naw alweth
   ny torsans chy

IIIs Miles
henna ny a vyn notye
le may thyllyn yn pup le
   certan y vos dasserhys
kepar del sevys a'n beth
the'n nef gans mur a eleth
   ny th'y weles yskynnys

Pilatus
teweugh awos lucyfer
a henna na geuseugh ger
   pypenagol a wharfo
ha why a's byth gobar bras
penryn yn weth ha hellas
   me a's re theugh yn luen ro

it is better you go yourself
   to those two fellows.

[*And then he shall go to the prison and not find them
   and Pilate will say:*]
Pilate
You do not speak unreasonably:
where are you Joseph, you monstrosity,
   and your comrade Nicodemus?
Oh, out, where are the prisoners?
If I do not find them, come to me immediately
   and you will badly need to say your prayers.

Servant
Sir, do not blame us.
   Were the keys not
in your keeping,
   and the doors secure?

Pilate
I admit you speak the truth:
   this is a miracle for sure,
for the doors were indeed secure
   and the walls too.

Knights, I do not blame you
for it would be dishonourable of me
   to do evil unto you.
The prisoners have gone
that were under nine keys:
   and they did not break out.

3rd Soldier
We shall make that known
wherever we go, everywhere,
   – for he has surely risen again –
how he rose from the grave
with many angels to Heaven,
   and that we saw him risen.

Pilate
Be silent, for Lucifer's sake!
Do not speak a word of this,
   whatever may come to pass,
and you shall have as a great reward
Penryn and also Helston,
   I shall give them to you entirely as a gift.

IVs Miles
aban osa mar gortes
   ny a wra del leueryth
ha pup onan ol iammes
   neffre parys thy's a vyth

17 'Nep a wruk nef' (Resurrexio Domini)

Mar. Mag
nep a wruk nef
   del eth yn beth
war y lyrgh ef
   mur ow hyreth
cryst clew ov lef
   pesaf y weth
may fy gynef
   orth ow dyweth

arluth ihesu
   ro thy'm an gras
par may feyf gvyw
   the gafos spas
gynes hythev
   sur yn nep plas
may bome vu
   ha guel a'th fas

del os formyas
   the'n nef ha'n lur
ha dysprynnyas
   thy'nny pup vr
cryst ow sylwyas
   clev mar a'th dur
thy's daryvas
   del garsen mur

dre mur hyreth
   ythof pur squyth
ha'm corf the weth
   yscarn ha lyth
ple ma haneth
   a wor den vyth
may caffen wheth
   cryst len a wryth

[*vadit ad ortum*]

4th Soldier
Since you are so generous
　we shall do as you say,
and each of us will be
　forever at your service.

17　Mary Magdalene and Jesus (The Resurrection of Our Lord)

Mary Magdalene
He who made Heaven,
　He who went into the grave,
great is my longing
　for Him.
Christ, hear my voice.
　I pray too
that you may be with me
　at my end.

Lord Jesus,
　give me the grace
that I may be worthy
　to have a place
with you today
　surely in some place,
that I may behold
　and see your face.

As you are the Creator
　of Heaven and Earth,
and our Redeemer
　every hour,
Christ, my Saviour,
　hear me if you care,
as I should greatly love
　to talk to you.

I am worn out
　by great longing,
and my body too,
　bone and limb.
Where is there tonight
　anyone who knows
where I might yet find
　Christ full of virtue?

[*She goes to the garden*]

Ortolanus (Jesus)
a vynyn ryth
  py le yth eth
rak kueth pygyth
  garme a wreth
na ol na scryg
  nep a whyleth
syghsys y treys
  gans the thyv pleth

Mar. Mag
arluth dremas
  mar cothas myr
cryst ow sylwyas
  ple ma the wyr
er y whylas
  rof thy's ow tyr
ihesu map ras
  clew ow dysyr

Ortolanus
a maria
  del won the bos
berth yn bys-ma
  onan a'y uos
a'n guelesta
  a thyragos
a alsesta
  y aswonfos

Mar. Mag.
galsen yn ta
  the'n kense fu
map maria
  henwys ihesu
rak na'n guela
  thy'm a nep tu
kueth a portha
  ny gansen tru

[*et tunc demonstrabat latus ejus ad mariam mag. et dicit:*]
Ortolanus
maria myr
  ov pym woly
crys my the wyr
  the thasserghy
thy's y whon gras

Gardener (Jesus)
O woeful woman,
   where are you going?
You pray out of grief,
   you cry out.
Do not weep or cry,
   He whom you seek,
you dried his feet
   with your two plaits.

Mary Magdalene
Lord, good man,
   if you have chanced to see,
Christ my Saviour,
   where He is indeed.
To find Him
   I should give you my land:
Jesus, Son of Grace,
   hear my longing.

Gardener
O Mary,
   as I know you are
of this world,
   and one of His blood:
if you saw Him
   before you
would you
   recognise Him?

Mary Magdalene
I would indeed,
   the former shape
of the Son of Mary,
   called Jesus:
for if I saw Him
   anywhere about
I would bear my grief,
   and not sing woe.

[*And then he will show his side to Mary Magdalene and say:*]
Gardener
Mary, look at
   my five wounds.
Believe that I did indeed
   rise again.
Thank you

    rag the thesyr
ioy yn ow gulas
    y fyth pur wyr

Mar. Mag.
a ker arluth
    eth yn grous pren
thy'm ny thogough
    amme the'th penn
me a'th pysse
    a lauasos
lemmyn amme
    vn wyth the'th tros

[*mulier noli me tangere*]

Ortolanus
a vynyn ryth
    na tuche vy nes
na na wra gruyth
    na fo the les
      ny thueth an prys
er na gyllyf
    the'n nef thu'm tas
may tewhyllyf arte thu'm gulas
      the gous worthys

Mar. Mag.
cryst clew of lef
    lauar an vr
may tuth a'n nef
    arte the'n lur
      the cous worthy'n
the thyskyblyon
    yv serrys mur
ha'n yethowon
    gans nerth pup vr
      yge kerhyn

Ortolanus
o maria
    lauar thethe
pur wyr me a
    the galile
      del leuerys
ha dres henna
    porth cof lauar
confort yn ta

    for your concern.
You will indeed have
    joy in my country.

Mary Magdalene
O dear Lord
    who went on the wooden cross,
I would not
    kiss your head
but I would ask you
    to allow me
now to kiss
    your feet just once.

[*Woman, touch me not*]

Gardener
O woeful woman,
    do not touch me at all.
No, it is useless
    and of no advantage.
        The time has not yet come
for me to go
    to my Father in Heaven,
whence I will return to my country
        to speak to you.

Mary Magdalene
Christ, hear my voice,
    tell me the hour
when you will come from Heaven
    to the Earth again
        to speak to us.
Your disciples
    are very sad,
and the Jews are gathered
    with great strength every hour
        round about them.

Gardener
O Mary,
    tell them:
In truth I shall go
    to Galilee
        as I said.
And, besides that,
    remember, speak
good comfort well:

   thy'mmo pedar
    mur yu kyrys

18   'Ow dewolow duegh gynef' (Resurrexio Domini)

Lucifer
ow dewolow duegh gynef
 warparth ol me agas peys
the kerghas gans y enef
 corf pylat gans mur a grys
yn tan whyflyn ef a sef
 ha paynys neffre a pys
ha'y gan a vyth ogh goef
 the'n bys-ma pan fue genys

Belsebuk
an corf-ma mylyges yw
 ytho ef a goth thy'nny
the vos yn dor nynsyw guyw
 nag yn dour nag yn hyly

Sathanas
yn dour tyber ef a fue
 yn geler horn gorrys dovn
ha myl den ef a wruk due
 yn dour-na rak vyth hag ovn

Belsebuk
gorhel vyth ny tremene
 an for-na na fe buthys
ny thyndylas lowene
 lemmyn yn tan bos cuthys

Lucifer
a'n dour y fue drehevys
 ha dreys arte the'n tyr mur
hag yn gorhel bras gorrys
 gynen may teffo the'n lur

Sathanas
goyl ha guern thotho ordnys
 may thelle yn mes a'n wlas
the vn carn y fue teulys
 par may cothas yn ow bras

Belsebuk
an carna a ygoras
 del o destnys thotho ef

Peter is greatly loved
  by me.

18   Pilate taken to Hell (The Resurrection of Our Lord)

Lucifer
My devils, gather
  together, I ask you,
to fetch along with his soul
  the body of Pilate with much strength.
In roaring fire he will remain,
  and in agonies that will last forever,
and his song shall be, oh, misery
  that he was ever born into this world.

Beelzebub
This body is accursed
  and so it is ours by right.
It is not fit to be in the earth,
  nor in water nor brine.

Satan
He has been put deep in an iron coffin,
  in Tiber's water
and a thousand men have perished
  in that water from fear and terror.

Beelzebub
Not a ship would pass
  this way and not be sunk.
He did not deserve bliss
  but rather to be covered in fire.

Lucifer
He was raised from the water,
  and taken onto dry land
and put in a great ship
  to come down to us.

Satan
Sail and mast were ordained for him
  to leave the country.
He was thrown onto a certain rock
  where he fell into my trap.

Beelzebub
That rock opened up
  as was fated,

rak pur wyr yth hepcoras
   dre y ober glascor nef
eno ny a'n receuas
   vthyk yw clewas y lef
tan ha mok ha potvan bras
   yn carna neffre y sef

Lucifer
potvan pup vr ha rynny
   skrymba bras a'n dewolow
ef a'n gevyth genen ny
   a pup drok maner ponow

Sathanas
ha ty corf bras mylyges
   the yfarn gans the enef
gynen y fythyth tynnes
   the cane a vyth goef

Belsebuk
lemmyn pup ol settyes dorn
   yn keth schath-ma th'y tenne
ha ty tulfryk pen pusorn
   dalleth thy'nny cane

Tulfryk
ye re gymmy tol ow guen
rak yn mes yma y pen
   sur pur hyr aves thu'm tyn
belsebuk ha sattanas
kenough why faborden bras
   ha me a can trebyl fyn

[*et sic finitur mors pilati*]

for surely he rejected
  by his deeds the Kingdom of Heaven.
There we received him,
  loud his voice is heard,
amidst fire and smoke and great heat,
  he will remain in that rock for ever.

Lucifer
Heat every hour of the day, and horror,
  great clamour from the devils:
he shall suffer every kind
  of cruel pain with us.

Satan
And you, great accursed body,
  your soul will be dragged
to Hell by us: your song
  will be, miserable me!

Beelzebub
Now let everybody set their hand
  to the boat to draw it in.
And you, Tulfryk, head of chorus,
  start singing for us.

Tulfryk
Yes, may you kiss my arse,
for his head is sticking
  a long way out of my arsehole.
Beelzebub and Satan,
sing a great bass
  and I shall sing a fine treble.

[*And thus ends the death of Pilate*]

Selections from Pascon agan Arluth (c. 1450)

19 'Tays ha mab han speris sans'

Tays ha mab han speris sans
wy abys a evn golon
Re wronte zeugh gras ha whans
ze wolsowas y basconn
Ha zymmo gras ha skyans
ze zerevas par lauarow
may fo ze thu se worthyans
ha sylwans zen enevow

Suel a vynno bos sylwys
golsowens ow lauarow
a ihesu del ve helheys
war an bys avel carow
Ragon menough rebekis
ha dyspresijs yn harow
yn grows gans kentrow fastis
peynys bys pan ve marow

Du sur dre virtu an tas
zynny a zyttyas gweras
En mab dre skyans bras
pan gemert kyg a werhas
han sperys sans leun a ras
dre y zadder may fe guris
Gozaff paynys pan vynnas
neb na ylly gull peghes

An dus vas a zeserya
zeze gulas nef o kyllys
gans aga garm hag olua
ihesus crist a ve mevijs
may fynnas dijskynna
yn gwerhas ha bos genys
gans y gyk agan perna
arluth du gwyn agan bys

Ihesu crist mur gerense
ze vab den a zyswezas
an vghelder may zese
zen bys desykynnas
Pehadoryon rag perna
o desevijs dre satnas
rag henna gorzyn neffra

Selections from The Passion of Our Lord (c. 1450)

19   Father and Son and Holy Ghost

> Father and Son and the Holy Spirit
> pray with a righteous heart
> that He may grant you grace, and long
> to listen to his passion,
> and grant me grace and knowledge
> to recall his words,
> that there may be praise to God,
> and the salvation of souls.
>
> Whosoever would be saved,
> let them listen to my words
> about Jesus, how He was hunted
> in the world like a deer,
> often punished for us
> and roughly abused,
> on the cross with nails fixed,
> tormented till He was dead.
>
> God certainly, by the power of the Father
> wrought help for us,
> the Son through great wisdom
> when He was born of a virgin,
> and the Holy Spirit full of grace,
> through His grace when He was made,
> to suffer pains when He chose,
> He who could not sin.
>
> Good people longed for
> the land of Heaven, which was lost.
> With their cries and lamentation
> Jesus Christ was so moved
> that He decided to come down
> into a virgin and be born,
> to redeem us with his flesh:
> Lord God, blessed are we!
>
> Jesus Christ showed
> great love for mankind.
> From the height where He was
> He came down to the world
> to redeem sinners
> deceived by Satan.
> For that, let us worship

ihesus neb agan pernas
An peynys a wotheuys
ny ve ragtho y honan
lemmyn rag pobyll an bys
pan vons y kefis mar wan
an ioull ze adam kewysys
an aval te kemer tan
a vell du y fethyth gurys
pan provas nyn io man

Warlergh mab den ze begha
reson prag y fe prynnys
yw ihesus crist ze ordna
yn neff y vonas tregys
y vos kyllys ny vynna
y doull ganso o tewlys
rag henna ze bob dyzgthya
forth a rug the vos sylwys

Kyn na goff den skentyll pur
par dell won lauaraff zys
yn tre du ha pehadur
accord del ve kemerys
rag bonas gonn pegh mar vur
mayn yn treze a ve gurys
eff o crist a theth dhen leur
mab du ha den yw kyffris

Ragon y pesys y das
oll y sor may fe gevys
gans y gorff dre beynys bras
agan pegh may fo prennys
mab marea leun a ras
oll y voth a ve clewys
ha kymmys a theseryas
zozo eff a ve grontis

20 'Dew zen crist a zanvonas'

Dew zen crist a zanvonas
ze berna boys ha dewas
an keth rena a spedyas
han soper a ve paris
crist worth an goyn a warnyas
dre onan bos treson guris
arluth du y a armas
py a yl henna bonas
Ihesus crist a worthebas

Jesus who redeemed us.
The agonies He suffered,
were not for himself,
but rather for the people of the world
who were found to be so weak.
The Devil spoke to Adam:
'The apple, take it,
you will be made godlike.'
But when he tried it, it was not like that at all.

When mankind sinned,
the reason that he was redeemed
was that Jesus Christ ordained
that he should dwell in Heaven.
He did not wish mankind to be lost.
His plan was laid,
to that end He prepared
a way to salvation.

Although I am not a very learned man,
I shall tell you what I know:
a reconciliation was made
between God and sinner.
Because our sin was so great,
an intermediary was made:
and He was Christ who came down,
the Son of God and a man also.

For our sake he prayed to His Father
that all His anger might be assuaged,
and with His body through great pain,
our sins might be forgiven.
The will of the Son of Mary,
full of grace, was heard,
and all that He desired,
was granted.

20 The Last Supper

Christ sent two men
to buy food and drink.
The two carried out their task
and the supper was made ready.
At the supper, Christ warned
that one would betray him.
'Lord God!' they cried,
'Who can it be?'
Jesus Christ answered,

ow tybbry genen yma
pup onan ol a ylwys
arluth du yv me hena
ha ihesus a worzebys
am scudel dybbry a wra
gwef vyth pan veva genys
a dor y vam zen bysma

Du a sonas an bara
ze rag y abestely
ow horf a ve yw henma
yn meth crist sur ragough wy
pernys a berth yn bysma
dyspresys haneth a vyth
an deppro gans cregyans da
gober tek eff an geuyth

Han gwyn esa war en foys
ef a rannas yn treza
yn meth crist hema yw goys
evough why pur cheryta
ganz dour gorris yn bazon
y wolhas aga garrow
hyyseas ys gureugh pur wyn
dell vynna du caradow

Henna pedyr a sconyas
ihesus ze wolhy y dreys
taw pedyr te ne wozas
yn meth crist pan dra raf zys
mar nyth wolhaff dre ow gras
yn nef ny vezyth tregis
ynmeth pedyr zym na as
troys na leyff na vo golhys

Ihesus crist leun a bete
a leueris zen dowzek
wy yw glan a bub fylte
mas nyn iough ol da na whek
bos Iudas ef a wozye
pur hager ha molozek
an ioul ynno re drecse
may fo gweth agis cronek

In delma crist pan wresse
ze iudas y leueris
te ke yn vn fystene
ze voth may fo colenwys

'He is eating with us.'
Every one called out,
'Lord God, is it me?'
And Jesus answered,
'He shall eat from my bowl.
Woe to him that he was born
from the womb of his mother into this world.'

God blessed the bread
in front of his apostles:
'This is my body,'
said Christ, 'certainly for your sake,
brought into this world.
Tonight it will be abused:
whosoever shall eat it in good faith,
he shall have a fair reward.'

And He shared between them
the wine that was on the table.
Said Christ, 'This is my blood:
drink it for love's sake.'
With water placed in a basin
He washed their legs.
He made them very clean
as beloved God ordained.

Peter refused to let
Jesus wash his feet:
'Be silent, Peter, you do not know,'
said Christ, 'what I shall do for you.
If I do not wash you by my grace,
you will not dwell in Heaven.'
Said Peter, 'Do not leave
a foot or hand unwashed.'

Jesus Christ, full of pity
said to the twelve,
'You are clean of every vileness,
but not every one is good or sweet.'
He knew that Judas was
very hideous and accursed.
The devil dwelt within him
so he was worse than a toad.

When Christ had finished
he said to Judas,
'Go, hurry
that your wish be fulfilled,

rag an termyn re deve
may fyth an begel kyllys
ha chechys yn tre dewle
han deves ze ves fijs

Kyn fallens ol me a veth
yn meth pedyr yth seruys
yn meth crist yn nos haneth
kyns ys boys colyek clewys
pedyr te am nagh tergweth
bythqueth arluth na vef zys
yn meth pedyr tan ow feth
nyth nahaff kyn fen lezys

In meth crist a ban rug zeugh
ternoth fernoth ow holye
daver vyth wy ny zecsyugh
ze worre trevyth ynne
betegens wy ny wozough
pan dra ezom agan be
arluth guyr aleuersough
y a gowsys yn treze

Mas lemmyn rys yv porris
bataylea kyns es coske
an geffo pows as gwyrzyns
ha zozo pernas cleze
sur yma dew zyn parys
y a leueris whare
hen yw lour na moy ny rys
du a leueris arte

21 'Han zewna pan vons squyth'

Han zewna bys pan vons squyth
war crist y fons ow cronkye
manna geve goth na leyth
na gesa worth y grevye
na war y gorff wek tam vyth
pur wyr henna o mur byte
ha whath moy wy a glewyth
a dormont crist del wharfe

In treze avel tus fol
garlont sperne a ve dyzgthtys
ha dre aga husyll ol
war y ben a ve gorris
may zo squardijs a dro ol

for the time has come
when the shepherd is lost
and placed under arrest,
and the sheep dispersed.'

'Although all others fail, I shall be,'
said Peter, 'in your service.'
Said Christ, 'This very night
before the cock is heard,
Peter, you will deny three times
that I was ever Lord to you.'
Said Peter, 'By my faith,
I shall not deny you even though I be killed.'

Said Christ, 'Since I made you
follow me, half-naked and barelegged.
You hadn't even a receptacle
to put anything in.
Nevertheless, you do not know
what need we had.'
'Lord, you said the truth.'
they said among themselves.

'But now it is necessary
to fight before sleeping.
Whoever has a robe, let him sell it
and buy a sword for himself.'
'Certainly, we have two ready'
they said soon.
'That is enough: no more is necessary.'
God said again.

21   The Scourging of Christ

And these two beat Christ
until they were worn out,
so that He had neither vein nor limb
that did not grieve Him,
nor any part of His sweet body.
Very truly, that was a great shame,
and yet you shall hear more
of the torment of Christ as it came to pass.

Amongst them, like madmen,
a garland of thorns was made,
and all advised
that it be placed on His head,
so that it was torn all round.

ay ben y oys o scolijs
hag ynno fest luhas tol
gans an dreyn a ve tellys

Gans den scyntyll a wozye
me a glewas leuerell
an arlont y ze denne
war y ben gans kymmys nell
ma teth an dreyn ha cropye
zen nempynnyon dre an tell
henno payyn a vur vylte
esa crist ow cozevell

A vyne gwarze yben
war y gorff bys yn y droys
squardijs oll o y grohen
hag ef cuzyz yn y woys
mur o an payn dar ken
ze vab du mur y alloys
del lever zyn an levar
kymmys payn ny ve ay oys

I a wyskis crist gant queth
han purpur rych o dyskis
rag y thry zen dor gans meth
yn ges y a leueris
mur a onour te afyth
te yw mygtern cvrvnys
hag yn y leff zyghow yn weth
gwelen wyn a ve gorris

Hag y thens ze ben dowlyn
hag y kewsens ze scornye
hag a gamma aga meyn
pup onon rag y eysye
lowene zys te yw zeyn
mygtern rys yw ze worzye
hen o zozo mur a bayn
may zezens worth y ranne

Onon gans an keth welen
yn leyff crist a ve gorris
an gwyskis lasche war an pen
bom pur gewar desezys
ha buxow leas hepken
ha tummasow kekyffris
ze gryst a dro ze zewen
gans nerth bras a ve syttis

From his head blood was shed
and in it there was many a hole
where the thorns pierced.

I heard it said by
a wise man who knew
that the garland was drawn
onto His head with so much force
that the thorns came to penetrate
the brains through the holes.
That was a pain of great vileness
that Christ suffered.

From the very top of His head
to his feet,
all His skin was torn,
and He was covered in His own blood.
Great was the pain beyond any other
for the Son of God,
as the Book tells us:
there was never such pain ever.

They dressed Christ in a cloth
and the rich purple was stripped off
to bring Him low for shame.
In mockery they said,
'Great honour you will have.
You are a crowned king.'
And in His right hand
a white staff was placed.

And they went on their knees
and spoke in mockery
and made faces at Him,
every one to scorn Him:
'Joy to you, you are
our king: we must worship you.'
It caused Him much pain
that they were rending it.

One struck Him a blow on the head
with the same staff
that was put in the hand of Christ,
a carefully aimed blow
and many buffets without cause
and strokes as well
on Christ's jaws
were struck with great strength.

Colon den a yll crakye
a vynha prest predery
an paynys bras an geve
han dyspyth heb y dylly
hag ol rag ze gerense
ihesus crist as gozevy
lymmyn gorqvyth y gare
ha gwyth denatar na vy

22 'Rag porrys rys o zozo'

Rag porrys rys o zozo
gase y ben zegregy
rag galse glan ze worto
y woys bewe ny ylly
war tu hay vam an pewo
y ben a vynnas synsy
hay eneff eth a nozo
gans garm eyn hag vghel gry

Ryp crows Ihesus y zeze
vn den henwys sentury
a vernans crist pan welse
kynuver tra marthusy
han enef del dascorse
erbyn natar gans vn cry
y leuerys heb scornye
hem yw mab du yredy
ha leas ganso ene
dozo a zuk dustuny

Nango hanter dyth yn wlas
po moy del yma scryfis
dorgris esa ha lughas
han tewolgow kekyffrys
veyll an tempell a squardyas
yn tre dew zen dor cozys
ena yn weth y torras
en veyn o creff ha calys

En bezow yn lower le
a pert a ve egerys
han corfow esa ynne
a ve yn ban dreheyvys
hag eth poran zen cyte
gans luas y fons gwelys

A man's heart would break
constantly to dwell
on the great pains He suffered
and the unearned contempt,
and all for love of you
Jesus Christ suffered it:
make sure you love Him now
and beware of ingratitude.

22   The Death of Christ

For He was compelled
to let His head hang,
for His blood had gone
from Him altogether, and He could not live.
He wanted to hold His head
towards his mother who recognised Him,
and His soul went from Him
with a cold shout and a loud cry.

Beside Jesus' cross there was
a certain man, a centurion.
At Christ's death he saw
so many miraculous things,
that when He gave up His soul
unnaturally, with a cry
he said without mockery,
'This is indeed the Son of God'
and many with him there
bore witness.

Then at midday or after
in the country, as it is written,
there was an earthquake and lightning
and darkness also.
The veil of the temple was torn
in two and fell to the ground.
And there also broke
stones that were strong and hard.

The graves in many a place
were opened wide,
and the bodies that were in them
were raised up
and went straight to the city.
This was seen by many

an gwyr ze zustynee
bos mab du neb o lezys

Dowr ha ler ha tan ha gwyns
houl ha lour ha steyr kyffris
a gryst ow cozaff mernans
anken y a wozevys
natur scyle me a syns
arluth da mar pyth peynys
ol y sogete kyn fons syns
rag y beyn ze vos grevijs

Enaff crist ze yffarn eth
hag a dorras an porzow
dre y nerth bras hay sleyneth
ena golmas dewolow
lucyfer kelmys yv whath
pur fast yn y golmennow
hag ef a dryk heb fynweth
yn yffarn yn tewolgow

23 'Mam Ihesus Marya wyn'

Mam Ihesus marya wyn
herdya an gyw pan wela
yn y mab yn tenewyn
dre an golon may resas
ha zen dor an goys han lyn
an nozo dell deveras
angus bras ha peynys tyn
ha gloys creff askemeras

Fest yn tyn hy a wole
ze wherzyn nysteva whans
hay dagrow a zevera
hay dew lagas pur zewhans
hay holon whek a ranne
me a leuer rag trystans
rag an grayth yn hy ese
nas gweze an spyrys sans

Dre y holon y zeth seth
y mab syndis pan welse
moreth an seth ha pytet
natureth a ha denseth
ha pen aral o pytet
tackis fast gans kerense

who bore witness to the truth
that it was the Son of God who was killed.

Water and earth and fire and wind,
sun and moon and stars also,
suffered disturbance
on account of Christ's painful death.
I believe that if a good lord is hurt
nature causes all his subjects,
even though they be saints,
to be afflicted for his pains.

The soul of Christ went to Hell
and broke down the gates.
There he bound up devils
by His great strength and skill.
Lucifer is still bound
very securely in his bonds,
and he shall abide without end
in the darkness of Hell.

23 The Price of Sin

The mother of Jesus, blessed Mary,
when she saw the spear thrust
into her son's side
so that it ran straight through His heart,
with the blood and the fluid
running from Him,
great anguish and terrible pain
and sharp ache she felt.

Very grievously she wept,
with no desire to laugh,
and tears dropped
quickly from her two eyes.
Her sweet heart would have split,
for sadness, I say,
had the Holy Spirit not held
the grace that was in her.

When she saw her son was hurt
an arrow pierced her heart.
Grief was the arrow, and sorrow,
that natural human feeling,
and on the other hand, pity,
fastened securely by love,

ny wozevys den bythqueth
kymmys peynys ow pewe

An seth yw rag leueris
as gwyskis tyn gans mur angus
war hy holon may crunys
dre nerth an bum fynten woys
ha hy a wolas kymmys
gans mar ver nerth ha galloys
an fynten may trehevys
ran yn ban du droka loys

an goysna dagrennow try
dre y ij lagas y zeth
ny go comfort na yly
a wrello y holon hueth
hay veynys mar drewesy
askemar ha kymmys cueth
yn oll an bys ny ylly
den cafos kymmys anfueth

I feynis o bras ha creff
yn ioy zezy trylys yw
rag mygternes yw yn nef
ze vos gorzijs hy yv gyw
Eleth ze rygthy a seff
leas myll y both a syw
hay mab as gorth del vyn ef
tecke ys houl yv y lyw

In corff Ihesus y zese
hag ef yn crows ow cregy
pymp myll strekis del iove
ha pedergwyth cans goly
ha tryvgons moy ganse
ha pymzek pur wyr ens y
hag ol rag pur gerenze
worth mab den ys gozevy

Pub tezoll neb a vynne
leuerel pymzek pater
a leun golon rag gorzye
pascon agan arluth ker
yn blyzen y a vye
ha bederow keneuer
hag a owleow ese
yn gorf Ihesus worth neuer.

no living body ever suffered
so much agony.

The aforementioned arrow
struck her fiercely, bringing great anguish
that settled round her heart
by the power of the five well-springs of blood,
and she wept so much
and with such force and power
that the well-spring was raised up
— God! what cruel pain!

Because of that blood, three teardrops
came from her two eyes.
There was no comfort nor balm
to make her heart whole,
and her agonies pitifully
gave her much affliction:
no one in the whole world
could suffer such misfortune.

Her pains were great and unrelieved.
They are turned to joy
for she is a queen in heaven:
she is worthy of worship.
Angels stand before her,
and many thousands will follow her,
and her son worships her as He pleases:
fairer than the sun is her colour.

On the body of Jesus
as He hung on a cross there were
five thousand stripes,
and four times a hundred wounds,
and three score more besides,
and with them were fifteen more,
and all for the pure love
of mankind He suffered.

Every day, whosoever would say
fifteen Our Fathers
with a full heart to honour
the Passion of our dear Lord,
in a year they would be
as many prayers in number
as wounds
in the body of Jesus.

Selections from Beunans Meriasek (1504)

24 'A das ha mam ov megyans'

Meriadocus
A das ha mam ov megyans
yv bos gorrys ze zyskans
   rag attendie an scryptur
gothvos ynweth decernya
omma ynter drok ha da
   yv ov ewnadow pupvr

Pater
Beneth du zys meryasek
pup vr ty yv colonnek
   parys rak dysky dader
meseger scon alemma
kegy gans ov map kerra
   bys yn mester a grammer

Primus Nuncius
Arlud ze voth a vyth gvrys
   my a wor pur wyre yn ta
py ma an mester trygis
   hag yzyv marthys densa
     sur worth flehys
meryasek pan vynnough why
an forth dalleth yredy
   ny a vyn ha pur vskys

Meriadocus
A das ha mam kekefrys
   pesef agis bannothow
maym beua the well grays
   benyza yn ov dyzyow
     desky dader
rag agis bennethow why
yv moy treasur zymmo vy
   es pyth an bysma neb vr

Pater
Ov mab wek zys benneth du
   ham benneth vy benyza
ny fylleth hedre ven bev
   ath porpos gene neffra
     lemmen squyer
kezegy gans ov map dy
ha gveyth warnotho defry

Selections from The Life of St Meriasek (1504)

24   The Education of Meriasek

Meriasek
O father and mother, my education
will be one of learning,
  to understand the Scriptures:
to know how to tell the difference
between good and evil,
  that is my constant desire.

Father
The blessing of God on you, Meriasek!
Every hour of the day you are ready
  and eager to learn goodness.
Messenger, quickly
go with my dearest son
  to a master of grammar.

First Messenger
Lord, your will be done.
  I know well
where the master lives,
  a wonderfully good man
    with children.
Meriasek, we will very quickly
get on our way
  as soon as you like.

Meriasek
O father and mother
  I shall ask your blessing
that I may have better grace
  all my days,
    to learn goodness,
for your blessings
mean more to me
  than all the wealth of the world ever.

Father
My sweet son, God's blessing
  and mine upon you for ever.
You will not fail in your aim
  while we live.
    Now, squire,
go with my son thither
and keep watch over him.

ena ty a yl dysky
  martegen the vrys mur dader

Mater
Ov map benneth varya
  dys ham bennath vy neffra
thethe ganov mannafi amma
  ewne yv zyn zeth leuf kara
    meryasek wek
my a dryst yn du avan
pan ven ny sur coth ha gwan
  gvreth agan revlys tek

Armiger Ducis
Meryasek alemma duen
gervyth a scryfe pluven
  whath me ny won ze redya
nag aswen ov lezerow
me a bys du karadow
  roy zynny ynta spedya

[*Hic magister pompabit*]

Magister
My yv mayster a grammer
gvrys yn bonilapper
  universite vyen
my a wor mur yn dyvyn
pan ve luen ov zos a wyn
  ny gara covs mes laten

Primus Nuncius
Honour zyvgh master worthy
  ha benytha mur reuerens
duk conan pur yredy
  y vab rag cawas dyskans
    sur danvenys
ateva zyugh doctor wek
dyskovgh ef yn maner dek
  ha wy a vyth rewardeys

Magister
Messeger na zovt an cas
my an dysk na vo yn glas
  gramarion vyth ay parow
devgh sezovg an flehys pur dek
  ma merovgh agis leffrov
pe dyth mynus kewsovghwy

And you may learn,
> perhaps, much goodness yourself.

Mother
My son, the blessing of Mary
> on you, and my blessing always.

I will kiss your mouth.
> It is only right for us to love you truly,
>> sweet Meriasek.

I trust in God above,
that when we are old and weak,
> you will do our bidding.

The Duke's Squire
Meriasek, let us go.
I do not know a single word of pen writing
> nor how to read,

nor even my letters.
I pray to beloved God
> that he grant us a safe journey.

[*Here the master will parade*]

Master
I am a master of grammar,
graduate of Bonilapper,
> a minor university.

I know much of rhetoric:
and when my glass is full,
> I will speak nothing but Latin.

First Messenger
Honour to you, worshipful master,
> and much respect for ever.

Duke Conan, truly,
> has sent his son
>> to get learning.

Here he is, dear doctor,
teach him in fine manner
> and you will be amply rewarded.

Master
Messenger, have no fear in the matter.
I shall teach him so well that there will not be
> anywhere a grammarian his equal.

Come, sit down, good children,
> and look at your books.

If you speak little,

let veth orth agis dysky
   ha mur nynsyv an gobrov

Primus Scolaris
Du ze gueras a b c
an pen can henna yv d
   ny won na moy yn liuer
ny vef yn scole rum levte
   bys ynnewer gorzewar
zum gothvas wosa lyfye
   me a zysk moy ov mester

Secundus Scolaris
E s t henna yv est
pandryv nessa ny won fest
   mur an reugh ov cronkya
rag my ny vezaf the well
vnwyth a caffen hansell
   me a russa amendie

Magister
Dyske moy gans ze coweza
pan vynnough eugh ze lyvya
   meryasek wek eugh gansa
rag wy yv tender yn oys
ha flehys yonk a gar boys
   ham bevnans vy yv henna

Meriadocus
Me a leuer zyvgh mester
   ha na vewy dysplesys
hezyv sur yv dugwener
   da yv sevell worth vn pris
   ha predery an ena
rag kerensa an passyonn
   a porthes ihesu ragon
   pynys hyzyv y fanna

   Ha pub gvener
a vo sur drys an vlyzan
gul peyadov my a vyn
   kyns eva na zybbry mevr

zen chappell me a vyn mois
ze crist a scolyas y woys
   ze vzyll ov peiadow
ha ze varye y vam
kyns eva na dybbry tam
   helma yv ov vsadow

it will hold back your learning,
   and the salary is not great.

First Scholar
God help me, a, b, c,
and the end of the song is d.
   I do not know any more in the book:
I didn't start school, by my faith,
   until yesterday evening.
After dinner I shall add
   to my knowledge, master.

Second Scholar
E, s, t, that is est.
I do not know what is next.
   Do not beat me too much
for I shall not be any better for it.
Once I have had breakfast
   I shall improve.

Master
Learn more with your friends.
Go to lunch when you wish.
   Dear Meriasek, you go with them,
for you are only young,
and young children love food,
   and this is my livelihood.

Meriasek
I must remind you, master,
   and please don't be angry,
that today, surely, is Friday:
   it is a good thing to abstain from one meal
     and think of the soul.
For love of the Passion
   that Jesus bore for us:
     I will do penance today.

     And every Friday
throughout the year,
I shall pray
   before eating or drinking.

I will go to the chapel,
to Christ who shed his blood
   to make my prayers,
and to Mary his mother
before drinking, or eating a morsel:
   as is my custom.

Magister
Ov map gvra ze vlonogeth
tevlys os ze sansoleth
   meriasek gon gvyr lemmyn
ke ha dues pan vy plesyes
myns may hallen sur esyes
   ty a vyth yn pup termyn

25 'Marners dorsona dywy'

Meriadocus
Marners dorsona dywy
the kernov mar segh defry
   mones genough y carsen
the ry nammur me numbus
sav me a beys crist ihesus
   thagys socra pup termen

Nauta
Wolcum oys genen dremas
ny ath wor the pen an gluas
   dre voth du kyn pen sythen

[*ascendit in navem*]

dus aberveth oma scon
hav marners tennogh dyson
   an goyl thym in ban lemen

Servus. Naute
At eve fast bys in top
nov mata make fast the rop
   yma an gvyns ov wetha
han mor ov terevl fol
me a greys kellys on ol
   ha buthys pur guir oma

Nauta
A gony pan vuen genys
warbarth ny a veth kellys
   ens pup the yes thy gela
nynsus oma forth nahen
ahanan ny vev vn den
   tru gony doys then pletma

Meriadocus
A betheugh a confort da
crist agen gueres a ra

Master
My son, do as you wish:
you are destined for sainthood,
  Meriasek, I now see in truth.
Come and go as you please.
I will do whatever I can to make
  things easy for you at all times.

25 Meriasek comes to Cornwall

Meriasek
Sailors, God's blessing upon you!
If you are going to Cornwall,
  I should love to go with you.
I have not much to give,
but I shall pray that Christ Jesus
  takes care of you at all times.

Sailor
You are welcome to go with us, good man.
We can get you to Land's End,
  if God will, before the end of a week.

[*He goes up into the ship*]

Come here quickly,
and, my sailors, quickly pull
  up the sail for me.

The Servant of the Sailor
There it is fastened to the masthead.
Now, mate, make fast the rope.
  The wind is blowing,
and the sea is madly rising.
I believe we are all lost,
  and drowned indeed.

Sailor
Oh, woe that we were ever born!
We shall all be lost.
  Let each of us confess to his comrade:
there is nothing left to do.
Not one of us shall live.
  Alas, woe that we have come to this!

Meriasek
Oh, be of good courage!
Christ will help us,

ha me a vyn y pesy
mar pe y voth indella
na rella den peryllya
in tyr na mor in bysma
    mar creya war crist ha my

Nauta
Meryasek gorthys reby
drethos ol sawys on ny
    a peryl sur in torma
kegy in tyr a dremas
in kernov the ihesu gras
    theth desyr ty re dufa

26 'A vreten sur then povma'

Meriadocus
A vreten sur then povma
dresen mor me re dufa
    del vynnas du ow desky
hag omma gul me a vyn
ryb chapel maria wyn
    thym oratry
us dour omma in oges
rag nefre nahen dewes
    nynsa om ganov defry

Domesticus
Dour yv mur ascant oma
reys yv polge da alema
    mones certan thy gerhes
corff bo gvyn a caffen vy
dour ny effsen eredy
    na ny vye rag ov lees

Meriadocus
North yst then chapel omma
me a vyn mos the guandra
    dour thymmo sur rag weles

[*Tranceat at pratum*]
   [*genuflectit*]

Ihesu arluth me ath peys
ihesu gront dovyr a wur speys
    ihesu dymmo der the graes

if that is his will
and I shall pray to him,
that no man be in peril
on land or sea in this world
   if he cry to Christ and me.

Sailor
Meriasek, all praise to you!
You have saved us now
   certainly from danger.
Now good man, go ashore
in Cornwall: thank Jesus
   that you wanted to come along.

26   Meriasek and Teudar

Meriasek
I have come from Brittany
across the sea to this country
   as God wished,
and here I shall make
by the chapel of the blessed Mary
   an oratory for myself.
Is there water close by?
Truly, no other drink
   shall pass my lips.

Servant
Water is very scarce here.
Truly, it is necessary to fetch it
   from a good way off.
I should not drink water for sure
if I could get beer or wine,
   nor would it do me much good.

Meriasek
Northeast of the chapel here
I shall wander,
   to look for water myself, for sure.

[*Let him go across to the meadow*]
   [*He kneels down*]

Jesus, Lord, I pray you,
Jesus, give me water soon,
   Jesus, through your grace,

del russys kyns the moyseys
   an men cales

[*her ye wyll sprynggyth up water*]

Domesticus
Densa benyges reby
dovr oma ov try thynny
   mar dek thagen confortya
kerys oys purguir gans du
prevys open oma vy
   theragon in teller ma

Homo Febricosus
A thu ellas pendrama
lader cleves thym yma
   a veth gelwys an seson
ganso me ambeth schorys
pup deth nansyv lues mys
   rag peyn feynt yv ov colon

Contractus
Me yv efrethek hep fal
du thym a sevya mal
   a pena marov an beys
yma tregys in cambron
den ov cul merclys dyson
   guel yv dyn moys dy uskys
hay besy a luen colon
   thynny ny guthyl guereys

[*transit ad meriadocum*]

Hom Febricosus
Lowene dys meriasek
ny yv dev then bohosek
   me grefijs gans an febyr
han keth den ma sur yv mans
na nyl susten na pegans
   ny yllen dendyl the guir
gura gueres dynny dyblans
   rag kerense ihesu ker

Meriadocus
[*genuflectit*]
Ihesu arluth neff han beys
   yehes dywy re grontya
ihesu arluth me ath peys

as you once did for Moses
   from the hard stone.

[*Here water springs up from the well*]

Servant
Blessed may you be, good man,
bringing sweet water
   to comfort us.
I am sure that
you are truly beloved of God
   before us in this place.

Feverish Man
O God, alas, what shall I do?
I have a virulent disease
   called the ague.
I have had attacks
every day for months:
   my heart is faint with pain.

Cripple
I am a cripple without a doubt:
God, how I long to be dead
   and no longer in this world!
There is a man in Camborne
performing miracles:
   we had better get there quickly
and beg him with a full heart
   to help us.

[*He crosses to Meriasek*]

Feverish Man
Joy to you, Meriasek!
We are two poor men.
   I am afflicted with fever,
and this man, for sure, is lame:
neither us us can earn
   food or sustenance at all:
please help us,
   for the love of our dear Jesus.

Meriasek
[*He kneels*]
Jesus, Lord of Heaven and the World,
   may he grant you health:
Jesus, Lord, I pray you

lemmen sav an keth tusma
maria mam luen a rays
   peys theth vap arluth ragtha
maria mam ha guerhays
   gueres ov pesy gena
sevugh inban a tus vays
   fetel omglowugh omma

Contractus
Gorthyans the crist me yv sav
yagh yv ov corff ham garrow
   kerthes heb greff me a yll

Homo Febricosus
ha me yv yagh the crist grays
meryasek wek luen a rays
   fortyn du dotho ny fyl
thy worthya ny yv senses
   hag a vyn awos peryl

Meriadocus
Grassegh the crist a tus vays
   adar travyth dymmo
omma lemen fondya plays
   dre voth ihesu a vercy
   sur me a vyn
awose helme eglos
the worthya crist deth ha nos
y feth omma thum porpos
   ryb chapel maria wyn

Morbosus
Ellas ellas pendrama
in ov fays cothys yma
   cleves vthyk num car den
in cambron me re gloways
yma prest vn methek brays
   ov sawya tus in certen
me a vyn moys the verays
   gul gueres dymo mar men

[*ad meriadocum*]
Lowene dis meryasek
thymo vy den bohosek
   awoys crist lemen gueres
in ov fays cleves yma
mana car tus an beysma
   neb lues sur ov gueles

save these people!
Mary, mother full of grace,
   pray to your son, the Lord, for them:
Mary, mother and virgin,
   help by praying with me!
Stand up, good people:
   how do you feel?

Cripple
Praise be to Christ, I am made whole,
my body and legs are restored to health:
   I can walk easily.

Feverish Man
And I am cured too, thanks be to Christ!
Sweet Meriasek, full of grace,
   God's favour will not fail him,
we are bound to praise him
   in spite of all danger.

Meriasek
Thanks be to Christ, good people,
   and not to me.
I will build a mansion here
   through the will of merciful Jesus,
      I will for sure.
And after that, there will be
a church to worship Christ in
day and night, as I intend
      by the chapel of blessed Mary.

Sick Man
Alas, alas, what shall I do?
A terrible disease afflicts
   my face: no one loves me.
In Camborne, I have heard,
there is a certain great doctor
   healing people.
I will go and see
   if he will cure me.

[*To Meriasek:*]
Joy to you, Meriasek!
For Christ's sake, help me,
   a poor man.
On my face there is a disease
that the people of this world cannot stand,
   nor anyone that sees me.

Meriadocus
[*genuflectit*]
Arluth neff reth weresa
naamam kyns es helma
   a sawyas an cleves mur
gans dour y raff the golhy
ihesu crist du a vercy
     theth gueres mar tuth an nur

Domesticus
Ty then gylleth boys lowen
sawys tek oys in certen
   grasse the meryasek wek
rak eff yv lenwys a grays
ha kerys gans du a rays
   del welyn letrys ha lek

Morbosus
Meryasek dywhy mur grays
me a beys crist luen a rays
   in neff thywhy ren tala
han wyrhes maria splan
du assus lues den gvan
   sawys genogh in bysma

[*tranceat*]
  [*hic teudarus pompabit*]

Teudarus
Tevdar me a veth gelwys
   arluth regnijs in kernov
may fo mahum enorys
   ov charg yv heb feladov
    oges ha pel
penag a worthya ken du
y astevons peynys glu
   hag inweth mernans cruel

Nuncius
Heyl dyugh ser arluth tevdar
   yma gena nowothow
saw ny vethe sur heb mar
   y covsel thyugh gans ganov
    na vethe nes
     del won inta
      war ov ena
    ny veth ov les

Meriasek
[*He kneels*]
May the Lord of Heaven help you,
as Naman cured this great disease
   in former times.
I shall wash you with water,
Jesus Christ, God of mercy,
   the time has come to help you.

Servant
Man, be happy,
you are restored to health, for sure,
   thanks to sweet Meriasek,
for he is full of grace,
and loved by God of grace
   as we all can see, both learned and laymen.

Sick Man
Meriasek, many thanks to you,
I shall pray to Christ full of grace
   in Heaven that he will reward you,
and to the glorious Virgin Mary.
God, how many frail people
   in the world are made whole by you.

[*Let him cross over*]
   [*Here Teudar will parade*]

Teudar
I am called Teudar,
   a lord who rules Cornwall.
My aim is that unfailingly
   Mahomet shall be honoured,
     near and far.
Whoever worships any other god,
shall feel sharp pain
   and a cruel death.

Messenger
Hail to you, Lord Teudar,
   I have news
that I do not dare speak of,
   for certainly, and without doubt,
     I know well
       on my soul
         it will not
      do me any good to speak of it.

Teudarus
Pyv an iovle us warfethys
  lauer thymmo ty lorden
ay covs ty falge negethys
  dar ny glov an plos iovden
covs unweth ty bothosek
  covs myscheff yth vryonsen
ay covs ty map molothek
  an iovl rebo the worfen

Nuncius
Yma oma in penwyth
  nebes a weyst the carnebre
vn pronter ov cuthel guyth
  sawya tus dal in bysme
    bother ha mans
ha pup cleves ol in beys
a thu ny vyn boys covsis
  mas a crist a thuk mernans
pan o marow dasserys
  y methe bue the vevnans

Teudarus
Out govy rag galarow
  py dol an iovle ythama
out govy na vuff marow
  kyns doys a dor ov dama
    govi rag schame
sovdoryan duen alemma
may hallen ganso rekna
    the develys name

Primus Miles
Ov arluth genough ny a
me re glowes an denna
  nansyv mysyow tremenys
tus dal eff a ra sawya
ha tus vother mageta
  inweth gul dethe cloweys

Secundus Miles
Tevdar dyugh me a leuer
an keth denna grueys yv muer
  purguir yn pow
mar ny vethe chastijs
a vahum ny veth sensys
  moy es ky heb feladow

Teudar

What the Devil has happened?
   Tell me, you blockhead –
hey, speak, false traitor!
   What! the filthy scoundrel does not hear.
Speak up, pauper!
   Speak! Damn your throat!
Speak, accursed son!
   May the devil take you!

Messenger

There is here in Penwith
   a little to the west of Carn Brea,
a certain priest doing work,
   making the blind see in this world,
     and the deaf and lame whole,
and curing every disease there is.
He will not speak of your god,
   but of Christ who suffered death,
and who rose again from the dead,
   to life, as he said.

Teudar

Out, woe is me, for agony –
   into what devil's hole shall I go?
Out, woe is me, I wish I had died
   before coming from my mother's womb!
     Woe is me, for shame!
Soldiers, let us go hence,
and settle up with him,
   in the devil's name!

First Soldier

My lord, we shall go with you.
We heard of that man
   some months ago.
The blind he makes whole,
and the deaf as well
   restoring their hearing.

Second Soldier

Teudar, I say to you,
truly, that man is being made much of
   in the country.
If he is not punished,
certainly, Mahomet will not be thought
   any better than a dog.

Teudarus
[*descendit*]
    Duen ny in kerth
    gans mur a nerth
      ov marogyon
    py ma tregys
    thym leferys
      bethyns dyson

Nuncius
    Sur me an guel
    arluth ryel
      enos in plen
    mes an chapel
      doys a ra len

Teudarus
Ty bagcheler treyl war tuma
the hanov thym lafara
    quik hath cregyans
    gothfes henna
    sur a vanna
      hath devethyans

Meriadocus
Meryasek yv ov hanov
  sevys a lyne conany
in crist ihesu caradov
  ytheseff prest ov cresy
    y vos lel du
genys ay vam maria
ha hy maghteth aywosa
  helma ov cregyans ythyv

Teudarus
Sevys oys a woys worthy
  meryasek beth avysyys
rag dovt cafus velyny
  na govs tra na fue guelys
    me a leuer
erbyn reson yv in beys
heb hays gorryth thymo creys
bones flogh vyth concevijs
  in breys benen heb awer

Meriadocus
Nynsesos ov attendya
  an laha del vya reys

Teudar
[*descends*]
    Let us go forth
    in strength,
      my knights.
    Tell me
    straight away
      where he lives.

Messenger
    Certainly, I see him,
    royal lord,
      yonder in the plain.
    He is coming faithfully
      out of the chapel.

Teudar
Young fellow, turn this way:
quickly, tell me your name
    and your faith.
    I want to know that
    for sure,
      and where you come from.

Meriasek
Meriasek is my name,
   from the line of Conan.
I believe at all times
   in beloved Jesus Christ,
     that he is the true God,
born of his mother Mary,
and that she remained a virgin:
   that is my belief.

Teudar
You are born of worthy blood:
   But Meriasek, beware
of falling into disgrace.
   Do not speak of anything imaginary:
     I'm telling you,
it is against all worldly reason,
believe you me, that without male seed
any child can be conceived
   in the womb of a woman.

Meriasek
You are not taking any account
   of the law as it was ordained

omma an genegygva
  a ihesu crist war an beys
    hay pascyon ker
avel hovle der weder a
heb y terry del wylsta
indella crist awartha
a thuth in breys maria
  heb mostye iunt vyth in suyr
der an sperys sans kerra
  concevis y fue the guir

Teudarus
Na wyle gene flatra
kynfes nefre ov clattra
  the ihesu ythese tays
mage lel avel y vam
nynsus ger guir malbe dam
  wath in ol the daryvas

Meriadocus
Du avan prest o y days
  a cothfes y attendya
rag prenna adam hay hays
  doys y fynnas then bysma
mernans tyn eff a porthas
  eneff map den gruk sawya
ese im colmen satnas
  eff as dros the lowena

Teudarus
Marso du avan y days
  me a leuer meryasek
eff a alse der y rays
  selwel rych ha bohosek
    heb boys marov
ath daryvas schame ythyv
pan othem o the vap du
  boys lethys avel carov

Meriadocus
Der pegh adam agen tays
  eff hay lynnyeth o dampnys
sav an devgys a vynnays
  arta y vones prennys
    the saluascon
an map a fue concevijs
ha densis a kemereys

regarding the birth
  of Jesus Christ on earth,
    and of His dear passion.
As you can see, the sun passes
through glass without breaking it,
so it was that Christ above
came into the womb of Mary
  without profaning any part, certainly,
He was truly conceived
  through the beloved Holy Spirit.

Teudar
Do not try to seduce me,
with your never-ending prattle,
  Jesus had a father
as surely as he had a mother.
There is not the slightest word of truth
  in any part of your story.

Meriasek
God above was always His Father:
  if you could only understand that
to redeem Adam and his seed
  He willed him to come into this world.
A grievous death He suffered,
  but He saved the souls of men
in thrall to Satan,
  bringing them happily together.

Teudar
If God above was His Father,
  I should say, Meriasek,
that He could through his grace
  save rich and poor
    without being put to death.
Shame on your story:
what was the need of the Son of God
  being killed like a deer.

Meriasek
Through the sin of Adam our father,
  he and his lineage were condemned,
but the Godhead willed
  that he should be redeemed
    for salvation.
The son was conceived,
and took the form of manhood,

rag na ylly an devsys
    gothe pasconn

Teudarus
Ny thue les agen argya
   kyn feny oma vyketh
meryasek crist denaha
   ha the cothmen me a veth
     may fo guelys
epscop worthy me ath ra
chyff peb les oll an povma
na moy me ny deserya
   mas gorthya mahum pup preys

Meriadocus
Ima guel forth es honna
grua thegy crist ker gorthya
   ken maner kyllys os suir

Teudarus
Vn ger na campol a gryst
ha mar qureth me ath wra trest
   wath coyl orthef ha beth fuir
rag pan deffen ha moys fol
an iovle a thue mes ay dol
   kyns es ov ruthy purguir

   Drok yv gena
   war ov ena
     meryasek wek
   gul dis mas da
   ha gorthyans grua
     thum dewow tek

Meriadocus
Theth dewow try mylwyth fy
rag sur dewlow ens y
   nys gorthya vy benytha
ortheff na wyla pythays
nahy mar mynnyth boys vays
   foyl oys mar trestyth inna

Teudarus
Out warnes ty fals jugleer
   defya ov dewow flour
ty a crek in cloghprennyer
   rag perel prence hag emperour
     omma the foyl

for the Godhead itself could not
    suffer passion.

Teudar
No good will come of our arguing
  though we were here for ever.
Meriasek, deny Christ,
   and I shall be be a friend to you
     so that all may see it.
And I shall make you a worthy bishop,
the chief of every court in the country.
I shall ask no more than
   you shall worship Mahomet at all times.

Meriasek
There is a better way than that:
You should worship beloved Christ,
   or you are surely lost.

Teudar
Do not mention a single word of Christ,
if you do I shall make you regret it.
    believe me and be sensible,
for if I were to go mad
the devil would come out of his hole
   before he scorches me, in truth.

    Upon my soul
    I am sorry
      sweet Meriasek
    to do you anything but good,
    just worship
      my fair gods.

Meriasek
Fie upon your gods, three thousand times fie!
for they are devils certainly.
   I shall never worship them.
Do not look for pity from me.
You must deny them if you want to be godly,
   you are mad to trust in them.

Teudar
Out, false trickster,
   for denying my superior gods.
You will hang here like a fool
   on the gallows for defying
     prince and emperor.

the voy nefre me ath cays
outlayer fyys ath wlays
covs vn ger erbyn ov rays
    ha ty an noyll

    Me yv emprour
    ha governour
      conquerrour tyr
    arluth worthy
    mur ov mestry
      gothfeth ha myr

Meriadocus
Tav thymo vy the clap sens
speyna a reth mur a gvyns
  oma sur in sevureth
guel yv dis bones cristyan
gorthya crist a luen golan
  ha my lemmen ath vygeth

Teudarus
Out govy gesugh thym spath
  alema quik rag feya
deve an iovle the rag ov fath
  ze vynnes ov begithia
marov off in kres an plath
  na pel mar trege omma
mahum darber hardygrath
  ze neb a ruk ov throbla

Tormentoris dugh in plen
tormentoris marsogh len
  tormentoris dugh dym scon
ay ay ay dar ny regh vry
reys yv aga herhes y
  pan yu mogh ol ov duwon

27 'Mayl at eua'

Doctor
Mayl at euva bargyn da
  maseger tek
lauer thymo in preytha
  them emper tek
    pendrus wervys

Secundus Nuncius
claff deberthys eff yv sur

I shall hate you for evermore,
brigand, outcast fled from your own country.
Speak one word against my faith
   and you'll be sorry.

   I am emperor
   and governor,
     conqueror of land,
   worshipful lord,
   great is my power:
     know it and take heed!

Meriasek
Be silent, hold your tongue:
you are talking such hot air.
   In all seriousness,
it is better for you to be a Christian,
and worship Christ with a full heart,
   let me baptise you.

Teudar
Go away, woe is me, leave me alone
   to flee this place.
The devil has come before my face
   wanting to baptise me!
I am as good as dead here
   if I stay any longer.
Mahomet, punish with evil
   he who plagued me.

Torturers, come into the plain,
torturers, if you are loyal,
   torturers, come quickly!
Oh, oh, oh — what? Do you not take heed?
It is necessary to go and get them
   as all my grief is in vain.

27   The Emperor's Doctors

Doctor
Damn it! Here is a good bargain,
   sweet messenger.
Tell me, I pray,
   what has happened
     to my dear emperor.

Second Messenger
A leper he is indeed.

ny welys in beys na mur
  denvith del ywa dyghtijs

Doctor
A haha me a wothya
bakcheler ienkyn in preytha
  heth ov lefer a fysek
dokhy indan the gasel
ha grua thegy ov gormel
  ov boys fesysyen connek

[*erthyn pott. ye bouke aredy And the urnell enspektad*]

Clericus Iankin
Rag esya an pedrennow
ha rag stopya tarthennow
  yma thywy forten tek
a caffogh sur benewen
polge ryb agis tenewen
  why a proffse den connek

[*descendit ad constantinum*]

Episcopus Poly
  Gorthyans in se
  ha lowene
    thyugh arluth gluas
  omma wharee
  ny redufe
    gans an gannas

Constantinus
A wolcum ser epscop flour
wolcum inweth ser doctour
  dugh inban me agis peys
ov cleves prest me a weyl
nynsyv grefons me an geyl
  a wothogh gul dym guereys

Doctor
Mannaff gueles agys dour
hag in vrna an empour
  angeveth gorthyb in cays

Justus
me a prederys henna
y vryn atta oma
  tovle in the wedyr glays

I have not seen in the world many
   men treated as he is.

Doctor
Aha! Aha! I knew it.
Bachelor Jenkin, I pray you,
   pass me my book of physic.
Carry it under your arm,
and praise me,
   for I am a smart physician.

[*Earthen pot. The book ready and the pot inspected*]

Clerk Jenkin
There is a good chance
that you will get relief for your buttocks
   and prevent eructation.
If you were to get a maid
beside you for a while,
     you would would know what to do.

[*He goes down to Constantine*]

Bishop of Poli
   Praise to the throne,
   and joy
     to you, lord of the country.
   We have come
   here directly
     with the message.

Constantine
O welcome, lord bishop supreme,
welcome to you too, sir doctor.
   come on up, I pray.
My illness you can plainly see.
It is no secret.
   Can you help me?

Doctor
I will inspect your urine,
and then emperor
     you will have a diagnosis.

Justice
I thought so.
Here is his urine:
   put it in your blue vial.

Doctor
Hoc vrum malorum
et nimis rubrorum
   aha me a wor inta
dus oma bacheler ienkyn
myr warvan drefe the vyn
   ay lok up byscherev tha

Annotho na gymmer glovs
kynthus ganso sawer pous
   gor dotho nes the frygow
helma yv mater tykly
lemen me a wor defry
   pendra yv an clevegov

Pendra vynnogh dym the ry
ha sawys pur eredy
   costentyn bethugh gena
dre weres ov du soly
me a vyn gul drynk dywhy
   mar cafa stoff the perna

Constantinus
Tan at omma thys *x* puns
in dalleth an rema syns
   grua vy sav hag y feth guel
benithe in the vevneyns
me ath ra parlet vhel

Doctor
Mayl an rema a ra les
me a vyn pesy cumyes
   rag mones dre
arta me a thue deth yov
oma dyugh gans dewosow
   a relle agis sawye

Doctor
There is a mixture of evils,
and too much ruddiness:
 aha! I know well what it is.
Come here, Bachelor Jenkin,
look, lift up your face –
 hey, look up, plague on you.

It will not harm you,
although it has a strong smell,
 put it near your nostrils:
this is difficult.
Now I know indeed
 what the diseases are.

What do you want me to give you?
I will make you well,
 Constantine, for sure.
With the help of my god Soli
I will make a potion for you
 if I get the funds for buying it.

Constantine
Here are ten pounds, take them.
Take these to begin with.
 Make me well again and I will see you
all right your whole life:
 I shall make you a high prelate.

Doctor
Damn it! These should do the job.
I will ask if
 I can go home.
I shall come to you again
on Thursday with drinks
 which should make you well.

28   'Me yv outlayer'

[*Exulatores hic pompabunt vel unus pro omnibus*]

Primus Exulator
Me yv outlayer in coys
moy reoute in ov oys
   bythqueth purguir numdarfa
pan vo due ov stoff achy
ware me a provy moy
   nynsyv marnes sportt raffna

Secundus Exulator
Nansyv preys aspya pray
due yv an mona rum fay
   mester in agen mesk ny
aspyen gvas gans pors poys
mar kyllyn den sans eglos
   whare y a kuntel moy

Primus Exulator
In sol matis duen in kerth
aspyogh gans mur an nerth
   py fo marchont ov quandra
y dalhenna na sparyogh
me a omgemer ragogh
   hagis menten benytha

[*descendit*]

Tertius Exulator
Me a weyl guas war geyn margh
na fella ny vanna pargh
   gene at eve sesijs
deyskyn then dor mata
ha the borse mes ath ascra
   me ambeth hath margh uskis

Mercator
A serys clowugh ov leff
dovtyogh drok thagis eneff
   pan dremennogh an bysma
agys sperys sur an pren
in anken ha mur a peyn
   a thu go ef an ene

[*ye prest aredy*]

28 Outlaws

[*Here the outlaws shall prevail or one for all*]

First Outlaw
I am an outlaw from the greenwood.
I never had, indeed,
  a grander life
since I began to garner wealth.
I shall try now to get some more –
  robbery is only a bit of fun!

Second Outlaw
It is time to watch out for our prey –
money has just arrived, by my faith.
  Boss, let us all
look out for a fellow with a heavy purse,
and if we cozen a holy churchman
  they will collect more soon enough.

First Outlaw
Get up, mates, and let's get going.
Keep an eye out,
  for a merchant may be wandering about.
Do not stop yourselves from getting hold of him –
I will look after you
  and keep you for ever.

[*He descends*]

Third Outlaw
I see a fellow on horseback,
I shall not suffer him to go further.
  Right, he is taken!
Let us get you down on the ground, mate,
and fetch your purse out of your bosom.
  I shall have you and your horse as well.

Merchant
O gentlemen, hear me!
Fear evil to your soul
  when you pass from this world.
Your spirit will pay for it
in great pain and tribulation –
  O God, woe to the soul!

[*The priest ready*]

149

Primus Exulator
Pur a wylste war an kee
eneff map den in bysmae
   ov repentya rag y throk
mar numkemer du certen
an iovle a ra purlowen
   maga fery avel hok

Quartus Exulator
Me a weyl guas in gon hyr
pronter ef a hevel suir
   yma mona gans henna
ser parson bona dies
me a vyn changye porses
   be my fay kyns mos lema

Presbiter
A te then preder ath du
y volnogeth byth nynsyv
   bones grueys in ketelma
terry y wormenadow
a regh why heb feladow
   gothvethugh y attendya

Primus Exulator
Neb a gemer ovn y thu
ny sewen henna neb tu
   mata orthen ny na set
sav dascor ol the vona
bo annyl the quartrona
   oma me a ra heb let

Presbiter
Galles genogh mens ambus
termen a thue crist ihesus
   interthon a ran an gvyr
prederugh helma deth brus
   pemont thymmo gruegh in suyr

Primus Exulator
A vethe preys bys deth brus
   ny thue henna in trogel
ty a gel moy an pyth us
   adro dyso dyogel
     streppyogh y queth
eff re ros thyn deth hyr lour
   an pement na hyns ny veth

First Outlaw
When did you ever see on earth
the soul of mankind
   repenting his evil on a hedge?
If God does not want me,
the devil will take me very happily,
   as merrily as a hawk.

Fourth Outlaw
I see a fellow in a long gown:
he looks like a priest to me,
   and he has money.
Sir, good day!
I will change purses,
   with you, by my faith, before I go.

Priest
O man, think of your God.
It is never his will
   for things to be like this.
You are breaking his commandments
you know:
   learn how to study Him!

First Outlaw
Whoever fears God
will not succeed anywhere.
   Mate, do not resist us,
give us all your money,
or else we'll quarter you
   here without hindrance.

Priest
You have taken all I have.
In time to come, Christ Jesus
   will share the truth between us.
Remember that on judgement day
   you will repay me certainly.

First Outlaw
Shall I risk it till the day of judgement?
   That is not something to affect the body.
You are concealing something
   about you for sure.
     Tear off his clothes –
he has kept us long enough today –
   you will not be repaid any sooner.

Secundus Exulator
At eve strepys in noth
in delma guthel y coth
   then guesyon astefe peth

29 'Me yv duk'

[*Hic Dux Cornubie pompabit dicens*]
Me yv duk in oll kernow
   indella ytho ov thays
hag vhel arluth in pov
   a tamer the pen an vlays
tregys off lemen hep wov
   berth in castel an dynas
     sur in peddre
ha war an tyreth vhel
thym yma castel arel
a veth gelwys tyndagyel
   henna yv ov fentregse

Leferys yv thymmo vy
   bones in keverang penweth
den grassyes pur eredy
dres an mor dy eff a thueth
   nynsyv na pel
ov styward a glosugh why
covs annotho in tefry
   leferugh dym dyogel

Senescallus Ducis
Clowys arluth galosek
eff yv gelwys meryasek
   den grassyes in y dethyow
gans pup ol ythyv kerys
inweth del yv leferys
   dadder mur y ruk in pov

Camerarius Ducis
Arluth me a leuer guir
gallas henna the ken tyr
   nansyv sythyn tremenys
gans vn den heb feladov
ny vue achy the kernov
   in neb le vythol guelys

Dux
Praga ytheth mes an pov
dremas o in y dethyov

Second Outlaw
Here he is stripped naked.
That's the way to treat
   those who have property.

29   The Duke of Cornwall challenges Teudar

[*Here the Duke of Cornwall shall parade saying:*]
I am Duke of Cornwall:
   as was my father before me,
and high lord in the country
   from Tamar to Land's End.
I live now, without a lie,
   at Castle-an-Dinas,
     in Pydar, certainly,
and in the High Territory
I have another castle
called Tintagel:
   that is my chief seat.

I am told
   that in the shire of Penwith
there is truly a man of grace.
Over the sea he came
   not long ago.
Seneschal, did you hear of him?
Tell me about him,
   and tell me surely.

The Duke's Seneschal
I have heard, mighty lord:
that he is called Meriasek,
   a man of grace apparently.
He is loved by all:
and it is said
   that he did good works in the country.

The Duke's Chamberlain
My lord, I say in truth
that he went to another country
   a week ago.
He has not been seen
by any man at all
   in Cornwall.

Duke
Why did he leave the country?
He was a good man in his time.

ny glowys ken leferel
ny govsy mas honester
pur guir a fur a thadder
   lues re ruk y gormel.

Camerarius Ducis
teudar pagan ongrassyes
in povma eff re dyrhays
   del glovsugh ha nynsyv pel
ny vyn gothe vn cristyan
in y oges pur certen
   marthys eff yv den cruel
meryasek ganso lemen
   helhys vue in kerth heb fael

[*finit*]

Dux Cornubiae
Out mylwyth war an ky plos
   prag na glowys helma kyns
ren arluth then beys am ros
   me a ra pur cot y guyns
kyns ys dumerher the nos
   eff a deerbyn trestyns
hag a guayn pur sempellos
   may kerna purguir y dyns

Bethugh parys ov meyny
ny vanna alowe ky
   pur certan achy thum tyr
eff an preveth hag in tyn
avodia sur mar ny vyn
   y woys a resek then luyr.

Senescallus Ducis
Parys on dywhy sur duk
mur a throk prest eff re ruk
   a pan duthe in povma
in menek in lestevdar
yma y penplas heb mar
   mur dotho ov resortya

Dux Cornubiae
Kyn geffo eff myllyow cans
purguir ythons the mernans
   dre voth ihesu us avan
me a vyn gothfes praga
y tuthe sur then povma

I haven't heard anything else.
He spoke nothing but decency:
very truly, many have praised him
   for his great goodness.

Duke's Chamberlain
Teudar, an ungracious pagan
has landed in this country
   not long ago as you have heard.
He would not suffer any Christian
to be around him, truly.
   He is a wondrously cruel man:
Meriasek was chased away
   by him for sure.

[*He finishes*]

Duke of Cornwall
Out, a thousand times on the foul dog!
   Why did I not hear of this before?
By the Lord who gave me to the world,
   I shall make his wind very short
before Wednesday night is out.
   He will be very sorry
and deserve his retribution
   so he will really gnash his teeth.

Be prepared, my retinue.
I will not allow such a dog
   to live within my land, for sure.
He will pay for it, and grievously.
If he will not depart,
   his blood will flow over the ground.

Seneschal
We are ready for sure, Sir Duke.
He has always done much evil
   since he came into this country.
In the Meneague, in Lesteudar,
is his headquarters, undoubtedly,
   many are rallying to him.

Duke of Cornwall
Though he may have a hundred thousand behind him
truly they will go to their deaths
   by the will of Jesus who is above.
I want to know why
he came to this country

heb ov lessyans in certan
ol warbarth duen alemma
  ov meny a luen golan

[*Dux descendit cum xxii armatoribus
with stremers*]

Dux
Leferugh ov arlythy
pythyv guel thynny sensy
  the vetya gans an turant
mar calla y tebel far
drefen y voys sur heb mar
  erbyn fay crist dyspusant

Senescallus
Tregys vue in lestevdar
  honna yma in menek
sav plas aral sur heb mar
  us then tebel genesek
    berth in povder
honna veth gelwys Godren
ena purguir an poddren
  thotho prest re ruk harber

Dux
the soyth ny a vyn sensy
  in hanov crist us avan
mar tryg in kernov defry
  ny a vet gans an belan
ov baner dyspletyoghwhy
  therago pur guir lemman
del goth the arluth worthy
  me a vyn moys ahanan

30 'Ser duk me a wel tevdar'

Senescallus
Ser duk me a weyl tevdar
ha parcel a throk coskar
  pur thevrey orth y sewa
covse ganso a vynnogh wy
ha govyn orto defry
  in povma pendra wyla

Dux Cornubiae
Manna purguir ov stywart
kynthus inno tebel art

without my licence, certainly.
Let us go hence together,
  my retinue, with a good heart.

[The Duke goes down with 22 men-at-arms with streamers]

Duke
Say, my lords,
what could be better for us
  than to meet with the tyrant
and his evil progress,
for he is undoubtedly
  contending against the faith of Christ.

Seneschal
He had been living in Lesteudar:
  in the Meneague,
but the evil-born one has
  another mansion, certainly,
    in Powder
called Godren:
there, truly, the corrupt one
  has made for himself a refuge.

Duke
We will head south
  in the name of Christ who is above.
If he dwells in Cornwall at all
  we shall meet the villain.
Display my banner
  before me very truly now
as is fitting for a worshipful lord:
  I will go forth.

30 The Great Battle

Seneschal
Sir Duke, I see Teudar
and an evil retinue
  following him, for sure.
Will you speak to him
and ask him indeed
  what he seeks in this country?

Duke of Cornwall
Seneschal, truly I will.
Although he has an evil art

byth ny vanna y thovtya
kynthusons ov thumwul creff
me a dava age grueff
   in age meske gruaff rovtia

[*ad stallum*]

Ty turant a thyscregyans
   pendryv the kerth in povma
tytel na chalyng dyblans
   aberth mam na tas oma
     purguir nyth us
ty re wores mes an gluas
meryasek neb o dremas
   acontis certen a zus

Teudarus
Me ath wor gy mes an pov
   kyn moys avel meryasek
mar corthyyth an plos myn gov
   neb a thuk peynis anwek
     sur in grovs pren
a vethe gelwys ihesu
rag vyngia purguir me yv
   war y servons eff certen
devethys of ty myn reyv
   thage dyswul of lemen

Dux
Ny seff henna yth galloys
   ty falge ky omschumunys
kynse me a scoyle the goys
   ha ty a veth devenys
     avel losow
rum ena the guthel covle
pagya merh es by my sowle
   me a glowes in ze pov
pendra deseff an map devle
   darvyngya war thuk kernov

Teudarus
Duk kernov hag oll y dus
indan ov threys me as glus
   poren kepar ha treysy
kynnago ov posceccyon
bras in meske sur ov nascyon
   me ren moghheys eredy
     conqueror off

I will never fear him.
Although they make out they are strong
I will touch their faces:
   I shall rule amongst them.

[*To the stage*]

You tyrant of unbelief,
   what right have you in this country?
You have no title nor clear claim
   through mother nor father
      very truly you have not.
You have chased Meriasek out of the country,
who was a good man
   respected by the people.

Teudar
And I shall chase you out of the country
   like Meriasek before I leave,
if you venerate that foul liar
   called Jesus, who surely bore
      a dreadful penance,
on the cross of wood.
Very truly I am here to retaliate
   against his servants.
I am here, greybeard,
   to exterminate them all right now.

Duke
That is not within your power,
   you false excommunicated dog.
Sooner I shall spill your blood
   and chop you up
      like vegetables,
on my soul, to make soup.
By my soul, you are a girl's bastard
   in your country, so I hear.
What does the devil's son expect?
   To take vengeance on the Duke of Cornwall!

Teudar
I shall skewer the Duke of Cornwall
and his crew under my feet
   like starlings.
And if my patrimony was not
great among my people,
   at least I have increased it.
      I am a conqueror,

    corff da in proff
    dovtijs in meske arlythy

Dux
Ny sensevy ath creffder
  ty turant vn faven guk
der an golen me ath ver
    mar nynseth in kerth war nuk
     quik mes am grond
predery a raff heb fal
in the pov ythesta gal
peys gevyans warna losal
   bo voyd am syght a pur hond

    Py fyn alyon
     war crustunyon
   omma deseves settya
me a ra ath pen crehy
may tevere an brehy
  ha pesy gueff ov metya

Teudarus
By my fay an we besen
  a latha margh a calla
indella ty gargesen
   drok thymo ty russa
    a mennen vy
purguir sevel in cosel
na vanna mes ty losel
yma myterneth ryel
   a thue thum gueres defry

Dux
The vyterneth schumunys
  theth gueres bohes a veth
galwy dis bras ha munys
   hag ol the varogyen keth
    hath arlythy
me agis gorte in plen
the crist del off servont len
   hag ol ov fobyl defry

Teudarus
   Ty vyl pen pyst
   na gampol crist
    the ragovy
   ha mar a qureth
   ty a feth meth

a good fellow indeed,
feared by lords.

Duke

I do not care one empty bean
   for your strength, tyrant.
I shall spit you through the heart
   if you do not get out
     of my land right now.
I think in your country
you are undoubtedly a rascal.
Beg forgiveness of me, you lout,
   or get out of my sight, you cur!

   Would an alien
     expect to attack
Christians here?
I shall make scab of your head
that the scurf may ooze out
   and you will cry 'Woe is me' when we meet.

Teudar

By my faith, the gnat
   would kill a horse, if it could.
So, you glutton,
   you would do me evil
     if I would
only stand quietly by.
I will not, you rogue,
for indeed there are royal kings
   who will come to my help.

Duke

Your excommunicated kings
   will be of little help to you.
Call them, great and small,
   and all your servile knights
     and your lords.
I shall await them in the field,
for Christ, whose loyal servant I am,
   and all of my people.

Teudar

   You vile blockhead,
   do not mention Christ
     to me.
   Shame upon you
   if you do,

    hath ost defry
  Plos marrek pour
    dar seposia
   prest a reta
omma settya orth emperour

Dux
Ea ty falge nygythys
me ny won the voys genys
  in bysma the pastel dyr
na deseff ty allyon plos
in ov hertons deth na nos
  ny rovtyyth pel gothfeth guir

Rag mellya gans tus vays
del o meryassek henways
  mur ty a far the lakka
by the dredful day off dome
me a leuer dys ty grome
  mas pur sempel nyth sensa

Teudarus
Ser duk ty a nagh the fay
bo neyl presner thymmovy
  eseth kens haneth the nos
mytern alwar ha tygys
mytern margh ryel keffrys
mytern casvelyn gewlys
  gans sokyr thymus ov tos

Dux
Dens an rena pan vynnans
  omma y a veth bohays
byth ny schappyons heb mernans
  re thu arluth mur a rays
kynfy omma myllyov cans
  ny a vyn ages gortays
in hanov crist thyn yma wans
  orth escar crist batalyays

Teudarus
Cryst ha ty me a thefy
hag omma ol agis fay
  atlyan kepar del ogh
rag mennes thymo settia
ov sovdrys gruegh heb lettya
  then crustunyon pennov trogh

and upon your host, as well.
A dirty little knight like you –
   what! do you presume
   just like that
to fight an emperor!

Duke
Yes, false reprobate,
I do not know that you were born
   in this world for a plot of land.
Do not expect, you foul alien,
my inheritance, day and night.
   Truly, you won't rule long.

For meddling with good people,
like Meriasek
   you will fare very much worse
at the dreadful day of judgement,
I say to you, you stableboy:
   very simply, I do not hold you good.

Teudar
Sir Duke, deny your faith
or you will be my prisoner
   before the night is out.
King Alwar and Tacitus,
royal King Mark also,
and a king called Casivellaunus
   are coming to my aid.

Duke
Let them come when they will:
   they will be but few,
and never will they get away alive.
   By the Lord God of great grace,
though there be hundreds of thousands
   we will await you:
In the name of Christ, I desire
   to do battle against the enemy of Christ.

Teudar
I shall defy both you and Christ,
and all your faith here,
   outlaws that you are,
for wanting to attack me.
My soldiers, don't hold back from giving
   the Christians broken heads.

Dux
rag mar quyk del vynny
in hanov crist a vercy
   theth gortheby parys off
ov sovdrys duen warnetha
pur thefry kyns tremena
   ahanan y a perth coff

[*gonnys. Hic praeliabunt*]

Teudarus
Ov sovdrys dregh thymo margh
[*horse aredy*]
na felle sur nynsus pargh
   dare ov fobyl yv marow
ha me tebelwolijs
da ythomleth a feyys
   an duk yv corff hep parov

Dux
Ho sovdoryon lemmen ho
galles an turant then fo
   nynso abel thum perthy
darum y bobyl yv marov
gorthyans the crist caradov
   grontia dym an vyctory

[*ascendit*]

Peys warbarth myns os omma
bevnans meryasek yma
   parte thyugh hythyv disquethys
dugh an ll a dermen
han remenant in certen
   dre gras du a veth guelys

Evugh oll gans anguary
ny a vyn agis pesy
   a luen golon
wy agis beth gor ha gruek
banneth crist ha meryasek
   banneth maria cambron
pybugh menstrels colonnek
   may hyllyn donsia dyson

Duke
I am ready as soon as you like,
in the name of Christ of mercy,
  to answer you.
My soldiers, let us go for them
before we leave:
  they will remember us.

[*Guns. Here they shall do battle*]

Teudar
My soldiers, bring me a horse!
[*Horse ready*]
There any resisting any longer –
  What! My people are dead,
and I am grievously wounded.
He fights well whom I disparaged –
  the Duke is a man without equal.

Duke
Stop, soldiers, stop now!
The tyrant has fled,
  he was unable to resist.
Some of his people are dead.
Praise to beloved Christ
  for granting me victory.

[*He goes up*]

Peace on all that are here!
Here the Life of Meriasek
  in part is shown to you today.
Come again and the rest
will certainly be revealed,
  by the grace of God.

Drink all of you with the play,
we ask of you
  with a full heart.
You will have, man and woman,
the blessing of Christ and Meriasek,
  the blessing of Mary of Camborne.
Pipe, hearty minstrels,
  that we begin our dance.

31 'Ellas ow holen yv trogh'

Mulier
Ellas ov holen yv trogh
ellas thym nynsese
   mas eff na confort in beys
maria gonys a raff
thy fesy gans colen claff
   rag ov map me a vyn moys

[*tranceat ad ecclesiam beate marie. genuflectit et expectat ibidem*]

Marya mam ha guerhes
   me a vyn the luenbesy
maria ov map gueres
   ha restoria thymo vy
maria me reth cervyes
   thum gallus bythqueth defry
maria wyn rag ov les
   y colmennov grua terry
maria mar a mynnes
   delyfrys bya surly

Tyrannus
Hov geylers golsovugh wy
   me a charg war beyn tenna
boys na dewes na regh ry
   the guas a ruk vy orna
the preson pur eredy
   an vorov rum lel ena
me a vyn prest y cregy
   y quartrona hay denna

Carcerarius
[*ad tyrranum*]
Arluth the voth a veth grueys
eff nefre ny veth goleys
   me a wor the guir henna
mar peth cregys an vorow
vastya boys heb feladov
   ny venen adro dotha

Mulier
Maria me reth pesys
   rag ov map sur lues guyth
maria wath ny vynsys
   thymo vy gul confort vyth

31 The Two Mothers

Woman
Alas, my heart is broken.
Alas, I had no other child
  but him, nor any comfort in the world.
I shall serve Mary:
I will go to pray to her
  with a sick heart for my son.

[*Let her cross to the church of the Blessed Mary. She kneels and waits in the same place*]

Mary, mother and virgin,
  I pray to you.
Mary, help my son
  and restore him to me.
Mary, I have always served you
  as best I can.
Blessed Mary, for my sake,
  break his bonds.
Mary, if you wish it,
  he would be delivered for sure.

Tyrant
Ho, gaolers, listen!
  I charge you on pain of disembowelling
to give no food or drink
  to the fellow that I ordered
to be thrown in prison.
  Straightaway tomorrow,
by my faithful soul, I will hang
  draw and quarter him.

Gaoler
[*to the tyrant*]
Lord, your will be done.
He will not be fed
  I know that for certain.
If he will be hanged tomorrow,
we will not waste food
  on him.

Woman
Mary, I have prayed to you
  for my son, surely, many times.
Mary, yet you would not
  give me any comfort at all.

maria me a weyl neys
   am creya vy fors ny reyth
maria mercy mar suys
   in nos praga nam clowyth
Maria nynsus nahen
   ny ammont ov peiadov
maria ov map certen
   yma in tyn colmennov
maria creys thym lemen
   rag ov flogh an caradov
maria the vap byen
   gene dre ytha hythov

Maria ater the vregh
   dulle them the vap ihesu
awoys ovn peryl na pegh
   eff a dre gena hythyv
     dus dus a vaby
farwel genes maria
ny vanna the annya
   oma na moy ov pesy

[*tranceat domum cum ihesu*]

Ihesu crist lowene dys
purker ty a veth guythys
[*cofyr aredy*]
   avel ov flogh ov honyn
hag in quethov fyn malys
in ov cofyr sur gorys
   oma alwethys certeyn
lemen me yw lowenhes
   moys the powes me a vyn

Maria
[*in celo dicit*]
Ihesus ov map caradov
myns us grueys heb feladov
   dalour y wothes certen
ha pendra us in golon
confort thum cervons dyson
     boys y carsen

Ihesus
A vam grua del vy plesijs
neb ath worth a veth esijs
   kyn fensi polge ov cortes
     theth servont myr

Mary, I see clearly
  that you take no notice of my crying.
Mary, if there is mercy,
  why do you not hear me in the night?
Mary, there is nothing left,
  my prayers count for nothing.
Mary, my son is truly
  in tight bonds.
Mary, trust me now,
  for my child's sake,
Mary, your little son, the beloved one,
  shall go home with me today.

Mary, from your arms
  give me your son Jesus.
In spite of sin and every danger
  he shall go home with me today.
    Come, come, O baby.
Farewell to you, Mary,
I will not trouble you
  here any more with my prayers.

[*Let her go home with Jesus*]

Jesus Christ, joy to you!
Very dearly I shall keep you
[*Coffer ready*]
  as if you were my own child,
wrapped in fine linen
and securely laid in my coffer,
  now locked.
Now I am joyful,
  I shall go to rest.

Mary
[*In Heaven she says:*]
Jesus, my beloved son,
you know unfailingly and only too well
  every action,
and what is in the heart.
I should like to be
  of keen comfort to my servants.

Jesus
O mother, do as you please.
Whoever worships you will find ease,
  although they may have to wait a while.
    Look to your servant,

grua the desyr
   ha both the vreyes

[*descendit maria cum ij angelis
ad carcerem*]

Maria
A then yonk fetel esta
mur yv the lavyr omma
   heb y dyndyl
sav a vo in bevnans da
grays du purguir the henna
   in dyweth certen ny fyl

Filius
Ihesu arluth thum gueres
byth ny alla omheres
   dyegrys off gans gvander
ny won rum caradevder
pendra yv an golevder
   us adro thym heb awer

Maria
Omconfort drefe warvan
kynthes gyllys feynt ha guan
   wath ty a veth confortys
in nos na gymer dyglon
me ath dylerff an preson
   oma y tuth rag the leys

Filius
Grovs crist benedicite
pyv re duth thymo ome
   han darasov ol degeys
nos tevle ytho nam nygen
ha lemen sur golvygyen
   adro thym yma cothys
hag yma forme a vynen
   myternes pur in y greys

Maria
Dore in mes the garov
the orthys an carharov
   prest me a den
ha dyso an darasow
vgoreff heb feladow
nynsus dyalwethy gov
   am guyth certen

follow your desire
   and the will of your mind.

[*Mary goes down with two angels
  to the prison*]

Mary
O young man, how are you?
Great is your travail here,
   without your deserving it.
But whoever lives a goodly life,
God's grace very truly for that one
   in the end certainly will not fail.

Son
Lord Jesus, help me,
I can never help myself.
   I am shattered by hunger.
I know not, by my charity,
what is the light
   that is all around me.

Mary
Take comfort, rise up,
although you have become feeble and weak,
   yet you will be comforted.
Do not be disconsolate in the night:
I shall release you from the prison,
   I came here for your sake.

Son
Cross of Christ, what blessings!
Who has come to me here
   though all the doors are shut?
It was a dark night just now,
but now for sure radiance
   has fallen around me,
and there is a form of a woman,
   a veritable queen at its centre.

Mary
Take out your legs:
Straight away I shall take
   your fetters from you,
and shall open the doors
for you without fail.
No mere keys will be able
   to prevent me.

Lemen ov map ke theth vam
ha lafer dethy heb nam
   maria theth delyfrya
ha spesly lauer dethy
drens hy ov map dymovy
ha gruens ov servia deyly
   arta awose helma

Filius Mulieris
Maria gorthys reby
maria guyff nynsen vy
   genes the vones ledijs
maria thyso mur grays
maria na ve the reys
   gon guyr y fyen dyswreys

Maria
Ov banneth genes heb nam
ham banneth y roff theth vam
   lauer in delle dethy
kyn thevely dethy pel
ov boys hep y clowes lel
   ny vennen y ankevy

[*finit*]

[*tranceat maria ad celum*]

Carcerarius
Out gony mata sa ban
haneth oll an beys gans tan
yma purguir ha presan
   ov colowhy
me a greys boys grueys forth lan
   ena defry

Garcon
An presnour in kerth galleys
han darasov oll degeys
   pyv an iovle revue oma
duen then turont leferyn
a molleth du in gegyn
   at oma sur drog athla

Carcerarius
[*ad tyrranum*]
A ser turant gony gony
an presner in kerth defry

Now my son, go to your mother,
and tell her truthfully
   that it was Mary who set you free,
and in particular tell her
that she should bring my son to me,
and that she shall serve me every day
   after this.

The Woman's Son
Mary, may you be praised!
Mary, I was not worthy
   to be guided out by you.
Mary, great thanks to you!
Mary, were it not for your grace,
   I know truly that I should have been destroyed.

Mary
My blessing upon you unblemished one,
and my blessings upon your mother.
   Say this to her,
that though I seemed distant to her,
that I could not hear her clearly:
   I would not forget her.

[*She finishes*]

[*Let Mary go over to heaven*]

Gaoler
Out, woe upon us, get up!
Tonight, all the world is on fire,
truly, and the prison
   shining.
I believe a clear path has
   been made indeed.

Boy
The prisoner has gone,
and the doors are all shut.
   Who the devil has been here?
Come, let us tell the tyrant —
O the curse of God in the kitchen! —
   here was an evil criminal for sure.

Gaoler
[*to the tyrant:*]
O sir tyrant, woe, woe upon us!
The prisoner this very night

    galles eff haneth in nos
golovder ganso revue
bythqueth moy ovn numdarfe
    re thu am ros

[*finit*]

Tyrannus
out govy harov harov
    py ma ov fresner feyys
why a feth purguir marov
    mara sywe dyenkys
        rum lel ena
an horsens revue methov
ha re ases tus an pov
    me a wor thy delyvrya

Garcon
Ay turant ke war the gam
molleth du the vap the vam
    yma ree ov leverel
heb ty vyth nag ovlya
delyfrys der varia
    fetel ywa dyogel
hagis boys wy de vlamya
    war vohogogyon cruel

[*finit*]
    [*yerde aredy*]

Tyrannus
Ay dar indelle vethy
    mal myscheff regis doga
ov sclandra mar mynnough why
    ha leferel ov bosa
        omma cruel
why an prevyth du in test
have that me agis lest
    rag desky drok thym covsel

Filius
Hebasca thywhy ov mam
    mur reverons the varia
thynny prest y fye cam
    mar ny rellen y gorthya
        in guelhe preys
hy re ruk ov delyfrya

has stolen away.
Radiance surrounded him.
By the God who made me
    I was never more frightened.

[*He finishes*]

Tyrant
Out, woe is me, harrow, harrow!
  where is my prisoner fled?
By my faithful soul
  if he has escaped
    you are as good as dead.
The sons of whores were drunk
and let the people
  deliver him, I know.

Boy
Hey, tyrant, take it easy,
God's curse to your mother's son!
  Some are saying,
without any oath-taking or false swearing,
that he was surely
  rescued by Mary,
and that you are to blame,
  for being cruel to the poor.

[*He finishes*]
  [*A staff ready*]

Tyrant
What! Is it so?
  Curses, May the devil take you!
To slander me
  and say I am cruel,
    I'll make you pay for it,
as God's my witness!
Take that! That will teach you
  to speak evil of me.

Son
Comfort to you, mother!
  Much respect to Mary:
it would be a wrong for us
  not to worship her
    for our good fortune.
It is she who has rescued me

mes a preson mam kerra
 le may theua drokhendelys

Mulier
Maria rebo gorthys
daswewys yv ov sperys
 ov map the gueles oma
fetel vusta delyfrys
laver thymo me ath peys
 ov map kerra

Filius
Maria thymo in nos
 purguir a thueth then preson
gans golov ha mur a tros
 in coske bo dufen dyson
 ny won esen
hy purguir am degolmas
han dares dym egoras
hag vfel am comondyas
 thum mam the dre may thellen
Inmethy lauer theth vam
me theth delyfrye heb nam
 sav thymo restoryans hy
ov map henna nynsyv cam
 pan vsy y flogh dethy

Mulier
The varya wyn mur grays
a vyna hy the guerays
 in dyweth ny veth tollys
y flogh me a gemerays
the orth y ysmach a rays
 drefen nages restorijs
 thymo gensy
marthys claff o ov holon
an flogh then ymach dyson
 my a vyn don eredy
Ha mos quik bys in eglos
oma atte guythys clos
 y aperia ny vynnys
maria lowene dis
maria dyso mur grays
 ov map dym dry pan vynsys

[*descendit ad ecclesiam beate marie cum ihesu*]

from prison, dearest mother,
   where I was badly treated.

Woman
May Mary be adored!
My spirit is restored,
   my son, seeing you here.
How were you set free?
Tell me, I pray you,
   my dearest son.

Son
Mary came to me in prison
   in the night, truly,
with light and much commotion.
   I did not know, honestly
     if I was sleeping or waking.
She certainly unbound me
and opened the door for me,
and gently bade me
   go home to my mother.
Said she: 'Tell your mother
that it was I who set you free without a second thought
   but let her restore my son
to me: there's nothing wrong with that,
   since she has her own son.'

Woman
Many thanks to blessed Mary!
Whoever she will help
   will not be disappointed in the end.
I took her child
from her holy image:
   wondrous sick was my heart
     because she had not
restored you to me.
I will hasten to the church
   and swiftly restore
the child to the image.
Behold it is closely guarded!
   I would never harm it:
Mary, joy to you,
Mary, many thanks to you
   for bringing my son to me according to your will.

[*She goes down to the church of Blessed Mary with Jesus*]

32 'Dugh why thym'

Meriadocus
[*in oratorio iacebat*]
Dugh why thym ov bredereth
corff ov arluth del deleth
   hythyv me re recevas
reys yv dyberth otyweth
   kyn fo tek an gowethas.
The ihesu rebo grasseys
gans mernans me yv tuchys
   reys yv mones an bysma
bredereth vsyogh dader
han vohosogyen pub vr
   bethugh sokyr an rena

Decanus
[*ad meriadocum*]
Arluth fetel vyth dynny
mar teberthyth eredy
   meryasek the orthen
me a wor in guir hep mar
benytho arluth ath par
   pur thefry nyngynbethen

Meriadocus
Yma an preys ov nesse
the crist me a vyn grasse
   thym y thadder in bysma
yesseys unctis communijs
off lemen the ihesu grays
the orth crist lel map guirhas
rag ov servesy in beas
   war thu pesy me a ra

[*genuflectit*]

Neb am gorth vy in bysma
   ihesu arluth gront dethy
gallus boys yesseys oma
   kyns es merwel eredy
corrf crist inweth receva
   ungijs gans henna defry
then vlas neff age ena
   may thella purguir then ioy

In le may feua gorthys
   peseff rag an keth rena

32 The Death of Meriasek

Meriasek
[*He was lying in the oratory*]
Come you to me, my brothers.
Today I received my Lord's body
   as is right and proper.
It is needful to part at last
   in spite of good comradeship.
Jesus be thanked!
I am touched by death,
   and it is time to go from this world.
Brothers, follow goodness
and, as to the poor, always
   be a help to them.

Dean
[*to Meriasek:*]
Lord, how will it be for us
if you go away
   from us, Meriasek?
I know indeed, for sure,
we shall not ever have
   a lord equal to you.

Meriasek
The time is drawing near:
I thank Christ
   for His kindness towards me in this world.
And now, thanks to Christ
I am confessed, anointed, and have taken communion.
From faithful Christ, son of a virgin,
I pray to God
   for my servants in this world.

[*He kneels*]

Whosoever reveres me in this world,
   Jesus, Lord, grant that
they be shriven here
   before I die,
and that they receive the body of Christ,
   certainly anointed with that,
so that their souls may go in joy
   to the land of Heaven.

That I may be revered on earth
   I pray that whosoever

maystefons y luen yeheys
  pesy warnaf a rella
ha sawys a pup cleveys
   aberth an corff han ena
susten maystefons kefrys
  ha lor pegans the vewa
In kernov me ambeth chy
  ryb maria a cambron
thum wyles neb a thue dy
  me as aquit purdyson
   kyn fo ov corff in ken le
in keth plasna neb a beys
gans ihesu y feth clowys
hay petyconn colenwys
  lafyll purgir mar pethe

Ov gol a veth suer
  in mes metheven
an kynsa guener
  rag nefre certen
   ov banneth vy
gans banneth crist pen an sens
the kemmys ov gol a sens
  y pese bys venary

prays for me
   may have full health,
and be made whole of every disease
   of the body and soul,
that they may have nourishment also
   and a sufficiency to live.
In Cornwall I shall have a house
   by Mary of Camborne:
and whosoever shall go there to visit
   I shall absolve him straight away,
     although my body is in another place.
In that same place whoever shall pray
to Jesus will be heard,
and his petition fulfilled,
   if truly it is lawful.

My feast will be
   the first Friday
in the month of June,
   and forever certainly.
     My blessing,
with the blessing of Christ, the head of the saints,
I shall pray forever
   for all those that keep my festival.

33 From **Homelyes XIII in Cornish by John Tregear** (c.1555–60)

De Creatione Homini: Ima an profet Dauit in peswar vgans ha nownsag psalme ow exortya old an bobyll the ry prayse hag honor the du ha thy servya in lowendar ha gans perfect colononow the reiosya in sight agan creator ha redemar. yma an profet dauid ow allegia helma kepar ha dell ewa sufficiant cawse again redempcion. *Scitote Quoniam Ipse Est Dominus. Ipse Fecit Nos, Et Non Ipsi Nos*, henna ew tha leverall in agan eyth ny. Gothvethow fatell ew du agan arluth ny, hag eff ew agan gwrer ny, rag ny ny russyn gull agan honyn. Rag in dede neb a rella predery an creacyoon a vabden ha pondra in ta in y remembrans a behan o agan dallath ny wore gull ken ys ry honor, lawde ha preysse the du neb o y gwrer ha creator. Rag in creacion a bub tra arell visible ny rug du an tas a neff mas commondya ha according thy blonogeth oll creators a ve gwrys gans an ger a thu. sow in creacion a vabden an tas a vseias solempnyty bras, ha lowre notabyll sicumstans. An kensa tra vgy ow tuchia an creacion a mad den, an tas a leverys *Hic Faciamus Hominem*, omma ny a ra gull den, an gerryow na o. an gerryow a thu an tas (kowses warlerth an maner an bobill) the thew an mab an second person ha then spuris sans an trissa person, kewses warlerth an maner an bobyll, pan vons y ow mois the wull nampith a ober bras, rag nyna tus a gymmer advisement bras kyns dallath aga ober inweth y ara ioynya gans an gwella han furra cosullyow a alla bos kyffes. An kyth cyrcomstans ma a alse bos geses in part du an tas rag eff a alsa creatya specially a thu an tas the vabden.

In Te Jhesu Spes Mea De Redemptione Humani Generis: I fe deswethys thewgh, tus vas, kyns lymma in kynsa homely fatell ve agan hendaaow ny, adam hag eve, dre an singular dadder han speciall favours a thu golosek, creatis nobyll ha worthy creature hag in stat a perfect innocencye y fe inweth dysquethis thewgn, fatell russens dysobaya aga gwrear, aga creator henno an tas a noff, ha rag henna y a thros aga honyn hag oll lynyath mabden then stat a thampnacion. Henew the vnderstondia agan redemption ny. Rag an vnderstonding a henna why a ra perfectly done in agys remembrans fatell ve an holl nature a then kyffrys in corffe hag in ena Defoylyn ha kyllys dre original pegh. Rag an ena, an pith ew an chyff part a vabden, a gollas dretha an especiall royow a race; ha gans an royowna ena madden o enduwyes in dalleth in y creacion inweth pelha agys henna ytho colynwis in royow a nature, henno reomembrans, vnderstonding, blonogeth, gans moy royow erall an parna, han corffe an pith ew an gwanha part a ve dres then stat a mortalite dre an meanys a orginall pehosow, dre henna maytho res thotha prys merwell, ha henna o dre pohosow agan hendasow ny. an corfe a ve gwrys gwan, ha drys the vos gustith the lyas kynda a cleves ha gwannegreth. favowre, ha then stat an bewnans heb deweth, pan ova in della

33 From **The Homilies by John Tregear** (c.1555–60)

On the Creation of Man: The prophet David in the ninety-ninth psalm, exorts all the people to give praise and honour to God and to serve Him in joy, and with perfect hearts rejoice in the sight of our Creator and Redeemer. The prophet David alleges this is sufficient for our redemption. *Know ye that He is the Lord. He made us and not we ourselves*, that is to say in our language, know that God is our Lord, and He our maker, for we did not make ourselves. For indeed, whoever might think of the creation of mankind and ponder well in remembrance of Him how small was our beginning could not do other than give honour, laud and praise to God who was his maker and creator. And in the creation of everything visible God, the Father from Heaven, only commanded and according to His will all creatures were made by the word of God. But in the creation of mankind, the Father used great pomp and enough noble ceremony. The first thing regarding the creation of mankind is that God said, *here we shall make man*, those were His words. The words of God the Father (spoken after the manner of the people) to God the Son, the second person, and to the Holy Spirit, the third person, spoken after the manner of the people when they go about some great work, for the people do not refuse to take good advice before beginning their work, but also they join with the best and wisest counsels that can be got. This same ceremony could have been left out by God the Father, because He could create and make mankind without it. But through it He declares the special favour of God the Father to mankind.

In Thee Jesus is my hope for the redemption of the human race: It was shown to you, good people, before this in the first homily how our ancestors Adam and Eve, through the singular goodness and special favour of almighty God, were created noble and worthy creatures and in a state of perfect innocence. It was also shown you, how they disobeyed their creator that was the Father of Heaven, and therefore brought themselves and the whole lineage of mankind to the state of damnation. That is to understand our Redemption. To understand you shall perfectly bring to your remembrance how the whole nature of man, both in body and soul, was defiled and lost through original sin. For the soul, which is the chief part of mankind, was lost through it, and the special gift of grace, with those fulfilled in gifts of nature; remembrance, understanding, the will, with others of the same kind, and the body, which was the weakest part, were brought to a state of mortality through original sin, because of which it was necessary for them sometime to die, through the sins of our forebears. The body was made weak, and caused to be subject to many kinds of sickness and infirmity. Therefore, God was not able through truth and justice, to receive mankind again to favour, and to the state of life without end, since he was thus defiled in both body and soul, through his defoylye kyffrys in corffe hag in ena dre y fowt y honyn, mas eff a vo kynsoll gwrys pure ha glane.

Jhesus De Primatina Ecclesie Militantis: Symon mab Joaness esta worth ow cara vy [?] pedyr a worthebys, Ea, arluth, te a wore fatell ra ve the care ge. crist a leverys, mage ow eyne ve. nena eff a goways thotha an tryssa trevath, Symon mab Joannes, esta worth ow care ve [?] pedyr a gemeras dewan, rag crist the leverell thotheff try torne, esta ge worth ow care ve [?] pedyr whath an gorthebys haga leverys, Arluth, te a wore pub tra, ha te a wore fatell re ve the cara, Eff a leverys the pedyr, gwra maga ow devis.

Sacrament an alter:
[An bara ha]n gwyn dir goir Dew ew trylis the corf ha gois chris[t]
Bara han gwyn dir geir Dew ew gwris corf ha [gois Christ]
Bara ha gwyn dir gyrryow Dew, Corf ha gois Christ gwris e thew

own fault, although man was at first made pure and clean.

Jesus on the primacy of the Church Militant: 'Simon, son of John, do you love me?' Peter answered him, 'Yes Lord, you know how I love you.' Christ said, 'Feed my lambs.' Then he spoke to him the third time, 'Simon, son of John, do you love me?' Peter became sad, for Christ had said to him three times, 'Do you love me?' Peter still answered him and said, 'Lord, you know everything, and you know how I love you.' He said to Peter, 'Feed my sheep.'

On the sacrament of the altar:
The bread and the wine, through the word of God, are changed into the body and blood of Christ.
The bread and the wine, though the word of God, is made into the body and blood of Christ.
The bread and the wine, through the word of God, the body and blood of Christ are made.

Selections from The Creacion of the World by William Jordan (1611)

34 Death and Lamech

Death
me yw cannas dew ankow
  omma dretha appoyntys
rag terry gormenadow
  tha adam gans dew ornys
    ef a verve hay ayshew
yn della ythew poyntyes
tha vyns a vewa in byes
    me the latha gans ow gew
adam na eva pegha
  ha deffan an tas terry
mernans ny wressens tastya
  mes in pleasure venarye
    y a wressa prest bewa
omma eve ytho poyntyes
  cheif warden war paradice
ha der pegh a coveytes
  oll y joye ythew kellys
    may fetha parynes ragtha
gans an Jowle y fowns tulles
der an serpent malegas
    dell welsowgh warbarth omma

[*Death departeth away*]

Lamec
[*in tent*]
peys I say golsowogh a der dro
  orthaf ve myns es omma
lamec ythew ow hanowe
  mabe ythove cresowgh thyma
    tha vantusale forsoth
o cayme mabe adam ythove
  Sevys an Sythvas degre
arluth bras sengys in prof
  nymbes pur suer ew bewa
    peb am honor par dell goyth
drog polat ove rom lowta
  na mere a dorn da ny wraf
mes pub eare oll ow pela
  a dues wan mar a callaf
    ow fancy yw henna

Selections from The Creation of the World by William Jordan (1611)

34 Death and Lamech

Death
I am Death, the envoy of God,
   appointed by Him here.
For breaking the commandments
   ordained by God to Adam
      he and his progeny shall die.
Thus it is ordained
to all things living in the world,
   that I shall kill them with my spear.
Had Adam and Eve not sinned
   and broken the Father's prohibitions,
they would not have known death,
   but would have constantly lived
      in pleasure forever.
He was appointed
   chief warden over Paradise
but through the sin of covetousness
   all his joy is lost
      and he shall be punished.
By the Devil they were deceived,
through the accursed serpent
   as you say together here.

[*Death departs*]

Lamech
[*in a tent*]
Peace, I say, gather round
   and listen to me all of you.
My name is Lamech:
   believe me, I am the son
      of Methushael, in truth.
I am descended from Cain, son of Adam,
   in the seventh degree,
and held to be a great lord.
   There is certainly no one living
      who honours me as is my right.
A bad lot am I, by my oath:
   I don't do much good,
but I am always fighting
   the weak if I can:
      that's what I like doing.

187

whath kenthew ow hendas cayne
  pur had dean lower accomptys
me an kymmar in dysdayne
  mar ny vethaf ve prevys
    whath mere lacka
moye es vn wreag thym yma
  thom pleasure rag gwyll ganssy
ha sure me ew an kensa
  bythqwath whath a ve dew wreag
han mowyssye lower plenty
  yma thym nyngens dentye
me as kyef pan vydnag ve
  ny sparyaf anothans y
    malbew onyn a vo teag
saw ythove wondrys trobles
  skant ny welaf vn banna
pew an iowle pandra v gwryes
  me ny won war ow ena
    na whath ny gavas gweras
an pleasure es thym in beyse
  ythew gans gwaracke tedna
me a vyn mos pur vskes
  than forest quyck alema
    ha latha an strange bestas
a vs kyck an bestas na
  na a veast na lodn in beyse
ny wressan bythqwath tastya
  na whath kyke genyn debbrys
    na gwyne ny vsyan badna
vyctuall erall theyn yma
  ha pegans lower tha vewa
gans krehen au bestas na
  me a ra dyllas thyma
    par del wrug ow hendadow
haw hendas cayme whath en bew
yn defyth yn myske bestas
  yma ef prest ow pewa
drevan serry an taes dew
  towles ew tha vyshow bras
rag drog polat par dell ew
  ha lenwys a volothowe

[*Bow and arw redy with the Servant*]

ow servant des mes omma
  haw gwaracke dro hy genas
me a vyn mos tha wandra
  bestas gwylls tha asspeas

Yet although Cain is my forefather,
  and very much considered a very bad man,
I shall take it amiss
  if I am not proved
    very much worse.
I have more than one wife,
  that I can have my pleasure of them.
And certainly I am the first
  to have had two wives.
And maids, many and plenty
  I have as well – they are not fussy.
I have them when I wish.
  I do not spare a single one
    if she be fair.
But I am sorely troubled,
  scarcely can I see anything.
    Who the devil is it? What's going on?
  I do not know, on my soul,
    nor is there any help for me.
One pleasure I have in the world,
  is to shoot with the bow.
I will very quickly go
  to the hunting ground from here,
    and kill the strange animals.
Is there meat of any animal
  in the world, wild or tame,
that I have not tasted,
  no meat eaten by us, nor wine
    of which we have not touched a drop?
Other food I have,
  and the wherewithal to live.
With the skins of those animals
  I shall make clothes for myself
    as my forefathers did.
And my forefather Cain
is still living in the desert
    amongst the animals.
Because he angered the Father, God,
  he is destined to come to great misfortune,
for he is a bad fellow,
  and filled with curses.

[*Bow and arrow ready with the servant*]

My servant, come here,
  and bring my bow with you.
I am going to roam about,
  to look for wild animals,

hag a vyn gans ow sethaw
   latha part anothans y

Servant
ages gweracke ha sethow
  genaf y towns y parys
me as lead bez yn cosow
  hag ena y fythe kevys
    plenty lower in pur thefry

[*depart Lamech. his servant leadethe hem to the Forest near the bushe*]

Cayne
gans pob me ew ankevys
  nyn aswon na mere a dues
cayne me a vythe henwys
  mabe cotha adam towles
    why a weall tha vysshew bras
whath ow holan ythew stowte
awos latha abell lowte
  na whath vs molathe an tase
    nymbes yddrack v in beys
why am gweall over devys
    ythama warbarth gans bleaw
ny bydgyaf bonas gwelys
gans mabe den in bysma bew
    drefan owboos omskemynes

Cayne
owne yma thym a bub dean
  ganso tha vonas lethys
saw an tase dew y hunyn
  y varck warnaf y settyas
    poran gans y owne dewla
    why oll an gweall

[*Shew the marcke*]

hag yth cowses yn delma
na wra dean vyth ow latha
    war beyn y thyspleasure leel
hag owe latha neb a wra
vij gwythe y wea acquyttya
    y cowses gans chardge pur greyf
saw whath wos an promes na
mere y thesaf ow towtya
    y bedna zym ny vyn ef

and with my arrows,
  kill a few.

Servant
I have your bow and arrows
  ready with me.
I shall lead you into the woods
  and there you will find
    plenty enough, for sure.

[*Lamech departs. His servant leads him to the forest
  near the bush*]

Cain
I am forgotten by everyone,
  not many people know me.
Cain is my name,
  the eldest son of Adam, destined,
    as I shall see, for great misfortune.
Yet my heart is set:
neither for killing that lout Abel,
  nor for my father's curse,
    do I have any regret in the world.
You see me completely
  covered with hair.
I do not pray to be seen
living by any man's son in this world,
    for I am excommunicated.

Cain
I fear every man,
  of being killed by him,
but God the Father himself
  put his mark on me
    exactly with his own hands:
    you all shall see it.

[*Show the mark*]

And it is thus you understand
no man shall kill me
  on pain of His sure displeasure.
And whoever shall kill me,
seven times he must shrive
  his conscience with a powerful penance.
But despite that promise
greatly I fear
  that he will not wish me his blessing.

[*Let hem hyde hem self in a bushe*]

rag henna war ow ena
me a vyn mos tha gutha
    in neb bushe kythew thym greyf

Servant
mester da der tha gymmyas
me a weall un lodn pur vras
    hanys in bushe own plattya
sera in myske an bestas
strange ythew eve tha welas
    merough mester pymava

Lamec
bythware thym na vova dean
  rag me ny allaff meddra
set ow seth the denewhan
  may hallan tenna thotha
    na berth dowt y fythe gwyskes

Servant
[*Let his man levyll the arrowe; and then shote*]
nefra na wrewgh why dowtya
ken es beast nagew henna
    ha strange yw tha vos gwelys
now yta an seth compys
  tenby in ban besyn peyll
pardell os archer prevys
  hag a lathas moy es myell
    a vestas kyns es lemyn

Lamec
now yta an seth tennys
  han beast sure yma gweskes
    y vernans gallas ganza

[*when Cayne is stryken lett bloud appear & let hem tomble*]

lead ve quyvke besyn thotha
may hallan ve attendya
    pan vanar lon ythewa

Cayne
owt aylas me yw marowe
  nymbes bewa na fella
gwenys ove der an assow

[*Let him hide himself in a bush*]

Therefore, on my soul,
I will go and hide
   in some bush, though it grieves me.

Servant
Excuse me, good master,
I see a very great beast
   over there crouching in a bush.
Sir, it is strange to see him
amongst the animals.
   Look, master, where he is.

Lamech
Take care it is not a man
   because I cannot get an aim.
Put my arrow alongside
   so I can get a shot at him:
     do not doubt that I will hit him.

Servant
[*Let his man level the arrow and then shoot*]
Have no fear that this
is anything but an animal,
   and a very strange one.
Now the arrow is straight,
   draw it up to the feathers.
You are an experienced archer,
   who has killed more than a thousand
     animals before now.

Lamech
Now the arrow is loosed,
   and the animal is shot for sure.
     He is dead.

[*When Cain is struck let blood appear and let him
   tumble*]

Take me to him directly
so that I may see
   what kind of animal he is.

Cain
Out, alas! I am dead,
   I can no longer live.
I am pierced through the ribs,

han segh gallas quyte drethaf
  pur ogas marow ythof

[*Lamec cometh to hem* & *fyleth hem*]

pardell vema vngrasshes
lemyn ythoma plagys
  dell welowgh why oll an prove

Lamec
owt te vyllan pandres gwryes
sure hema ew dean lethys
  me an clow prest ow carma

Servant
ow karma yma an beast
  me an gweall ow trebytchya
gallas gona hager feast
  roy y grohan thym I pray tha
    tha wyell queth thym tha wyska
blewake coynt yw ha hager
  ny won pane veast ylla boos
yth falsa orth y favoure
  y bosa neb bucka noos
    ba henna y fyth prevys

[*hear Lamech feleth hem*]

Lamec
goria gas vy the dava
  drefan gwelas mar nebas
pew osta lavar thymma
  marses den po beast bras
    dowte ahanas thym yma

Cayne
a soweth vmskemymes
  me ew cayne mabe tha adam
genas y thama lethys
  molath theis ow thas ha mam
    haw molath ve gans henna

Lamec
pewa te ew cayne mab tha adam
  ny allaf cregye henna
defalebys os ha cabm
  overdevys oll gans henna
    ythos gans bleaw

and the arrow has gone straight through me:
  I am very near death.

[*Lamech comes to him and feels him*]

As I am without grace,
I am suffering now,
  as you can see: you all will experience it.

Lamech
Out, you scoundrel! What has happened?
This is a man killed for sure:
  I hear him shouting.

Servant
The animal is crying out:
  I see him stumbling.
He has taken a fearful blow.
  I pray you give me his skin
    to make a garment for me to wear.
Strange he is, hairy and ugly.
  I do not know what kind of animal it is.
He could be, by the look of him,
  some Bucca of the night,
    and that will be shown to be true.

[*Here Lamech feels him*]

Lamech
Wait, let me touch it,
  because I see so poorly.
Who are you? Tell me,
  are you a man or a great beast?
    You frighten me.

Cain
Oh, woe! Outcast!
  I am Cain, son of Adam,
I am killed by you.
  My father's and mother's curse upon you,
    and my curse along with it.

Lamech
Who? You are Cain, son of Adam?
  I don't believe it.
You are changed and bent over
  and quite overgrown
    with hair.

prag yhosta in delma
yn bushes own crowetha
   marth bras ythew
me ny allaf convethas
y bosta ge ow hendas
   na care y thym in teffry

Cayne
am corf ythos devethys
  hag a adam tha hendas
lemyn ythos melagas
  ha vij plag te hath flehys
   a v[yth] plagys creys a ve
marche dew warnaf ew sethys
  te an gweall in corne ow thale
gans dean penvo convethys
  worthaf ve serten ny dale
   bos mellyes a vs neb tra

Lamec
te a weall veary nebas
banna ny allaf gwelas
   tha vos accomptys lowta
prag y wruge dew settya merck
  in corn tha dale thym lavar
kyn verhan warnas mar stark
  ny welaf mere ath favoure
   na merke vetholl yth tale

Cayne
me a levar heb y dye
genaf dew a wrug serry
hay volath in pur theffrey
  thym a rose
drefan latha ow brodar
abell o henna predar
  mara mynta y wothfas
der henna me a thowtyas
  gans peb a fethan lethys
saw dew thyma a wrontyas
  war y thyspleasure ef ryes
   ny vethan in keth della
ha pennagle a wra henna
plages y fetha ragtha
hay verek y settyas omma
  in corne ow thale rag token
ha tha ganas she omskemynys

Why are you like this
lying in the bushes?
    It is a great marvel.
In truth I cannot believe
that you are my relative
    or any kinsman to me at all.

Cain
Of my body you are come
  and of Adam, your forefather.
Now you are accursed
  and you and your children
    will be plagued with seven plagues, believe me.
God's mark is set on me :
  you will see it in the horn on my forehead:
It should be understood
  that no man ought to interfere
    with me in any way.

Lamech
You see very little:
I can hardly see anything
    of any account, by my oath.
Why did God place a mark
  on your forehead? Tell me!
Though I am looking at you so carefully,
  I do not see what you look like,
    nor any mark on your forehead at all.

Cain
I tell you, without swearing an oath
that God became angry with me,
and put his curse
  on me for certain,
because of killing my brother:
Abel was the one,
  if you did but know it.
For that reason I feared
  that I would be killed by anyone,
but God granted,
  on pain of his displeasure
    that it should not be so.
And whoever might do it
would be punished,
and his mark he placed here as a sign
  in form of a horn on my forehead.
And may you be cast out!

o me tha vo[na]s lethys
  en ath dewlaga[s] lemyn

Lamec
a soweth gwelas an pryes
genaf y bosta lethys
    marsew ty cayne ow hendas
ow boya o tha vlamya
ef a ornas thym tenna
ha me ny wellyn banna
    me nebas pur wyre in faes

Cayne
a lamec drog was ythos
  ha me in weth mear lacka
hemma o vengeance pur vras
  ha just plage ornys thyma
    soweth an pryes

Lamec
cayne whath kenthota ow hendas
  tha aswon me ny wothyan
na ny wrugaf tha wellas
  nangew sure lyas belthan
    drefan bos dafalebys

Cayne
defalebys ove pur veare
  hag over devys gans bleawe
bewa ythesaf pub eare
  in tomdar ha yender reaw
    sure nos has dyth
by bydgyaf gwelas mabe dean
gans ow both in neb termyn
  mes company leas gwyth
    a bub beast!
oll an trobell thym yma
an chorle abell rag latha
    hemma ew gwyer thymo trest.

Lamec
prag ye wrusta ye latha
hag eve tha vroder nessa
    henna o gwadn ober gwyres

Cayne
drefan eve thom controllya
ha me y vroder cotha
    ny wrug refrance thym in beys

Oh, that I should be killed
   now in front of you!

Lamech
Oh, woe, that I should live to see
you killed by me,
   if it is you, Cain, my kinsman.
My servant was to blame:
he commanded me to shoot,
and I scarcely saw a thing
   very well at all.

Cain
O Lamech, you are a bad lot,
   but I am much worse.
This was great vengeance
   and a just punishment for me:
      alas the hour!

Lamech
Cain, even though you are my kinsman
   I did not know how to recognise you.
Neither have I seen you
   for many years,
      because you have changed.

Cain
I am very greatly changed,
   and covered with a pelt.
I live constantly
   in heat and coldness of frost,
      night and day for sure.
Not to look upon the sons of men,
at any time is my desire,
   but many times the company
      of every beast.
All the trouble falls on me
for killing Abel:
      that is true, trust me.

Lamech
Why did you kill him
your closest brother:
   that was a bad deed.

Cain
Because he ordered me about,
and I am his elder brother.
   He gave me no respect in the world.

der henna me a angras
ha pur vskys an lathas
   nymbes yddrag a henna
molath dew ha tas ha mam
gallas genaf ve droag lam
   poran rag an ober na
ow holan whath ythew prowte
   kynthoma ogas marowe
mersy whelas yma thym dowte
   thymo rag an oberow
me a wore y vos dew stowte
   thymo ny vidn ef gava
   na gevyans me ny whelaf
yethesaf ow tremena
   theso ny vannaf gava
ow ena ny won pytha
   tha effarn ew y drigva
     ena tregans gwave ha have

Lamec
ah soweth gwelas an pryes
   cayne own hengyke ew marowe
ragtha ty a vyth lethys
   a false lader casadowe
     squattys ew tha ampydnyan

[*kill hem with a staf*]

Servant
owt aylas me ew marow
haw fedn squatyes pur garow
   why an gweall inter dew ran

Lamec
rag henna moes a lemma
my a vydn gwell a gallaf
ny amownt gwythell duwhan
   lemyn ragtha

[*depart away*]

I Devyll
yma cayne adla marowe
devn the hethas tha banowe
   han pagya lamec ganso

Because of that I became indignant
and very quickly killed him.
  I do not regret it.
The curse of God, and father and mother,
have followed me, and evil circumstance
  precisely for that deed.
My heart is still arrogant,
  although I am all but dead.
I fear seeking mercy
  for my deeds:
I know that He is a resolute god:
  He will not forgive me,
  nor forgiveness shall I seek.
I am dying:
  I will not forgive you.
I do not know where my soul will go:
  hell is its dwelling place –
    there let it dwell, winter and summer.

Lamech
Oh, alas, that I should see the time!
  Cain, my kinsman is dead.
You shall be killed for it,
  O false hateful thief.
    Your brains are scattered!

[*Kills him with a staff*]

Servant
Out! Alas, I am dead,
and my head very rudely split.
  Here it is in two halves.

Lamech
I shall go from this place
as best as I can.
It is not worth lamenting
  for him now.

[*Departs*]

1st Devil
Cain the outlaw is dead.
Let us fetch him to his torments
  and young Lamech with him.

II Devyll
deas a ena malegas
theth vroder te a lathas
   abell neb ib dean gwirryan
yn tane te a wra lesky
han keth pagya ma defry
   yn effarn why drog lawan

[*the devills careth them with great noyes to hell*]

35 The Flood

Noy
now an lester ythew gwryes
   teake ha da tham plegadow
a bub chan a vestas
   drewhy quick ym orthe copplow
chattell ethyn kekeffrys
   dew ha dew benaw ha gorrawe

[*The arck ready and all maner of beastis and fowles to be putt in the arck*]

Sem
nynges beast na preif in beyse
   benaw ha gorawe omma
genaf thewhy yma dreys
   in lester ytowns ena

[*Let rayne appeare*]

Cham
a dase lemyn gwrewh parys
   an lyw nangew devethys
yma lowar dean in beyse
   kyns lemyn sure a gowas
     ages bos why gucky
pan wressowh gwyl an lester
   omma prest in creys an tyer
     moer vyth nyngeza defry
       the doen in ker

Japheth
geas a wressans annotha
dowie sor dew nyngessa
   thothanns nena me a wore gwyer

2nd Devil
Come, O accursed soul
   to the brother who you killed,
      the innocent Abel.
You shall burn in fire
in Hell, and this youth too,
     to be full of sorrow.

[*The devils carry them with great noise to hell*]

35 The Flood

Noah
Now that the vessel is made,
   handsome and good and pleasing to me,
Quickly bring to me in twos
   every kind of creature,
cattle, birds too,
   two by two, male and female.

[*The Ark ready and all kinds of animals and birds to be put into the Ark*]

Shem
There is no beast nor worm in all the world,
   female or male
not brought to you here by me.
   Behold them in the vessel.

[*Let rain appear*]

Ham
O father, make ready,
   now that the flood has come.
There are many men in the world,
   who said you
     were foolish.
When you made the vessel
right here in the middle of the land,
   there was no sea, certainly,
     to bear her away.

Japheth
They made mockery of it,
they did not fear God's anger
   I know for sure.

Noy
an lywe nangew devethis
   may thew da thyne fystena
pub beast oll ymma gyllys
   in lester thaga kynda
      dell yw orngys thymo ve
Kewgh abervath ow flehys
   hages gwregath magata
ogas an Noer ew cuthys
   der an glawe es awartha
te benyn abervath des
ow der bethy a vynta

Noy's Wife
res ew sawya an pyth es
nyn dale thym towlall tho veas
   da ew thyn aga sawya
I costyans showre a vona
an keth tacklowe es omma
   noy teake te a wore hedna

Noy
[*a raven & a culver ready*]
nangew mear a for pur wyer
aban gylsen sight an tyre
   rag henna thym ke brane vrase

[*let the raven fle and the culver after*]

nyedge in ker lemyn ha myer
   terathe mar kyll bos kevys
hag an golam in pur sure
   me as danven pur vskys
      sight an noer mar kill gwelas

Father in Heaven
marowe ew pub tra ea
   sperys a vewnans vnna
me a worhemyn whare
   than glawe namoy na wrella

[*The culver cometh with a branch of olyf in her mouthe*]

Noy
Then tase dew rebo grassyes
an golam ew devethys
   ha gensy branche olyf glase
arall bethans delyverys

Noah
Now that the flood has come
  it is good for us to hasten.
Every beast has gone
  into the vessel according to their kind,
    as I was instructed.
Go inside, my children,
  and your children too.
The Earth is almost covered
  by the rain from above.
You, woman, come inside,
or do you want to drown?

Noah's Wife
We need to save whatever we can –
it doesn't pay to throw anything away:
    it is good for us to save them.
They cost a good deal of money,
those things there:
    fair Noah, you know that.

Noah
[*A raven and a dove ready*]
Truly, it is a long way
since we got out of sight of land,
    so go, raven, for me.

[*Let the raven fly, and the dove after*]

Fly away and see
  if any dry land can be found,
and certainly I shall send
  the dove very quickly,
    to see if she can get sight of land.

Father in Heaven
Everything that had
  the spirit of life in it is dead.
Soon I shall order
  the rain to rain no more.

[*The dove comes with a branch of olive in its mouth*]

Noah
To God the Father, thanks!
The dove has come back
  with a green olive branch.
Let another be sent!

   does ny vydnas an vrane vras
     neb caryn hy a gafas
nangew ogas ha blethan
   aban dallathfas an lywe
marsew bothe dew y honyn
   neb ew gwrear noer ha neef
     tha slackya an kyth lyw brase
y vothe rebo collenwys
omma genan ny pub pryes
     kekefrys ha mabe ha tase

Father in Heaven
noy me a worhemmyn theis
   ke in meas an lester skon
thethe wreag hathe flehys keffrys
   ethyn bestas ha pub lodn

Noy
meare worthyans thyes arluth nef
te a weras gwadn ha creaf
   in othom sure panvo reys
den in mes bean ha brase
chattall ethyn ha bestas
   myns a ve in lester dres

[*An alter is redy veary fayre*]

yn dewhillyans pehosow
   grwethill alter me a vydn
me a viden gwythyll canow
   ha sacryfice lebmyn
radn chan a bub sortowe
   keffrys bestas hag ethyn
     gans henna thy honora

[*Some good church songes to be songe at the alter and frankensens*]

   ha rag hedna gwren ny cana
   in gwerthyans zen tase omma

Father in Heaven
hebma ythew sawer wheake
   hag in weth Sacrifice da
pur wyer noy ef thybma a blek
   a leyn golan pan ewa
     thyma ve gwyres
rag hedna sure me a wra

The raven would not return,
   it found some carrion.
No, it is nearly a year
   since the flood began.
If it is the will of God,
   the maker of Heaven and Earth,
     to cease this great flood.
May His will be done,
by us here always,
   Son and Father.

Father in Heaven
Noah, I order you,
   to leave the vessel quickly,
your wife and children,
   birds, animals, and every bullock.

Noah
Much glory to you, Lord of Heaven.
You help the weak and strong
   in need, for sure, when necessary.
Let us come away, great and small,
cattle, birds and beasts,
   all that were brought into the vessel.

[*A very handsome altar is made ready*]

As an atonement for sin
   I will make an altar.
I will now make songs
   and sacrifice,
one of every kind,
   beasts and birds,
     to honour Him.

[*Some good church songs to be sung at the altar and frankincense*]

   And therefore let us sing
   in glory to the Father here.

Father in Heaven
That is a sweet smell
   and a good sacrifice.
Truly, Noah, it pleases me,
   as it was made for me
   with a full heart.
Surely therefore I shall

Benytha woa hebma
    in ybbern y fyth gwelys

[*a Rayne bowe to appeare*]

an gabm thavas in teffry
   pesqwythe mays gwella why hy
remembra a hanaf why
  me a wra bys venarye
    trestge thyma
distructyon vythe an parna
benytha der thower ny wra
wos destrea an bysma
   ha rag hedna
cressowgh collenwouh keffrys
  an noer vyes a dus arta
pub ehan ha beast in byes
   puskes in moer magata
     a v[yth] thewgh susten omma
nynges tra in bysma gwryes
   mes thewhy a wra service
bethowh ware na vo lethys
   mabe dean genawhy neb pryes
ha mar petha in della
me a vidn ye requyrya
a thewla an kethe dean na
y woose a theffa scullya
yn havall thymma obma
ymadge dean gwregaf shapya
mar am kerowgh dell gotha
why a wra orthaf cola

Noy
ny a vidn gwyll in della
   del ewa dewar theny
ha thethe worthya rag nefra
   par dell ew agan dewty

an kethe jornama ew de
  en tase dew rebo grassyes
why a wellas pub degre
   leas matters gwarryes
     ha creacon oll an byse
In weth oll why a wellas
  an keth bysma consumys
der lyvyow a thower pur vras
   ny ve udn mabe dean sparys
     means noy y wreag hay flehys

give a blessing after this.
   It will be seen in the sky.

[*A rainbow to appear*]

Truly the rainbow,
   each time you see it,
will remind you of me.
   I shall be for ever:
     trust me.
I shall never again make
any like destruction by water,
for fear of destroying the world,
    and so
increase, fill up
   the world with people again,
every kind of beast in the world,
   and fish in the sea
     will be there for your nourishment.
There is nothing in this world made
   but to do you service.
Beware lest there be killed by you
   a son of man at any time.
For if it were to be
I would require
from the hands of that same man
who came to spill his blood.
I fashioned man
in my own image.
If you love me as is right
you will believe me.

Noah
So we will do
   as is required of us,
and worship you for ever
   as is our duty.

The day is over,
   thanks be to God the Father.
You oversaw every step,
   many things performed,
     and the whole creation of the world.
Also you saw
   this world consumed
by great floods of water.
   Not a single son of man was spared
     except Noah, his wife and his children.

dewh a vorowe a dermyn
　　why a weall matters pur vras
ha redempc[y]on granntys
　　der verey a thew an tase
　　　tha sawya neb es kellys
mynstrels growgh theny peba
may hallen warbarthe downssya
　　　del ew an vaner han geys

[*Here endeth the Creacion of the worlde with noyes flude wryten by William Jordan: the XII the August 1611*]

Come the morrow:
   you will see great things,
and redemption granted
   through the mercy of God the Father
     to save those who are lost.
Minstrels, pipe for us,
so that we can dance together,
   in the proper manner and style.

[*Here ends the Creation of the World with Noah's Flood written by William Jordan: the 12th of August 1611*]

36 One Parson's Certificate to Another, to Marry a Couple, whose Banns had been called, from Mr. Drake, Vic. of St. Just, to Mr. Trythal, Cur. of Sennen by William Drake (c.1636)

> Drake Proanter Eest, the Toby Trethell.
> Demytho Jowan an dean
> Tha Agnez an benen;
> Rag beneas an gy.
> En eglez ny Zelio Tri:
> Ha hemma urta ve, rago why
> Ha henna demithe gy.

37 John of Chyanhor by Nicholas Boson as transcribed by Edward Lhuyd (c.1665)

1 En termen ez passiez thera trigaz en St Levan, dên ha bennen en teller kreiez Tshei an hÿr.
2 Ha an huêl a kÿdhaz skent: Ha medh an dên dhÿ e urêg; me a vedn mÿz dha huillaz huêl dhÿ îl; ha huei el dendel 'gÿz bounaz ÿbma.
3 Kibmiaz têg ev kÿmeraz, ha pel dha êst ev a travaliaz, ha uar an dûadh e 'ryg dhÿz dhÿ tshei tîak; ha 'ryg huillaz ena huêl dha 'uîl.
4 Panna huêl allosti guîl medh an tîak; pÿb huêl ÿlla medh Dzhûan. Ena dzhei a varginiaz rag trei penz an vledhan guber.
5 Ha pa thera diwadh an vledhan, e vêster a dhisguedhas dhÿ dho an trei pens. Mîr Dzûan medh e vêster; ÿbma dhÿ gûber: Bez mar menta rei dhem arta, me a dheska dhîz kên point a skîans.
6 Dreu hedna medh Dzhûan: Na medn a vester rei dhem, ha me a vedn laveral dhîz: kemereu' dhan medh Dzhûan. Nenna medh e vêster: Kemer uîth na 'rey gara an vôr gôth frag an vôr noueth.
7 Nenna a dzhei a varginiaz rag bledhan moy, rag pokâr gwber. Ha pÿ thera dhiuadh an vledhan e vêster a dhrôz an dri penz. Mîr Dzhûan mêdh e uaster, ÿbma dha guber; bez mar menta rei dhem arta, me a dhÿska dhîz ken point a skîans.
8 Pa'n dreu' hedna mêdh Dzhûan; Na medh e vêster rei dhem ha me vedn lavarel dhîz: Kemereu' dhan medh Dzhûan. Nenna medh e vester; Kebmer uîth na ray ostia en tshei lebma vo dên kôth demidhyz dhÿ bennen iy(*ng*)k.
9 Enna dzhei a vargidniaz rag bledhan moy. Ha pa thera diuadh an vledhan e uaster dhrôz an trei penz. Mîr Dzhûan medh e vester: ÿbma dha guber: bez mar menta rei dhem arta me a dheska dhîz an guelha point a skîanz ôl.
10 Pa'n dreu hedna medh Dzhûan. na medh e vêster rei dhem; ha me a lavar dhîz: Kemereu' dhan medh Dzhûan. Nenna medh e vester: Bedhez guesgyz dhiueth, ken gueskal enueth, rag hedna yu an guelha point a skîans oll.

36 One Parson's Certificate to Another, to Marry a Couple, whose Banns had been called, from Mr. Drake, Vic. of St. Just, to Mr. Trythal, Cur. of Sennen by William Drake (c.1636)

> Drake the Priest of St Just, to Thomas Trethell.
> Marry John the Man
> to Agnes the woman;
> For their banns have been read,
> in our church on three Sundays:
> And that from me, for you
> and therefore marry them.

37 John of Chyanhor by Nicholas Boson as transcribed by Edward Lhuyd (c.1665)

1 In the time that is past, there were living in St Levan a man and a woman in the place called Chyanhor.
2 And the work fell scarce. And the man said to his wife, 'I will go to seek work and you can earn your living here.'
3 He took fair leave and far to the east he travelled, and at last he came to the house of a farmer, and sought work there.
4 'What work can you do?' said the farmer. 'Every kind of work,' said John. And they bargained for three pounds a year wages.
5 And when it came to the end to the year his master said, 'Here are your wages. But if you will give them back to me I shall teach you a point of knowledge.'
6 'What is it?' said John. 'No,' said his master, 'give them to me, and then I will tell you.' 'Take them then,' said John. Then his master said, 'Take care not to leave the old road for a new road.'
7 And they bargained for another year for the same wages. And when it came to the end of the year his master brought him the three pounds. 'Look, John,' said his master, 'here are your wages. But if you give them back to me I will teach you another point of knowledge.'
8 'What is it?' said John, 'No,' said his master, 'give them to me and then I will tell you. 'Take them then,' said John. Then his master said, 'Take care not to lodge in the house of an old man married to a young woman.'
9 And they bargained for another year. And when it came to the end of the year his master brought him the three pounds. 'Look, John,' said his master, 'here are you wages. But if you will give them back to me I will teach you the best point of knowledge of all.'
10 'What is it?' said John. 'No,' said his master, 'give them to me and then I will tell you.' 'Take them then,' said John. Then his master said, 'Be struck twice before striking once, and that is the

11 Lebmen Dzhûan e na vendzha servia na velha, bez e vendzha mÿz teua dha e urêg. Na medh e vêster reu' mÿz hidhu, ha ma gurêg vî a pobaz metten; ha hei'ra guîl tezan ragez, dhÿ dhÿz dre dhÿ dha 'urêg.
12 Ha an dzhei a uýraz an naw penz en dezan. Ha po 'riga Dzhûan kýmeraz e kibmiaz, ýbma medh e vêster, ma tezan ragez dhÿ dhÿn dre, dhÿ dha 'urêg: Ha po tî ha dha urêg an moiha lûan uarbàrh; nenna g'reu' tèrhi an dezan ha na henz.
13 Kimiaz têg e kemeraz, ha tiwa ha tre e travaliaz; ha uar an dhiuath e rig dÿz dha Gûn St. Eler Ha enna ev a vettiaz gen trei vertshant a Tre rîn (Tîz plêu) tÿz dre mez an fêr Karêsk.
14 Ha Dzhûan amedh an dzhei, diou gennan nei: Lûan oan nei dhÿ 'gýz guelaz huei. Pòlîa ve ti mar bèl?
15 Amedh Dzhûan, me a ve servia ha lebmen theram mÿz drê dhÿ a urêg. Ha medh an dzhei, ewz bàrha nei; ha uelkom ti a vêdh.
16 An dzhýi a kymeraz an vòr noueth, ha Dzhûan a guithaz an vor gôth.
17 Ha mÿz reb Kêou Tshoy Uûn, ha nagô an vartshants gillyz pèl dhoart Dzhûan; bez leddarn a glenaz ort an dzhei.
18 Ha an dzhýi a dhalladhaz dhÿ 'uîl krei: Ha genz an krei a 'ryg an Vartashants guîl; Dzhûan a greiaz auêth; Leddarn, leddarn!
19 Ha genz an krei a 'rîg Dzhûan guîl, an ledran a forsakiaz an Vertshants: Ha po 'ryg an dzhei dhÿz dhÿ Varha Dzhou, enna an dzhei a vettiaz arta.
20 Ha Dzhûan amedh an dzhei: Sendzhyz ôn nei dhÿ huei: Na vîa ragoh huei nei a vîa tîz oll dizurêyz Dîz barha nei, ha uelkym ti a vêdh.
21 Ha po 'ryg an dhzei dhÿz dhÿ'n tshei lebma gôth fîa an dzhei ostia; amedh Dzhûan me dal guellaz an ôst an tshei.
22 An ost an tshei amedh an dzhýi: Pe'ntra venta guîl gen an ôst an tshei? ýbma ma gen ostez nei ha yý(ng)k eu hei: mar menta guellaz an ôst an tshei, kî dhÿ'n gegen, ha enna ti an kâv.
23 Ha po 'ryg e dhÿz dhÿ'n gegen; enna e uelaz an ôst an tshei; ha dên kôth o ê, a guadn, a trailia an bêr.
24 Ha amedh Dzhûan, ýbma na vadna vi ostia bez en nessa tshei. Na huâth mêdh an dzhei. Gurâz kona abarhan nei, ha uelkym tî a vêdh.
25 Lebmen an hostez an tshei, hei a kýnsiliaz gen nebyn vanah a erra en tre, a dhÿ destrîa an dên kôth en guilli en termen an noz, a resta a dzhýi sýppozia; ha gýrra a fout uar an Vertshants.
26 Ha po Dzhûan en guilli, therra tôl an tâl an tshei; ha eve a uelaz gulou. Ha e savaz am'àn amez e uili; ha ev a gýzýuaz, ha e glýwaz an manah laveral. Ha trailiaz e gein dha an tÿl; martezen (amedh ev) ma nebônen en nessa tshei, a 'ryg uelaz agen hager oberou. Ha genz hedna, an guadn-gyrti genz e follat a dhestrîaz an dên kôth en guili.
27 Ha genz hedna Dzhûan genz e golhan, trohaz (der an tol) mêz a kein gûn an manah pîs pyr-round.

best point of knowledge of all.'

11 Now John would not serve any longer, but wanted to go home to his wife. 'Do not,' said his master, 'go home today. My wife is baking this morning and she will make a cake for you for your wife.'

12 And they put the nine pounds in the cake. And when John took his leave, his master said, 'Here is a cake for you to bring home to your wife. And when you and your wife are most happy together then break the cake and not before.'

13 He took fair leave and travelled homewards, and at last he came to St Hilary Down. There he met three merchants of Treen (fellow parishioners) coming home from Exeter fair.

14 'Oh John,' said the three, 'come with us. We are glad to see you. Where have you been so long?'

15 Said John, 'I was serving, and now I am going home to my wife.' And said they, 'Go with us, and welcome you will be.'

16 They took the new road and John kept to the old road.

17 And he went by the hedges of Choon. And the merchants were not long gone from John, when thieves seized them.

18 And they started to cry out. And with the cry that the merchants made John cried also, 'Thieves! Thieves!'

19 And with the cry that John made the thieves let the merchants go. And when they came to Marazion they met once more.

20 'Oh John,' they said, 'we are beholden to you. If it weren't for you we should all be murdered Come with us, and welcome you will be.'

21 And when they came to the inn where they should lodge, John said, 'I ought to see the host of the house.'

22 'The host of the house?' they said. 'What do you want with the host of the house? Here is our hostess, and she is young. If you want to see the host of the house, go to the kitchen, and you will find him there.'

23 And when he came to the kitchen he saw the host of the house, and an he was old man, weak, and turning the spit.

24 And John said, 'I will not lodge here, but in the next house.' 'Not yet,' they said, 'Have supper with us, and welcome you will be.'

25 Now the hostess of the house, she planned with a certain monk in the house to destroy the old man in bed at night and to put the blame on the merchants.

26 And when John was in bed, there was a hole in the gable of the house and he saw a light. He stood up in his bed and listened, and he heard the monk speaking. Turning his back to the wall, he said. 'Perhaps there is somebody in the next house to see our dirty deed.' And with that the bad wife and her companion murdered the old man in his bed.

27 And with that John with his knife cut (through the hole) a fair-sized round piece from the back of the monk's gown.

28 And the next morning the bad wife started to cry that her good

28 He nessa metten an guadn-gyrti, hei a dhalasvaz dhÿ 'wîl krei ter dhÿ e thermâz hei destrîez: Ha rag na erra dên na flôh en tshei bez an vertshantz, an dzhei dhal krêg ragta.

29 Enna an dzhei a vea kemeryz, ha dha an klox-prednier dzhyi a ve lediyz: Ha war an diuedh Dzhûan a dhêth uar' a go phidn.

30 Ha Dzhûan medh an dzhei ma kalliz lùk dha nei: Ma agen ost nei destrîez nehuer ha nei dal krêg ragta.

31 Huei ôl? mêr a huei an lutîziou (a medh Dzhûan) gyr tero an dhiz rag riman a 'ryg an bad-ober?

32 Piua ÿr medh an dzhei? pîu a 'ryg an bad-ober? Piu a 'ryg an bad-ober? medh Dzhûan: mar nyz medra dheffa previ peu a 'ryg an bad-ober; mî a vedn krêg ragta.

33 Laverou' dhanna medh an dhzhei. Nehwer medh Dzhûan, po thera vi itta 'o guili, mî a uelaz gulou, ha mi a savaz am'àn: ha thera tol en tâl an tzhei.

34 Ha nebyn Mânah a trailiaz e gein uar bidn an tùll. Martezen medh ev ma nabonnen en nessa tshÿi a el guelaz agen hager-oberou.

35 Ha genz hedna gen a holhan me a trohaz pîs, der an tol mez a kein gûn an manah; pîs pyr-round. Ha rag gîl a giriou-ma dhÿ vÿz prêvez; ÿbma ma an pis et a phokkat dhÿ vÿz guelyz.

36 Ha genz hedna an Vartshants a vî frîez: ha an vènin ha'n manah a vî kemeryz ha kregys.

37 Nenna an dzhei a dhêth uarbàrh mez dha Varha Zhou; Ha uar an diuadh dzhei 'ryg dÿz dhÿ kûz karn na huìla en Borrian.

38 Nenna thera vòr dhiberh; ha na Vartshants a vendzha arta dhÿ Dzhûan mÿz dre barh an dzhei; bez rag an termen e na vendzha; mèz e vendsha mÿz dre dhÿ e urêg.

39 Hapo dho ev gilliz dhort an Vartshants ev a dhelledzhaz an termen mal dha va prêv erra e wrêg guitha K´ympez et i gever: erra po nag erra.

40 Ha po 'ryg e dÿz dhÿn darraz, ev a vendzha klouas dhên aral en guili: Ev a uaske e dÿrn uar a dhàgier dhÿ dhestria an dhêau. Bez e brederaz ter gotha dhodho bÿz aviziyz dhiueth ken guesgal enueth.

41 Ha ev a dhêth a mês arta; ha nenna e gnakiaz. Peua ez enna en bar' Deu amedh hei.

42 Thera vi ÿbma medh Dzhûan: Re Farîa pîua glow vi medh hyi. Mar sô huei Dzhûan, dîaw tshÿi. Dowoy an gòlou dhanna, medh Dzhûan: nenna hei a dhorôaz an golou.

43 Ha po 'ryg Dzhûan dÿz tshei, mêdh ev po 'ryg avî dÿz dhÿ'n dÿrraz, me a venzhÿ klÿwaz dên aral en guili.

44 He Dzhûan medh hyi, po 'rygo hwei mÿz ker, thera vi gillyz trei mîz gen 'hlôh; ha lebmen ma dhÿ nei mepping huêg en guili, dhÿ dheu robo gor zêhez.

45 Medh Dzhûan me vedn laveral dhiz. A vester ha vestrez roz dhem tezan ha lavèraz dhem; Pan vo mî ha'm g'rêg an moyha lûan uarbàrh dho terri an dezan, ha na henz: ha lebman ma kaz dhÿ nei

man had been murdered. And as there was neither man nor child in the house except the merchants, they should hang for it.
29 They were taken and led to the gallows. And at last John met them.
30 'Oh John,' they said, 'we have had bad luck. Our host was murdered last night and we must hang for it.'
31 'All of you? Look for the justices,' said John, 'to bring before them those who did the evil deed.'
32 'Who knows,' they said, 'who did the evil deed?' 'Who did the evil deed?' said John. 'If I cannot prove who did it, I will hang for it.'
33 'Say then,' they said. 'Last night,' said John, 'when I was there in my bed I saw a light and I stood up and there was a hole in the gable of the house.'
34 'And a certain monk turned his back against the hole. "Perhaps," he said, "there is somebody in the next house to see our dirty deed."'
35 'And with that I cut with my knife through the hole a fair-sized piece from the back of the monk's gown. And to prove it I can show you the piece in my pocket.'
36 And with that the merchants were released, and the woman and the monk were taken and hanged.
37 Then they all came together to Marazion and at last they came to Coose Cornwilly in Buryan.
38 There was a forked road, and the merchants wanted John to go home with them again. But for the time being he would not, but would rather go home to his wife.
39 And when he had left the merchants he span out the time so that he might see whether his wife was staying faithful to him, was she or was she not.
40 And when he came up to the door he thought he heard another man in the bed. He pressed his fist on his dagger to murder them both. But he remembered that he had been warned before striking once.
41 And he went outside again and knocked. 'Who is it in God's name?' she said.
42 'I am here,' said John. 'By Mary, who do I hear?' said she. 'If you are John, come in.' 'Bring the light then,' said John. And she brought the light.
43 And when John came in, he said, 'When I came to the door I thought I heard another man in the bed.'
44 'Oh John,' said she, 'when you set off I was three months gone with child; and now we have a sweet little son in the bed, thanks be to God.'
45 Said John, 'I will tell you. My master and mistress gave me a cake and said to me, "Break the cake when you and your wife are most happy together and not before." And now we have cause to be happy.'

rag bÿz lûan.

46 Nenna dzhei a dorhaz an dezan, ha thera nâu penz en dezan. Ha an mona an dzhei a gavaz; ha'n bara dzhei a dhabraz; ha na ve iden frôth na mikan na trauaran nôr vez. Ha an della ma diuadh me daralla dhodhans.

38 Nebbaz Gerriau Dro Tho Carnoack by Nicholas Boson (c.1675)

Gun Tavas Carnoack eu mar pu gwadn hez, uz na ellen skant quatiez tho ewellaz crefhe arta, rag car dreeg an Sausen e thanen en pow idden ma an kensa, an delna ema stella teggo warno tha hep garra tho tha telhar veeth buz dro tho an Aulz ha an more, el eu a va clappiez lebben oggastigh en durt pedn an wollaz tho an karrack looez, ha tuah Poreeah ha Redruth, ha arta durt an Lizard tuah Helles ha Falmouth: ha an powna, an idna deu Codna (teer ez) en fester a dro tha iggans moldeer, ha buz quarter, en po hanter an lester na; en telhar idden ma ha gul ma mouy Sousenack clappiez dre eza Curnoack, rag radden el bose keeves na el skant clappia, na guthvaz Curnoack, buz skant Denveeth buz ore guthvaz ha clappia Sousenack; rag hedna he volden kallick eue tho gweel dotha gurtaz ha dose a dro arta, rag ugge an Teez tho merwal akar, ny a wele an Teez younk tho e clappia le ha le, ha lacka ha lacka, ha an delna eue a vedden beha durt Termen tho Termen. Rag an Tavaz Sousenack clappies mar da vel en telhar weth en wollaz tavaz an metherwin an [... .] na na gu an Pobel Coth tho bose skoothez war noniel, kar dre vedno why gwellaz urt hemma dro tho an Empack Angwin an brossa ha an cotha Fratier mesk ul an clappiers Carnoack, a dewethaz rag guffiniez tho dismiggia, Gevern Anko, eue a reeg peverre war Gever, ha meskeeges dro tho Anko, eue levarraz droua Gever ul, eue a wya dro, Gevern buz nekovaz dro an geer ko dewethaz durt per hen ko. Tra an pa [....] Me a glowaz dro tho an Karack Mean Omber; rag hedna mar peth travith gwrez tho gwetha Curnooack, eue a dale bose gen kine eu ginnez ubba, ha Deskez da, kevez buz mennau; rag na genz buz nebbas buz deu po try a orama anetha, mesk an gy wonen eu gwenhez ha Deskez, drez ul an rerol ane derarta enge polta, po vedn dose ugge va drez lirkland an delna eu penaveth [....] ab peth gwrez, lebben it an scant vedna bose gwrez uggehemma, vos deshava marveer Guthaz an l[....]az Tavaz pokarra tha Greckian, Hebran; [....] Me a glowaz lever [....] Markressa, an Dean deskez teer na gwellaz hemma [....] a venya kavaz fraga e ouna en skreefa composter, &c. Whath hemma el mose rag bonogath leig; rag na rigga ve beska gwellaz skreef Bretten Coth veeth; an Letherau war an Mean beath ez en Eglez Burian na oren pendra tho weel anotha, ha Mean orrol en Madern en Gunneau Bosolo henwez Mean scriffez tho an Jorna ma tegge na orren panna Letherau noniel; an peth eu gwellez gen a vee tho bose guthnethez ha dismiggiez en lawar Coth gwnez war Cota Dean broze en Arganz hunt

46 They broke the cake, and there were the nine pounds inside. And the money they kept, and the cake they ate. And there was no quarrelsomeness or spite between them in the world. And this is the end of my story about them.

38 A Few Words About Cornish by Nicholas Boson (c.1675)

Our Cornish tongue is so weakened that we can scarcely hope to see it revive again. For the English drove it into this narrow country in the first place, and that still has a bearing on it, without its remaining in any place but about the cliff and the sea. It is spoken these days nearly from the end of the land to the grey rock, and towards St Ives and Redruth, and again from the Lizard towards Helston and Falmouth: and as to that country, the narrower two necks of land are about twenty miles long, and but a quarter, or half that wide. And in that narrow place there is more English spoken than Cornish, for there are some to be found who can hardly speak or understand Cornish at all, but there is hardly anyone who does not understand and speak English; therefore, it will be hard to keep it and revive it, for after the old people die off, we see young people speak it less and less, and worse and worse, and so it will decrease as time goes on. For the English Tongue is spoken well in every place in the countryside [....] the old people are not to be relied upon either, as you will see from this concerning the learned Angwin, the greatest and eldest scholar amongst Cornish speakers, and lately asked to explain Gevern Anko. He thought of *an Gever* [goat] and was confused about *Anko* [death], and said that it was 'Goats all', he knew about *Gevern* [shire, hundred] but forgot that the word *ko* was from *park en ko* [remember]. I heard something of the same kind about the Logan Stone; so, if anything is to be done to retain Cornish, it must be done by those who are born here, and well educated, but seldom found, for they are but few. I know of two or three; amongst them there is one who is sophisticated and learned beyond all others before him, or who will come after him in all likelihood; so, if something is not done now, it will scarcely be done later, as he knows so many languages, Greek, Hebrew; [....] I heard say [....] If that learned and wise man should see this [....] he would find many reasons to correct the orthography &c. But this is just a layman's opinion, for I never saw any old British writing: I did not know what to make of the letters on the gravestone in Buryan Church; and another stone in Madron on Bosullow Downs, named Mean Scriffez [Men Scrifa – writing stone] to this day bears we know not what letters either; what I saw and understood after working it out was a sentence of letters in silver over a hundred years old on the coat of arms of a great man, now a knight in the west end of the land of Devonshire, and lost (it seems) by his clerk, going tho Canz bloath Coth lebben marrack en pedden west pow Densher, ha kellez (kar dre hevol) gen e Mab leean, mose tuah e Bargenteer en Pedden an wollas; eue ve kevez a dewethaz gen wonen reeg gweel Ke, ha gwerhez; an gwaz reeg e perna, a re [....] slanen tho an kensa skon [....] an Choy na igge tri [....] nez tho an karrack glooz en Cooze. An Gerriau war no [....] Car Dey res pyb tra, lebben nebbaz kene cowzez mar dewethaz (kar dre hevol) thera Curnooack en powna, ha lebben na gez buz nebbaz en powna an peth; ez gweel terem Creege drevednaua doweth akar. Rag me a hunnen ve gennez en Collan an Powna eu an Curnooack mouyha Cowzes, ha whaeth may kothem penaz oma buz dro tho wheeath Bloah Coth, na olgama e clappia, na skant e guthvaz; an where thera ma pedeere tho durt Seeanz a Dama tesna an Pobel-choy, ha an Contravagian tho clappia traveeth tho Ve buz Sousenack. Ma kothem cavaz tra an parma en lever Arlyth an Menneth dro tho e deskanz Latten. Hag ubba mar peth ama kibmiez tho gweel Semblanz gun Aulsen Coth Brose:

> Parvum Hoerediolum Majorum regna meorum
> Quod Proavus, quod Avus, quod Pater excoluit.
>
> *Nebbaz gun Teer, gun Treveth, ha bean Reveth,*
> *Telhar a Seera, Seera ... hinge a weth.*

[....] enna mose a lez tho Sc[....]ha ugge hedda mose tho Frenk, na gez kothem tho guthva meer en Tavaz Curnooack, lebna tose tho gawaz tra-gweele en Bez; ha lebben thera Ma toula tho gwellaz mar pel itna oggastigh vel leez an Controvagian, ha ma them mar veer crenga rarta; buz na ellam ry tho tha mouy tre guffia them; rag theu e skant tounack tho bose gwellez en leeaz Gerreau, a dael bose gwrez aman durt an Latten, po an Sousenack: ha na ore den veeth durt peniel reeg an kol ma kensa dose durt an Romans meskez gen a Brittez, po ugge hedna durt an Sausen, metessen durt an dew; buz thera ma wheelaz en skreefma (mar mere drel a ma) tho gurra an geerna a treneuhan ra dismiggia gun Tavaz ny senges tho rerol; ma lever bean rebbam dro tho an Arlothas Curnow skreefez rag an Flehaz nab Blethanniau a lebma, dro tho [....] deag wariggans, le [....] ma leverres gen [....] aorama dro tho an Tavaz Curnooack, Fat la eue a reeg dose t[....] mose a leez an Bretten, ha an Kembreeanz, ha an Curnowean, mesken gy na eue likland dre vidna gaz pel hep merwal akar, ha dose tho travith; therama suppoga an delna tho an lita, rag an Bretten ha an Curnowean: Voz an Frenkock feen parrez tho cummeraz telhar wara niel, ha an Sousenack nobla war e gilla; na orava drel an Kembreean gweel rag tho gwetha ge Tavaz; buz Me a aore hemma, urt a hoer an Curnoack, druava talvez buz nebbaz tho bose gurrez, war barrha gen an Sousenack, an peth eue parrez tho ry polta gwel tho tha, dre gava Cummerez durta; ha whaeth an Sousen metessen olga gawaz maga nebbaz Skeeanz vel an Brittez it ge clappia ge for, nereegan d[....]e drez ubba an kensa dalleth lebma gun towards his estate at Land's End; it was found recently by someone making a hedge and sold; the fellow who bought it sent it to the nearest branch of the House near the Grey Rock in the Wood [St Michael's Mount]. The words on it are 'Love God above everything', now said slightly differently. Recently (it seems) there was Cornish in that country and now there is hardly any in this country; which makes me think it will disappear. For I myself was born in the heart of the country where Cornish is spoken most, but even so I have no memory of it after I was about six years old, so I could hardly speak or understand it; the problem I think was a whim of my mother who forbade the servants and neighbours to speak anything but English to me. I remember seeing something of the same kind in the book of Lord Montaigne about his Latin. And here if I have leave to make a reference of our ancient great Ausonius:

> Parvum Hoerediolum Majorum regna meorum
> Quod Proavus, quod Avus, quod Pater excoluit.
>
> *Little our land, our estate, and small wonder,*
> *Father's place, grandfather's also.*

[....] then in going away to School, and after that going to France, I have no memory of the Cornish tongue much, until I came to business in the world; and now I reckon to see as far in it as most of my neighbours, and I have as great a love for it; but I cannot give more to it than I should; for it is incomplete in many words, which must be made up from the Latin, or English: and no man knows how this loss first came about, from the Romans mixing with the Britons, or after that with the English, perhaps from both; but by writing this I am looking (as far as I can) to refute the argument that shows our language to be beholden to others; there is a little book written by me about the Lady of Cornwall, written for the children some years ago, about [....] thirty, where [....] is said by [....] what I know about the Cornish tongue, how it came to split from the Breton and Welsh; and Cornish, as one of them, is not likely to remain long without dying out and coming to nothing; I assume so, at least as far as the Breton and Cornish are concerned, because fine French is ready to take on the one, and noble English the other; I do not know what the Welsh can do to keep their tongue; but I know this, from its sister language Cornish, that it is worth so little in comparison to English, which can give it much more than it receives in return. And yet the English might have found as little knowledge as the Britons in speaking their own way when they first came over here, until our better climate and the benefits of our good island raised them to a higher level. If anyone should say that the old tongue of the Britons could be raised to the same level if it were more favoured, I am so far from denying the tongue of my mother and my mother country, that for love of it I am

gwel neaue ny, ha an Gwayne gun Enys de reeg ge dro tho an u whelder ma [....] martra wonen ve [....] lever ol drolga tavaz an Brittez cooth tose th [....] ewhelderma, a we [....] marpee angy maou fortidniez, thera ve ma pel durth naha an dadn an Tavaz a Dama ha a pow, uz rag e Crenga dro ma parrez tho leverol an delna a weah, ha descunta leh dressa lever an Have an Arlothas Kernow bose kevez en dula a Flehaz ugge hemma, radden olga bose parrez tho leverol drerama gweel nebbaz aga a Curnoack, voz dre vengama gweel a hunnen tho bose devethez drez Maur, buz ma bose gun ollez gen panna Collan da therama leverol ul an Sompel rag an Curnooack; eue a dael bose Ankou e hunnen a vedden pedeere drerama creege hedna tho bose gweer eu skreefas enna, rag travith orrol buz tho gweel weez, ha lebben dru a devethez ita Brez, mea vedn gweel Duath an Skreefma durt an dewetha reem vez an Kensa Caon Horace,
    Quod si Me lyricis Vatibus inseres
Sublimi feriam Sydera Vertice.

Mar pethum Francan-belgan ma ra bose
Po car dru Sousen-Curnow vith anar vrause.

ready to declare this as well, moreover, that were a book of 'The Duchess of Cornwall's Summer' to be found in my children's hand after this, some might be prepared to say that I was belittling the Cornish, because I should be making myself like someone come from over the sea. Nevertheless, it can be seen with what a good heart I am declaring the whole matter of Cornish, and it must be Death itself that will think that I believe this to be true, for no other reason but to make mockery, and now that it comes into my mind, I will make an end of this writing by writing the last verse of the first song of Horace,

Quod si Me lyricis Vatibus inseres
Sublimi feriam Sydera Vertice.
[O that you would place me among the harp-playing prophets and that I would touch the stars with my head.]

If I shall have it, Franco-Belgian I shall be,
or as is Anglo-Cornish, will be great honour.

39 'Menja Tiz Kernuack buz gasowas' by John Tonkin (c.1693)

Menja Tiz Kernuack buz gasowas
tha kanna vee gy el e glowas
Rag fyr ha mescack thew a gwreze
Ubba en Tale gullas en Beze

Rag me a venja cowas na peath
della na vee a denneth tha weath
Rg an pocar ez en pedd'n
ha peege gungans mee a vedd'n

Ma tha ni Materne da
ha maternes maga Ta
Besca Rig dane Roul en Gwalaze
buz nag ew an Poble vaze

Eve Rig doaz thurt pow e whonnen
Tiz da gunja Leeas wonnen
Gorolyon da droaze e war dower
Sowias E vownans kerra vel ow'r

pereeg eve gurra Trooze war Tir
Eve welcumbes me ore Gwir
ha tha vethes tha Careesk
maga sowe besca ve pesk

Enna na rig eve Trigas pel
Buz eath tha wheelas an peath o gwel
an Jooal rag gurra war e bedd'n
   ha e weetha eve a vedd'n

Mattern James rig quachas e stoppia
bus E na allja e theath tha gloppia
Eva rig quachas moaze tha an gwella ternuan
bus e gothas drez an ne wharn

Ha ul e poble poonias tha Gova
Hemma e bra gwarre why na gova
Ha e tha worthen eath e whonnen
rag cowas gen e gare Trip-Cunnen

Enna e wraze Lowar wheal tha weel
Bowneege kelles Leeas meel
buz materen Wille wraze an wheal
ha fesias gy car vez an gweal

39 'If Cornish people would but listen' by John Tonkin (c.1693)

If Cornish people would but listen
to the song of mine they can hear
for wise and foolish it is made
here at the arse end of the world.

For I would have one thing
by which no one would be the worse
for how it is in the end
and I will pray for them

We have a good King
and queen as well
Never did a man rule a kingdom
if the people were no good

He came from his own country
with many people to serve him
ships to bring him over the water
saved his life, more precious than gold

When he set foot on land
he was welcomed I do truly know
and when came to Exeter
he was as safe as a fish

There he did not long remain
but went to see what was better
The devil did put into his head
and he will keep him.

King James tried to stop him
but he could not trip him up
He tried to go the best way
but he fell over

And all the people ran to him
his brave play do you not remember
and went to Ireland himself
to speak with his friend Tyrconnell

There he found many tasks to perform
Many thousands of lives lost
but King William carried out the task
and chased them from the field

Nenna e eath car rag Frink
rag debre an Tacklow ewe per trink
ma enna whath eve me ore gwir
ha plodia gen an hagar veer

ha enna ni e ved'n e ara
amesk an poble ez e gara
ha moaz tha wellaz an peath ez gwreze
en poww an Flemmen amesk an Tiz

Enna ma Leeas wonnen kelles
Kana geegans tha boaze gwelles
ha muy dale moaz tha an gletha stella
an lacca berra a mesk an gwellah

Ma Materen ni doaze Tre beddn wave
ha moaze car arta pe teffia have
Dewe reffa e sowia Tre ha leaze
ha gweel a vownans mear a heaze

menja e buz gweel dua
an Streef ter ni ha'n Creege thua
Materen Frink thera vee a menia
na venja hedda whath gun greevia.

40 'Ni Venja pea a munna seer' by John Tonkin (c.1695)

Ni venja pea a munna seer
ez boaze whele es car thurt an Tir
ca veca a Vlethan veth mar hir
ni veea plaises me ore gwir

Ma Leeas peege etha dirria pel
buz peea dua a veea gwel
ni veea preeze da rag an stean
ha rag an Hearn thurt Wille Mean

Buz Lebben preze ewe rag gweel dua
ha clappia tyrrah whath rag trua
rag leeas mascogna ma laveres
ha an gwella ewe nakeves

Dewe reffa Sowia an Egles ni
ha an Prounterian da eze et angy
ha gweel than gy ul servia Dewe
an Poble en kaniffar Plewe

Then he went away to France
to eat things that are bitter
There he remains I know
and pleads with the ugly-looking one

And there we will leave him
with the public who love him
and go to see what is going on
in the land of the Flemings amongst the people

There, many a one is lost
to sing with them to be improved
and I still have to go to the sword yet
the worst and shortest amongst the best

Our King is coming home by winter
and going away again when summer comes
May God preserve him at home and away
and make his life very long

If only to make an end of
the strife between us and the recent belief
It is the King of France that I mean
That would not yet grieve us.

40 A Cornish Song, to the Tune of the Modest Maid of Kent by John Tonkin (c.1695)

We would pay the money certainly
that is being sought from far afield
although the year might be ever so long
we should be pleased, I know indeed.

Many are praying for it to last long
but would be better if there were an end to it
we should have a good price for tin
and pilchards from William Mean.

But now it is time to make an end
and speak more wisely out of pity
for many a foolishness is spoken
and the best forgotten.

May God save our churches
and the clergy in them
and make them all serve God
and the people of every parish.

an Prounter ni ez en plew East
grouns e broaze carra Apostle Chreest
magga pel ter el eve heathes
ha nenna Dewe e vedd'n e worras

ha ni an Poble ul dale gweel
an peath eggee e Lal tha ni da zeel
ha rie gun gwella scovarn dortha
na dale ni gurra ul tha gotha

Lebben Dewe reffa gun Sowia ul
nenna na geath denneth tha gul
Glaze Neave than enna ni veath a heaze
mar ta ni gweel da war an Beaze

41 'Ha mî ow môs en gûn lâs' by Noel Cater (1698)

Ha mî ow môs en gûn lâs
Mî a-glowas trôs an buscas mines
Mes mî a-droucias ün pesk brâs, naw ê lostiow;
Ol an bôbel en Porthîa ha Marghas Jowan
Nerva na wôr dh 'ê gensenjy.

42 'Pela era why moaz, moz, fettow teag?' by Edward Chirgwin (1698)

Pelea era why moaz, moz, fettow, teag,
  Gen agaz bedgeth gwin, ha agaz blew mellyn?
Mi a moaz tha'n venton, sarra wheag,
  Rag delkiow sevi gwra muzi teag.

Pea ve moaz gen a why, moz, fettow, teag,
  Gen agaz bedgeth gwin, ha agaz blew mellyn?
Greuh mena why, sarra wheag,
  Rag delkiow sevi gwra muzi teag.

Fatla gûra ve agaz gorra why en dowr,
  Gen agaz bedgeth gwin, ha agaz blew mellyn?
Me vedn sevel arta sarra wheage,
  Rag delkiow sevi gwra muzi teag.

Fatla gûra ve agaz dry why gen flo,
  Gen agaz bedgeth gwin, ha agaz blew mellyn?
Me vedn ethone, sarra wheag,
  Rag delkiow sevi gwra muzi teag.

Our vicar in the parish of St Just
may he act like an apostle of Christ
as far as he can manage it
and God will help him with the rest.

And we the people should all do
what he tells us to do on Sunday
and give our best ear to him
We should not let it all drop.

And now may God save us all
and then nobody shall be lost
The Kingdom of Heaven is entirely for our souls
if we do good on the world.

41 'As I went on a green plain' by Noel Cater (1698)

As I went on a green plain
I heard the noise of tiny fish
But I found one big fish with nine tails;
All the people in St Ives and Marazion
could never get hold of him.

42 'Where are you going pretty fair maid?' by Edward Chirgwin (1698)

Where are you going pretty fair maid,
   With your white face and your yellow hair?
I'm going to the well, sweet sir,
   for strawberry leaves make maids fair.

Shall I go with you pretty fair maid,
   With your white face and your yellow hair?
Do what you want, sweet sir,
   for strawberry leaves make maids fair.

How if I put you on the ground,
   With your white face and your yellow hair?
I will stand up again, sweet sir,
   for strawberry leaves make maids fair.

How if I get you with child,
   With your white face and your yellow hair?
I will bear it, sweet sir,
   for strawberry leaves make maids fair.

Pew vedn a why gawas rag seera rag guz flo,
   Gen agaz bedgeth gwin, ha agaz blew mellyn?
Why ra boz e seera, sarra wheag,
   Rag delkiow sevi gwra muzi teag.

Pen dre vedd a why geil rag lednow rag 'as flo,
   Gen agaz pedn du, ha agaz blew mellyn?
E feera veath trehez, sarra wheag,
   Rag delkiow sevi gwra muzi teag.

43 Two Poems of Advice by James Jenkins (c.1700)

Ma leeaz Greage. Lacka vel Zeage.
Gwel gerres. Vell commerez.
Ha ma leeaz Bennen. Pocare an Gwennen.
Eye vedn gwrrez de gu Teez. Dandle peath an beaz.
Fleaz hep skeeanz. Vedn gweel gu Seeaznz.
Bur mor crown gy pedery. Pan dall gu gwary.
Ha madra ta. Pandrigg Seera ha Damah.
Narehanz moaz dan Cooz. Do cuntle gu booz.
Buz gen nebbes lavirrians. Eye venjah dendel gu booz
   dillaz.

Cousow do ve che dean more ferre
De leba es meare a peath ha lease Teer
Ha me reeg clowaz an poble compla
Fa Ethreaz do chee Eithick gwreage dah
Hye oare gwell padn dah gen hy glane
Ha et eye ollas hye dalveha gowas tane
Na dalle deez perna Kinnis war an Sawe
Na moase cuntle an drive dro dan Keaw
Rag hedna vedn boaz couzese dro dan pow
Gwell eye veeha perna nebas glow
Ha hedna vedn gus tubma a theller e aragg
Ha whye ell evah cor gwella more sease du bragg
Na dale deiw gwell treaven war an treath
Dreath hedna why vedn kelly meare a peath
Buz mor mennow dereval worbidn an pow yeine
Why dalveha gowas an brossa amine
Ha ryny vedn diria bidn moar ha gwenz
Nagez drog vyth gwres lebben na kenz.

Who will you have as father of your child,
   With your white face and your yellow hair?
You will be his father, sweet sir,
   for strawberry leaves make maids fair.

What will you do for clothes for your child,
   With your black head and your yellow hair?
His father will be a tailor, sweet sir,
   for strawberry leaves make maids fair.

43   Two Poems of Advice by James Jenkins (c.1700)

There are many wives worse than chaff,
Better left than taken,
And there are many women like the bees,
They will help their men to earn worldly wealth.
Children without wisdom will do their whim,
But if they think what their play is worth
And take careful note of what father and mother did
They will not need to go to the wood to collect their food
But with a little labour they would earn their food and
   drink.

Listen to me you man so wise
who has a great deal of wealth and land
for I have heard the people mention
that to you is given a fearfully good wife.
She knows how to make a good cloth with her wool
and in her fireplace she deserves to have fire.
You should not buy fuel by the load,
or go to gather the brambles about the hedges
for that will be spoken of about the country.
It would be better to buy some coal
and that will warm you behind and in front
and you can drink best beer if you have malt.
It is not worth you building houses on the beach.
Through that you will lose a lot of wealth,
but if you will build against the cold country
you should get the biggest stones
and those will last a year against sea and wind.
There is no harm done now and before.

44 In Obitum Regis Wilhelmi 3tii Carmen Britannicum, Dialectu Cornubiensis; An Normam Poetarum Seculi Sexti by Edward Lhuyd (1703)

Kôth-davas Brethou hows dewedhaz,
Kosgasow pel, devinow nebaz;
Devinaz an wrma peb gwlaz:
An bys nith glowas mêz wzaw;
Lemmyn lavar, ha nevra taw.

Lavar Lemmyn, genz ewhal lêv,
Hannadzian down, ha garm krêv;
Golsowez d'ola pen perhen trêv.

Lavâr lemmyn, ha Dew pyza,
Rhag Gwlaz Kernow, triwath gomera:
Hi thir dho gwith, hai' hredzianz dha.

Gwlâz Kernow rygollaz hy mâer;
Ry gollaz an enizma arluth tâer;
An byz gwir-gredzians rygollaz y gledhvaer.

Gwlâz Kernow regollaz y gweraz;
Rygollaz Enys Brethon y Threvdaz:
Ha 'Rhedzians gwir Dadloyar brâz.

Kosgardh an dowr, squattyow goz rwzow,
Goz golow, goz revow, goz oll skaphow;
Seith mledhan ne dhibryw vor-bozow.

Kosgardh an Stên, rowmann goz bolow;
Gwlezow, ravow, palow, pigolow:
Komero' gostanow, marhow, ha kledhow.

Tiz meskat, praga rew gware?
An dedhma dho horlya neb vâz his kare;
Menz godhez reson, rhag galar re.

Sevowh a mann, ha klew'mo lavarow:
An hwidlow yw genniv ent re hagarow;
Re wir, re revedh, ha pel re harow!

Sevowh a mann, ha sqwattyow goz dillaz,
Ha gwllow goz bolow genz dowr an lagaz;
Ha gwarrow goz pennow genz lidziw glâz.

44 On the Death of King William III, a British Song in the Cornish Dialect; according to the pattern of the poets of the sixth century by Edward Lhuyd (1703)

The sun of the ancient tongue of the Britons has set,
You have slept long, you have scarcely awoken;
Now has every kingdom awoken:
For many ages the world has not heard you;
Now speak and never again be silent.

Speak now, with loud voice,
Deep sighs, and strong cry;
Let the head of every household hear your weeping.

Speak now, and pray to God,
For the Kingdom of Cornwall, may He have mercy upon it
To keep its land, and its good faith.

The Kingdom of Cornwall has lost its guardian;
This island has lost a vigorous lord;
The world of true faith has lost its swordsman.

The Kingdom of Cornwall has lost its help;
The Island of Britain has lost its Patriarch;
And true religion, a great advocate.

Fellows of the water, scat your nets,
Your sails, your oars, all your boats;
For seven years do not eat sea-food.

Fellows of the Tin, abandon your mines;
Picks, shovels, spades, pick-axes:
Take shields, horses and swords.

Foolish people, why do you play?
This day no decent person cares to go hurling;
Whoever knows reason, will be mourning too much.

Arise, and hear my words:
The tidings that I have are too horrible;
Too true, too astounding, and far too evil!

Arise, and scat your clothes,
And wash your cheeks with the water of the eye;
And cover your heads with grey ash.

Galarvi ni odhaz bez Dew e honan;
Gorewhal Dhew, yw trey a wonan:
Ev ôr klevaz pen kolan wan.

Gwan an gwenzvi, ha kelmyz yw'n havaz:
Yn skovarn ny'hlew; ny wêl yn lagaz;
An dallow rag own dhan dôi me kodhrz!

An Màhtern William an byzma eskaraz:
Re vâz dhan dôr Dew nêv ai kemeraz:
Kemerez nei keffrys dhoy triwath, hai 'raz.

An Màhtern William yw marow soweth!
Devêrez Ûn lemma genz ewhal elaeth;
Gwae nei an byzma, ni dal tra veth!

An Màhtern William val eal yw gwryz;
An urma mi wêl porth nêv ageryz:
Pella ni olav mwy vel ryg colyz.

Wz dên nag yw hir, nag yw dâ;
Màhtern ha pohodziak dhan vernaz yn trâ;
Dhan vewnaz vâz, vedh marnaz gwella.

Oilsow lawr; galarwisg; row man:
Dew rygemeraz yn whedhan;
Gorthrodhez aral, Maternez Ann.

Hy gwredhan yw down; hy hôrf krêv;
Hy skyriow byz tyvyz a mann dhan nêv:
Byz own rhag henna war pêb pel trev.

Dhort henna war Frank, ha war Spân byz owan:
Biz Elzabeth ail: pyr yw I holan
Dhan Zowzan kovaithak, ha leal Brethon.

Penzivik Kernuak, an skrefna ry gwelaz,
Ownow anodha pûb gêr nag yw vâz:
Rhag pel tir Powys dhort Por-Enaz.

None know my sorrow but God himself;
Most high God, who is three and one;
He knows the sickness of every feeble heart.

Weak my spirit, and bound is my tongue:
In my ear there is no hearing; there is no sight in my eye;
Ah, hold me for fear I should fall to the earth!

King William has left this world:
Too good for the earth, God has taken him to Heaven:
May he take us also through his mercy, and his grace.

King William is dead alas!
Lifted up on high with the angels:
Woe is us, this world is worth nothing!

King William is made like unto an angel;
Now I see the gate of heaven opened;
No more shall I weep now I have ceased.

The age of man is not long; it is not good;
King and pauper come to death in the same way;
Whoever has a good life, will have the best death.

You have wept enough; cast aside mourning garb:
God has taken one tree;
He has substituted another one, Queen Anne.

Her root is deep: her body strong:
Her branches grow up to Heaven:
Let there be fear therefore in every distant town.

Because of this, may there be fear in France and Spain:
May she be a second Elizabeth: Pure is her heart
to the wealthy Saxons and the faithful Britons.

Noble Cornish, who have seen this writing,
Correct every word of it that is not good;
For distant is the land of Powys from Mousehole.

45 A Cornish Proverb by William Allen (1704)

    Kensa blethan, byrla a' baye,
    Nessa blethan, lull a' laye,
    Tridgya blethan hanna drubba,
    Peswarra blethan, mol a Dew war ef reeg dry hy uppa

46 'Ma Canow vee wor Hern gen Cock ha Rooz' by John Boson (1710)

    Ma canow vee wor Hern gen Cock ha Rooz.
    Kameres en zans Garrack glase en Kooz.
    Poth'u an Coocoe devithes Treea
    Durt Moar Tees Por Dega dega Creea
    Ha kennifer Bennen oggas e Teen
    Gen Kawall ha Try Cans Hern wor e Kein.
    Th'a gweel Barcadoes en Kenifer Choy
    Gen Ganow leaz Hern, Hern, Holan moy
    Po the'ns Salles da, idden Mees worbar
    Pres eu tha Squatcha Man ha tedna Kar
    Udg hedda, Goula glaneth en dour sal
    E vedn Ri Hanou da tha Muzzy ol
    Gorra spladn en Balliar, Pedden ha Teen
    Gobar ha Tra broaz Enz rag Varshants feen
    Meero why rag Gwethan heer Tarthack Troos
    Gorras war hedda Minow pemp canz pooz
    Try termen en death meero why dotha
    Rag hanter Mees durta saim vedn cotha,
    The'u hemma vor guir an Hern tha parra
    En Marras Gwella ghy vedn wharra
    Blethan wor blethan Gra Gorollion toas
    Ha gen Hern lean moas ort Dour Gawvas
    Wor duath Gra Gwenz Noor East wetha pell
    Rag an Poble pow tooben debra ol
    Ma Peath Hern pokar ol an Beaz
    Moy Poble Bohodzack vel poble Broaz.

45   A Cornish Proverb by William Allen (1704)

> First year, hugging and kissing,
> Second year, billing and cooing,
> Third year, coming to blows,
> Fourth year, the curse of God on who brought her here.

46   The Pichard Curing Rhyme by John Boson (1710)

> My song concerns pilchards with boat and net
> Taken in the bay of the Grey Rock in the Wood.
> When the boats came home
> From the sea people cried, 'Tithe! Tithe!'
> And every woman near her husband
> With a basket and three hundred pilchards on her back
> To smoke pilchards in every house
> With mouth wide open, 'Pilchards! Pilchards! More salt!'
> When they are well-salted one month together
> It is time to break them up and draw a cart
> After that, clean them in salt water
> They will give a good name to all the girls
> Who put them properly in a barrel, head to tail.
> A reward and a big thing they are for fine merchants.
> Look for a long tree of thirteen feet
> Put stones of five hundred pounds on it
> Look at them three times a day
> For half a month oil will fall from them
> That is the proper way to prepare the pilchards.
> They will sell in the best market.
> Year after year ships will come
> And they will leave Gwavas Lake full of our pilchards
> At last, the North East wind will blow far
> For the people of hot countries will eat them all.
> The wealth of pilchards is like the world
> More poor people than rich.

47 'An [Why] poble hui, en pow America' by William Gwavas (1710)

An [Why] poble hui, en pow America, uncuth dho nei, huei dho gurria an Deu guir a'n nev k'an doar Neb g'ryk an Houl, an Lur, ha an Steren Rag porth a'n Tiz war an Tir, ha g'ryk kynifara tra en Dallath ha Eu Deu, olghallnzack dres ol an Beyz.
                 Bounaz hep Diueth.
                 Amen.

En Blethan a'n Deu Arlueth nei, 1710   W. Gwavas.
          a an Tempel K'res en Loundres
          En Pow a'n Brethon.

48 Letters in Cornish by William Gwavas and Oliver Pender (1711)

Nag o ve whath Hanter Dean kernuack da, tha screfa do why, leb ez Dean Broaza, ha pylta gwell skientek en Tavaz-ma – mez hemma ew rag deskians ve.
               William Gwavas

                       Durt Newlin in Bleau Pawle
                           22 East, 1711.

Sara Wheage,
      Me rig fanja guz Lether zithan lebma, buz nagerra termen dem de screffa du straft arta: Rag nag ez buz lebban duath dem dro d'an hollan kear, marastha Dieu tha augutti ull gwerres; ma owne du vee ma duath do nisau blethan dro d'an Hern, nages prize veethes moase whath ragt'angi; an hern gwave vedn geele droeg d'an hern have, rag ma dro da deux mill Hosket whath in Falmeth, gwerres ha de boas gwerres; ha mouns screffa inna warbedden ni.
      Memto Orlenna { Na Gwitha Hern ree pell
                      { Ken Gwarra; rag prijse da eu gwell
                          (Adheworth Newlyn, e'n Blew Paul,
                             on 22ves mys Est, 1711.
     Rag na algia ea clappia na screffa Curnoack precarra why. Thera moy Gembrack peath rig ea gweele.
               Oliver Pender

47 'You people in the Land of America' by William Gwavas (1710)

You people in the land of America, unknown to us, you have learnt to worship the true God of heaven and earth, Who made the sun, the moon, and the stars for the help of people on earth, and made everything in the beginning and is God almighty over all the world.
Life without end.
Amen.

In the year of the God our Lord, 1710   W. Gwavas.
From the Middle Temple in London
in the land of the Britons.

48 Letters in Cornish by William Gwavas and Oliver Pender (1711)

I am not yet half a good Cornishman to write to you, who is a greater man, and much more learned in this tongue – but this is for me to learn by.
William Gwavas

From Newlyn in the Parish of Paul
22nd August 1711

Sweet Sir,
I got your letter a week ago, there was not time for me to reply to you quickly: it is only now that I have finished with the matter of the dear salt, great thanks to God, which is nearly all sold; I am afraid there is an end to the pilchards until next year, but there is not a price set for them yet; the winter pilchards will do harm to the summer pilchards for there are about two thousand hogsheads still in Falmouth, sold or to be sold; and they are writing there against us.
Momento Orlenna {Not to keep pilchards too long
{Before selling; for a good price is better.
(From Newlyn in the Parish of Paul
22nd August 1711.
Because he could not speak or write Cornish like you. There was more Welsh in what he did.
Oliver Pender

49 'En Lavra coth pa vo Tour Babel gwres' by John Boson (1711)

> En levra coth pa vo Tour Babel gwres
> Scriffas, Gomar mab Japhet vo en Beas
> Ha Dotha tavaz Karnooack vo Res.
>
> Lebbn duath Tavas coth ny en Kernow
> Rag kar ny Jenkins gelles durt an Pow
> Vor hanow taz ny en Eue tha Canow.
>
> Descans ony gen hemma, an Brossa es
> Desces en Tavazow ha dotha Bres,
> Ha Pedn ffeerha ha Moy Skeeans Res.
>
> Ancho vedn gweel an Dean eu wella
> Cotha dadn Daor pokare an Ezella
> Meer a kol – Ry termen them tha Hoola.

50 'Padn an mean, ma Deskes broaz Dean' by William Gwavas (c.1711)

> Padn an mean, ma Deskes broaz Dean,
> En tavaz Kernuack gelles.
> Termen vedn doaz rag an Corfe tha thoras
> Mes Tavas coth Kernow ew kelleys.

51 Advice to a Friend by John Boson (c.1711)

> Kymero 'wyth goz lavarak pouz,
> goz argan, ha guz aur;
> Ma Ladran moz, en Termen Noz,
> Reb vor Loundres Tur.
> An hagar musi, ma ens vâze
> The-ens en Kinever Tol,
> Dha meraz, rag an peth es moaz.
> Komero 'vyth goz kal.

52 On the Death of Mr. John Keigwin by John Boson (1716)

> En Tavaz Greka, Lathen ha'n Hebra,
>   En Frenkock ha Carnoack deskes dha,
> Gen ol an Gormola Brez ve dotha
>   Garres ew ni, ha Neidges Ewartha.

49 An Elegy on the Death of James Jenkins by John Boson (1711)

> In old books, when the Tower of Babel was made
> it is written that Gomer, son of Japheth, was in the world
> and to him the Cornish tongue was given.
>
> Now is the end of our old tongue in Cornwall
> for our friend Jenkins is gone from the land
> in the name of our Father in Heaven to sing.
>
> We learn by this, that the greatest who is
> learned in tongues and has judgement,
> and the wisest head and more knowledge given.
>
> Death will make the man who is highest
> fall under the earth like the lowest.
> Much loss -- give time for me to weep.

50 Epitaph for the Death of James Jenkins by William Gwavas (c.1711)

> Beneath the stone is gone a man
> greatly learned in the Cornish language.
> A time will come for the body to rise
> but the old tongue of Cornwall is lost.

51 Advice to a Friend by John Boson (c.1711)

> Take care of your heavy trousers,
> your silver and your gold,
> there are thieves going in the night-time,
> by the road of the Tower of London.
> The wicked girls are not good
> They are in every hole
> on the lookout for what is going on.
> Take care of your cock.

52 On the Death of Mr. John Keigwin by John Boson (1716)

> In the Greek, Latin and Hebrew language,
>   In French and Cornish well-learned,
> With all the praise of mind that was his
>   We are left while he has flown upwards.

53 On a Lazy Weaver by William Gwavas (c.1728)

> Why ladar gweader,
> Lavarro guz pader,
> Ha ro man do higha an cath:
> Gra owna guz furu,
> Hithow, po avorou,
> Ha whyew boz dean dah whath.

54 Verses on the Marazion Bowling-Green and Club by William Gwavas (c.1728)

> Ny ol devethes war tyr glaz,
> Dho gware peliow, rag gun ehaz;
> Dibre tabm dah, hag eva badna,
> Mal nag wunnen, moaz gwadn trea,
> Mez ol krêv, en karensa vâz,
> Dho ara tyr, ha gunnes hâz.

55 Advice to Drunkards by William Gwavas (c.1728)

> Na reugh eva re,
> Mez eva rag guz zehaz;
> Ha hedna, muy, po le,
> Vedn gwitha, corf, en ehaz.

56 A Cornish Riddle by William Gwavas (c.1728)

> Flô vye gennes en Miz-merh,
> Ni-trehes e bigel en miz-east;
> E a roz towl
> Dho Proanter Powle,
> Miz-du ken Nadelik

57 'Chee dên krêv' by William Gwavas (c.1728)

> Chee dên krêv leb es war tyr,
> Hithew gwr, gen skîans fyr;
> Ha'n Dew euhella, vedn rye,
> Peth yw wella ol rag why.

58 'Hithow gwrâ gen skîanz da' by William Gwavas (c.1728)

> Hithow gwrâ gen skîanz da:
> An gwiraneth ew an gwella,
> En pob tra, trea, po pella.

53   On a Lazy Weaver by William Gwavas (c.1728)

>You thief of a weaver,
>Say your prayers,
>   and give up playing with the cat:
>Straigthen your ways,
>today or tomorrow,
>   and you will yet be a good man.

54   Verses on the Marazion Bowling-Green and Club by William Gwavas (c.1728)

>We have all come onto green land,
>to play bowls for our health;
>to eat a good morsel, and to drink a drop,
>so that not one goes home weak,
>but all strong in friendship,
>to plough land and plant seed.

55   Advice to Drunkards by William Gwavas (c.1728)

>Do not drink too much,
>   but drink for your health;
>and that more or less,
>   will keep body in good health.

56   A Cornish Riddle by William Gwavas (c.1728)

>A child was born in March,
>We cut his navel in August
>He gave a fall
>to the Parson of Paul
>in November before Christmas.

57   Advice to all Men by William Gwavas (c.1728)

>You strong man, who is on land,
>today act with wise knowledge,
>and God on high will give
>that which is best of all for you.

58   'Today act with good knowledge' by William Gwavas (c.1728)

>Today act with good knowledge
>the truth is the best,
>In everything, at home, or far away.

59 'Cara, Gorthya, ha ouna Dêw' by William Gwavas (c.1728)

> Cara, Gorthya, ha ouna Dêw,
> An Materyn, ha'n lahez, en guz plew:
> Ouna Dêw, parthy Materyn;
> Ha cara goz contrevogion.

60 War an Lavar gwir a'n Dewthack Tiz pêg a'n Pow Middlesex; ha an Brêz a'n padgwar Braneriow enna – Gwavas versus Kelynack (1728)

> Pengelly Broaz, ha dowthack tîz,
> Rag pusgaz dêk an gyroz brez:
> Fraga? Gwîran ath yw an gwella
> En pob tra, trea, po-pella.
> Ha nessa, Hale têg, gen lavar fyr,
> Ol Poble gwrêz dho adzhan gwîr;
> Hellier tubm e helfias reb pul:
> Comyns skîentek vye glan ol.

61 'Contrevack Nicholas Pentreath' by William Gwavas (c.1728)

> Contrevack Nicholas Pentreath,
> Pa reffo why doaz war an dreath
> Gen puscas, comero whye weeth
> Tha geel cumpas, hedna ew feer;
> Ha cowz meaz, Dega, Dega,
> Enna ew oll goz dega gweer.

62 William Bodinar's Letter (1776)

Bluth vee eue try egance a pemp. Thearra vee dean boadjack an poscas. Me rig desky Cornoack termen me vee mawe. Me vee de more gen care vee a pemp dean moy en cock. Me rig scantlower clowes eden ger Sowsnack cowes en cock rag sythen warebar. No riga vee biscath gwellas lever Cornoack. Me deskey Cornoack mous da more gen tees coath. Nag es moye vel pager pe pemp en dreav nye ell clappia Cornoack leben, poble coath pager egance blouth. Cornoack ewe oll neceaves gen poble younk.

59 'Love, worship and fear God' by William Gwavas (c.1728)

> Love, worship and fear God,
> The King, the laws and your parish:
> Fear God, respect the King;
> And love your neigbours.

60 On the verdict of the twelve honest men of the County of Middlesex; and the judgment of the four Barons therein – Gwavas versus Kelynack (1728)

> Great Pengelly, and twelve men,
> for fish tithe gave the word:
> Why? Truth is the best
> in everything at home and far away.
> And next, fair Hale with wise saying
> Help all people to know the truth,
> A warm hunter chased by a pool:
> Learned Comyns, was all clean.

61 To Neighbour Nicholas Pentreath by William Gwavas (c.1728)

> Neighbour Nicholas Pentreath,
> When you come onto the beach
> With fish, take care
> to do fairly what is wise
> and speak out, 'Tithe! Tithe!'
> That is your true tithe.

62 William Bodinar's Letter (1776)

My age is three score and five. I am a poor fisherman. I learned Cornish when I was a boy. I went to sea with my father and five other men in a boat. I hardly heard a single word of English spoken in the boat for as much as a week together. I never saw a Cornish book. I learned Cornish going to sea with old men. There are no more than four or five in the village who can speak Cornish now, old people four score years old. Cornish is all forgot by the young folk.

63 'Coth Doll Pentreath' by Thomson (c.1777)

Coth Doll Pentreath cans ha deau
Marrow ha kledyz ed Paul pleû,
Na ed en Egloz, gan pobel braz
Bes ed Egloz-hay, coth Dolly es.

64 Proverbs and sayings from Archæologia Cornu-Britannica by William Pryce (1790)

1 Gwrâ chee gofen skîans a Dêw.
2 En Hâv, perkou Gwâv.
3 Gwrâ kelmy ow colon dez.
4 Betho why fyrah nessa.
5 Gurra ny tedna pokiar.
6 Bethoh fyr, ha heb drok.
7 Ena, ha corf, finzhow lahes Dêw.
8 Bethes gwaz vâz, ha leal.
9 Gwrêz dah, chee gwaz vâz, ha leal.
10 En metten pan a why fevel, why rez cawse tha guz taz, ha guz damma, wor a guz pedndowlin – Bednath Deew, ha an bedneth war a vee, me pidge thu Deew.
11 Der taklow minniz ew brez teez gonvethes, avelan tacklow broaz: dreffen en tacklow broaz, ma an gymennow hetha go honnen; bus en tacklow minnis, ema an gye suyah hâz go honnen.
12 Gwrâ, O Mateyne, a tacklow ma, gen an gwella krêvder, el boaz pideeres an marudgyan a go terman; ha an tacklow vedn gwaynia klôs theez rag nevera.
13 Po rez deberra an bez, vidn heerath a seu; po res dal an vor, na oren pan a tu, Thuryan, houl Zethas, go Gleth, po Dihow.
14 Dibre mor-gi en mîz Mea, rag dho geil maw.
15 Goribow ol pub onyn.
16 Hithow gwrâ, gen skîanz da.
17 An Lavor gôth ewe laver gwîr,
Ne vedn nevera doas vâs a tavaz re hîr;
Bes dên heb tavaz a gollas e dîr.
18 Ez kêz? ez, po neg ez; ma sêz kêz,
Dro kêz; po negez nêz, dro peth ez.
19 Sâv a man, kebner tha li, ha ker tha'n hâl;
Mor-teed a metten travyth ne dâl.
20 Karendzhia vendzhia,
Ravaethiaz na vendzhia.
21 Cowsa nebaz, ha cowsa da;
Mêz cowsa nebaz an gwella.
22 Cusal ha têg, sîrra wheage, Moaz pell.
23 Re a ydn dra ny dal traveth.

63 Epitaph for Dolly Pentreath by Thomson (c.1777)

>Old Doll Penteath, aged 102,
>Deceased and buried in Paul parish too,
>Not in the Church with people great and high,
>But in the churchyard doth old Dolly lie.

64 Proverbs and sayings from Archæologia Cornu-Britannica by William Pryce (1790)

1. Ask wisdom of God.
2. In Summer, remember Winter.
3. Bind my heart to you.
4. Be wiser next time.
5. Let us draw equally.
6. Be wise and without evil.
7. Soul and body hold the laws of God.
8. Be a good and faithful servant.
9. Well done, you good and faithful servant.
10. In the morning when you rise, you must say to your father, and your mother, on your knees, the blessing of God, and a blessing on me, I pray to God.
11. Through small things the minds of men are understood, just like the big things: because in the big things they stretch themselves, but in small things, they follow their own nature.
12. O King, do these things with the best strength that can be thought of and the marvel of their time; and these will win you praise forever.
13. When you leave the world, longing will follow; when you begin the way, it is not known whether it is to the East, West, North or South.
14. Eat a dog-fish in May to make a boy.
15. Answer everyone.
16. Today act in good knowledge.
17. The old saying is a true saying,
No good will be counted to come from too long a tongue;
But a man without a tongue lost his land.
18. Is there cheese? Is there, or isn't there, if there is cheese, bring cheese; if there isn't cheese, bring what there is.
19. Get up, take your breakfast, and walk to the moor;
the morning tide is not worth anything.
20. Love would,
Greed would not.
21. Speak little and speak well;
but to speak little is best.
22. Quiet and fair, sweet sir, goes far.
23. Too much of one thing is not worth anything.

65 Padar a'n Arluth from Archæologia Cornu-Britannica by William Pryce (1790)

Agan Taz leb ez en nâv, benigas beth de hanno, gurra de gulasketh deaz, de voth beth gwrâz en' oar pokar en nâv. Ro dony hithow agan pyb dyth bara; Ha gava an gy leb es cam ma war bidn ny: Ha na dege ny en antail, buz gwitha ny dort droge: Rag an mychteyrneth ew chee do honnen, ha an crevder, ha an âworryans, rag bisqueth ha bisqueth. An dellma ra bo.

66 Cornish Family Mottoes (no date)

1 The Earl of Godolphin — Frank ha leal etto ge.
2 Polwhele — Karenza Whelas Keranza.
3 Tonkin — Kenz ol Tra, Tonkin, Ouna Dêu Matern yn. Deske tha vos daa.
4 Noye — Teg yw hedowch.
5 Harris — Car Dêu reyz pub tra.
6 Carminow — Cala rag Whethlow.

67 Two Poems by Georg Sauerwein (c.1865)

Ker Mr. Edwin Norris
A aswon war an nor-vys
Pup cufdra cufa cufyon,
Hag yu gwywa, dre henna
Dhe dhon an hanow penna
A Edwyn, hen yu 'aswon'.

Woge lettys dydhyow hyr,
Cafaf hydhew ow dysyr –
yllyf arte dheugh skrepha:
Mar a pe ow lether ber,
Gyfeugh a rag four amser,
Mar re hyr – coskeugh yn ta:

Lyas houl a yth a ler
Aban dheugh a res ow ger,
Tro my skrephen arte'n scon:
Mar dhewedhes collenwel
Tra ambosys dheugh mar bel
Dhymmo yu meth, y gon.

Dyffry ny vydh powesva
Dhymmo, hep an newodh da
A'gas gyffyans lyen a ras:
Gyfeugh dhymmo, cowydh ker,

65 The Lord's Prayer from Archæologia Cornu-Britannica by William Pryce (1790)

Our Father, which art in Heaven; Hallowed be thy Name; Thy Kingdom come; Thy Will be done, On Earth as it is in Heaven. Give us this day our daily bread, And forgive us our trespasses as we forgive those who trespass against us. And lead us not into temptation; But deliver us from evil. For Thine is the Kingdom, the Power and the Glory, For ever and ever. Amen.

66 Cornish Family Mottoes (no date)

1	The Earl of Godolphin	Free and faithful art thou.
2	Polwhele	Love seeks love.
3	Tonkin	Before everything, Tonkin, Fear God and King, Learn to be good.
4	Noye	Fair is peace.
5	Harris	Love God above everything.
6	Carminow	A straw for stories.

67 Two Poems by Georg Sauerwein (c.1865)

Dear Mr. Edwin Norris,
Whom I know in this world
With the kindest kindness of kind ones
And who is most worthy, for that reason
To bear the most excellent name
Of Edwin, that is, 'to know'.

After frustration for many days,
I get today my desire –
I can again write to you:
If my letter be short,
Forgive it for lack of time,
If too long — sleep well!

Many suns have gone down
Since I gave you my word,
It is time for me to write quickly again,
So late to fulfil,
A thing promised you for so long
It is shame for me I know.

In truth, there will be no rest,
For me, without the good news
Of your forgiveness full of grace:
Forgive me, dear friend,

Gwelaugh vy rageugh war ler,
Dreheveugh vy, ow Syr mas

Dreheveugh ve arte'n ban
Dh'agas kynse grasow splan,
A fue dhymmo dysquethys,
Pan yn Loundra, 'n agas chy
Ymysk agas ol deilu,
Geneugh kousel a yllys.

Pandra wrussyn leverel?
Pup tra, ha trao erel:
Gerryow whereow, gerryow whek,
Am bup tavas pel po oges –
Ow gul omladh, ow gul cres –
Ogh, an amser lowen, tek!

Lemmyn ny'm bydh moy nep dra
Hep ow hof a'n dydhyow da,
Gof, ha hireth y'm calon.
Hireth bras, ha hireth down,
Hag, yn teffry, doubt hag own,
A dhewyllyf dres an don!

Gwylsough'n wlas – my a'n aswon –
G'las an meyn a-ugh an don,
G'las lowene, tekdra, marth,
Wodheugh why, pa'n g'las a'n pow!
G'las Tre-pen-pol, g'las Kernow!
Yno ny a a warbarth!

Lemmyn gwylyow lowena
Yn agas tre, yn Loundra,
Dheugh why, ha dh'agas teilu:
Blydhen newodh dha yn whyth,
Lowena newodh pup dyth,
Ha hydhew, farwel dheugh why!

―――――――

Cowyth ker, dhe dhen claf
Trist yu pu tra, kyn fe'n haf,
Kyn fe'n houl ha'n stergen glan:
Lemmyn. Kyn a pup tra'n nos
Ny ellough why'ndella mos.
Kepar ha'n houl ha'n stergan
'Ma 'gas cufder ynof splan
Gans y wolow y honen
Pan a's cofiaf y'm colon:

See me low before you,
Lift me up my dear sir.

Lift me up again
To your kind of wonderful graciousness,
Which was shown to me,
When in London, in your house,
Amongst all your family
I was able to speak with you.

What did we say,
Every thing and other things
Bitter words, sweet words,
About every language far or near –
Making conflict, making peace –
Oh, the happy fair time!

Now I do not have anything more
Apart from my memory of the good days
Memory and longing in my heart.
Great longing and deep loving
And indeed anxiety and fear
That I shall not return over the wave.

You saw the country – I know it –
The land of the stones above the wave,
Land of joy, beauty, wonder,
Do you know what land in the kingdom?
The land of Tre, Pen, Pol, the land of Kernow!
There we shall go together.

Now may there be festivals of joy
In your home, in London,
For you, and for your family:
A Happy New Year also,
New joy every day,
And today, farewell to you!

———————————

Dear friend, to a sick man
Everything is sad, although it be summer,
although the sun and the starlight be bright:
Now. Although everything becomes night
You cannot be thus.
Like the sun and the starlight
Your kindness is bright within me
with its own light
When I remember you in my heart:

Duw a's bynyga pup deyth
Hag a'm gra vy cuf yn wheyth
Dhe skrepha kepar del gon!

68 'A Grankan, a grankan' by John Davey (1891)

A grankan, a grankan,
A mean o gowaz o vean
Ondez parc an venton
Dub trelawza vean
Far Penzans a Maragow
Githack mackwee
A githack macrow
A mac trelowza varrack.

God bless you every day
and make me kind also
to write in the way I know!

68 The Crankan Rhyme by John Davey (1891)

O Crankan, O Crankan!
Beyond the fields of the spring
you give but little
– only three shoots by the stone.
The road between Penzance and Marazion
is very green
and a whole lot fresher
– three shoots grow for every passing horseman.

Complementary texts

69   From **The Bodmin Manumissions (c.960)**

This is the name of that woman Ælfgyth whom Æthælflæd freed for her soul and for the soul of her lord Duke Æthælwerd on the bell of Saint Petrock in the town which is called Liskeard in the presence of these beholding witnesses, Æthælstan the priest, Wine the priest, Dunstan the priest, Goda the thane, Ælfwerd Scirlocc, Æthælwine Muf, Ealdred his brother, Eadsige the writer, Prudens the priest, Boya the deacon, Wulfsige the deacon, Bryhsige the clerk, so that she may have freedom forever.

Here is made known on this book that Æilsig had bought a woman Ongynedhel and her son Gydhiccael for half a pound at the church door in Bodmin and paid to Æilsige the portreeve and Maccos the hundredsman four pennies for tax. Then Æilsige did as he had intended to the persons he had bought and freed them on Petrock's altar forever free of liability. On the witness of these good men: Isaac the mass-priest and Bledcuf the mass-priest and Wunning the mass-priest and Wulfger the mass-priest and Grifiudh the mass-priest and Noe the mass-priest and Wurthieidh the mass-priest and Æilsig the deacon and Maccos and Tedhion Mordred's son and Kynlim and Beorlaf and Dirling and Gratcant and Talan. And if anyone breaks this freedom may he have Christ's protection withdrawn. Amen.

These are the names of the sons Wurcon, Aedhan, Iunerdh, Wurfodhu, Guruaret whose sons and nephews and all their descendants have defended themselves by an oath, by permission of King Edgar, for by the accusation of evil men their fathers were said to have been serfs of the King: witnessed by Comoere the Bishop, witnessed by Ælfsie the Earl, witnessed by Dofagan, witnessed by March, witnessed Ælfnodh, witnessed by Byrhtsie the priest, witnessed by Mitcwdh the priest, witnessed by Abel the priest.

This is the name of that man whom Cenmenoc freed for his soul on the altar of Saint Petrock, Benedic, in the presence of these beholding witnesses, Osian the priest, and Morhaitho the deacon.

70   From **The History of the Kings of Britain by Geoffrey of Monmouth (1136)**

While I was thinking about these things and many related matters, Walter the Archdeacon of Oxford, a man very learned in the art of public speaking and the history of distant lands, brought me a certain very old book in the British tongue which set out the acts of all the Kings of the Britons from the first one, Brutus, right down to Cadwaladr, son of Cadwallon in a continuous and very elegant narrative. Prompted therefore by his request, even if I would not gather ornate words in the gardens of other men, but satisfied with the rustic style of my own pen, I took great care to translate that book into the Latin tongue.

Now Corineus called the part of the kingdom that had been allocated to him by lot, Kernow, after his own name: and the people are called the Cornish after their leader, although he could have had his choice of the provinces, before all the others who had come, he preferred that region which is now called Cornwall, either because it is the horn of Britain, or by the corruption of the aforesaid name. Now, it pleased him to wrestle against giants, of whom there were many more in that place than in any of the provinces which had been shared out amongst his colleagues. There was amongst the others, a certain repulsive one called Gogmagog, eighteen feet tall, who had so much strength that once he had shaken an oak tree he could pull it out as if it were a hazel rod. On a certain day when Brutus was celebrating a festival to the Gods in the harbour where he had landed, Gogmagog and twenty other giants fell on him and made a great slaughter amongst the Britons. But the Britons at last assembling from all around defeated them: they killed all of them apart from Gogmagog. Brutus ordered him to be spared, wanting to see a wrestling match between him and Corineus who delighted in encountering such creatures. Therefore Corineus hopping up and down with joy, girded himself up and, having thrown down his weapons, challenged Gogmagog to a wrestling match. The contest began as Corineus and then the giant took up his stand, and each wrapped the other about with his arms and the air shook with their gasps. Immediately, Gogmagog grasped Corineus with all his strength and broke three of his ribs: two on the right side, and one on the left. Wherefore Corineus, driven to anger, summoned his strength, put him on his shoulders, and, with as much speed as the weight permitted, ran to the nearest coast. From there, having climbed to the top of a very high cliff, he threw him down, and cast the aforesaid deadly monster that he was carrying on his shoulders into the sea: and he, falling onto steep rocks was torn into many fragments: and he stained the breakers with his blood. That place took its name, from the the throwing down of a giant, as Lamgogmagog, that is, the Leap of Gogmagog.

71   The Prophecy of Merlin by John of Cornwall (c.1150)

O East wind, your seed uproots the South Wind
from our gardens, and the tithed follows the example of the tither;
there shall be borne across in timber, keen and encased in iron,
fighting in the fields in threefold armour,
a people fierce in wars, burning for the slaughter of the Saxon.
Afterwards those who gave their effort to rakes and ploughs,
will not spare their mother and will reach into her entrails.

Every wrong that makes a yoke of slavery for a people
they owe to Treachery; let me not be troubled to remember it.
How many years will the Prince have lived to restore our
people? Twice over seven you will reckon the same number,
cruel Northern France, parent of a fertile soil, rejoicing
that twin heirs of an avenger are growing up as dragons.
First, a bow is bent for the destruction of one;
the other laughs under the melancholy shadow of a name,
he will be feared four times twice and five years.
But the lion of justice, to whom all things indeed
are fulfilled, that lion lasts twice seven over eight;
clipping the claws of hawks and the teeth of wolves,
he gives all forests and all harbours everywhere.
Every nine this one rears up, the town eroded by the Seine
trembles, and in the Atlantic each island of Dragons.
Then the curly-headed one will put on a many-coloured cloak
and his clothes will not protect him from the misdeeds of an unsound
mind; then there will be squeezed from the narcissus and the thorn
and gold will flow from the horns of the grazing cattle.
Therefore, willing or not, with a foot cut off, the barking one
will make a treaty with the stag. The appearance of money is split
to this; also the form of half a circle is added.
Henceforth, the Aarau, the most famous flying creature,
will seize its nest and Scotland will weep for its snatched cubs.
Alas! what crime of the sea will the third bring forth!
The one unmoved by that was ransomed for his threefold fierceness.
On seven French-born of the blood on one mother
a sad, ruddy-throne, having suffered so many deaths, so many ends,
cries out and declares: 'Normandy, do you know what is going on?'
Recently I too suffered, recently I poured out my entrails;
only through these destructions can destruction be relieved.
O wide island, you are swimming with tears! There is scarcely me,
and all are kings today because the sword is used too sparingly.
From now on, this one is the possessor surrounded by unfilial terror;
With his face covered in shadows of night, the lion's
progeny, hostile once more, will shine against the stars.
A broken law will call an eagle to anger with a cub
and those who skulk in the woods hunting to the very walls,
that the bulls will sometime hate those whom they fear.
No love of brothers or true faith of allies,
or very little calm, over willows climb brambles.
Alas, too great a licence is given to wolves and kites.
Three times six revolutions shall this age last.
You, House of Arthur, a subjected faith-breaking people,
then you will see the seizure of cattle of the plains of Reont.
But what are you doing in defiance? O Victorious one, wait a while;
why, effeminately painted with make-up and with curled hair,
lost people, why do you use a dress with rings, why do you love

to make yourself vulgarly familiar with the trivia of Venus?
You are punished: one plague, one pain condemns us all;
Abandoned you will lie, unless you can bring comfort.
Flame, hunger, diseases or whatever new upheavals, your fates
conspire against you, these things also whip others.
Behold, in the pillaging of his father, with lightning, round the hard
head, girdled about and bringing low the crest of the helmeted one,
the pale adopted one shall walk round the springs of Periron.
What is his standing? What hope in our seed?
Let him serve or let him perish, or let him lose wealth and name,
the translateral hills of Scotland will approach;
in the land of Arfon the brass plague is being forged;
a bird of prey reins in a boar and reveals the ancestral time.
This third nest will fall apart again;
a year will come, London will yield up the remains of the sceptre.
I was amazed at first, I am amazed that he stood forth second,
or fourth, or fifth. Soon there will arise from the citadel of the Britons
so that he may grow, so that the javelin may be made into a lance,
make a tomb for all will be raised up as a sad machine;
death will be envied, nor will the shape of money be simple.
      Learn the way at last, Cornwall, learn the work.
And our cradles shall bring back the Saxon mourning.
Why is our hand so generous? Who thereafter will be thought free?
      Where the Great Bear looks, where the Tamar flows to the
South, by the yoke of Brentigia the French lord it everywhere,
if you would continue to live, O queen, you will so unplough,
out of which rat-catchers and buck goats are multiplied in value.
The fury of the winds and every revolt against the citizens
will rage until the sad anger of the thunder ceases.
Therefore, let the unfortunate common people share the favour,
and in the meantime for itself it will make unimportant prayers.
Religion weeps, the frocked one prays vainly,
he who turns the heaven, who forges the lightning listens.
In the past, Ireland lies down for the sixth;
also the offspring of the West reach out for the North.
And why so late paying the menacing castle?
When the shield was permitted it was useful to pay the fare.
Is he more praiseworthy for his piety or his prowess in arms?
Demolishing fortifications, reducing groves to level ground,
he will make the hills naked, he will renew the statutes and laws.
He who will put on to his side wings previously cut off
and also with a lion's mane placed in his locks,
more sure in affection, he will reach into high places by flight,
for indeed he will separate the temples of holy men,
and the dragon will not send alert kings into the pastures.
He will bedeck cloaks with cities and attractive jewels
and joyously bestow his own favours on virgins;
then seeking one, he will gladly marry her.

His years will be few and swift for the little ones.
Go, days of the Lynx! May you be ashamed, German worm,
that you and your gods crossed our frontiers.
It will anger and act for itself, why did Northern France burn more slowly? And like an old keystone England will place its old name.
Thus may she go to hers, may my race eradicate hers.
        May the weather be fine. Conan will sail the waves
and may he who commands the East support Cadwaladr.
A horseman whiter than snow loosening the reins of his mount,
all for duty having passed the whirlpool of Periron, with a whitening rod snatches the streams in the middle of a circle,
and measures a mill over it.
After so many disasters and often stormy labours,
the Severn will hear so many trumpets, so many of its
battles to be mixed, your rivers will laugh, O Tevi!
And the thorns tremble, the twins pitch their tents.
Now there, now in another place, the first things are owed to Reont. The enemy will receive lances, stakes, swords and darts in their warm flanks; gore flows and stains everybody;
I bear witness that the waves are happy, the sands are happy.
The German tyrants would have been happy had they ceased before. Whoever are worthy of their horses and close in handling spears, they will learn to conquer, few will desert the standards.
For shame! Eight and ten thousand there just now.
Four turn back in ignoble disgrace.
Behold what Gwynedd wanted, and it rises again
to its golden head and leads the people back together,
a woman will change fleeces for purple cloths,
a man brings silver until the City of the Legions has squeezed;
the valleys burst out and the oaks are green,
the mountains of Arfon reach the clouds with their peaks.
Posterity will lift up the crown of the Great Briton;
the good appearance of the leaders extends to deserved honours,
the appearance of the two extends to ordinary customs.
Three times twenty, three times a hundred finish the years,
golden freedom and age the same colour in heaven.

Here endeth the Prophecy of Ambrosius Merlin
about the seven kings.

72 *From* **The Cornish Glosses of the Prophecy of Merlin by John of Cornwall (c.1150)**

(46)   [*He lasts*] He lasts in an aforesaid rhythm that is eight and they all make thirty-five; which is again divided in this manner; that is twenty-five years and a half; by that is not to be understood a half of a half, but rather a half of twenty, namely ten.

(61) [*Three-fold fierceness*] For he was partly Norman, partly Scots, and partly descended from the direct nobility of the Cornish.

(63) [*Solium*] The Kingdom that is Cornwall, which in history is called the House of Coronius because that man Coronius got it by lot from Brutus in ancient times; the House is also called the Kingdom of Arcturus because he arose as the greatest of Kings amongst them.

(66) [*He now*] He now, then etc. All this was brought about when the Viscount Frewin and other Cornishmen conspired in his punishment and they killed them at a town which is called Treruf and even more things are said here that I shall pass by lest my speech be seen.

(87) [*Flame and hunger*] Flame, that is copious burning. Hunger. That hunger sometimes rises from the menacing greed of the despoilers and sometimes from barbarity. For in that time the wind raves like one possessed, so that it leaves the prayers of the husbandmen unfulfilled. This evil he calls in the British tongue the wind of the leaves, which means the shaking out of the wind.

(91) [*Canus adoptatus*] This is what is said in the British tongue; a King grey like his mare. Of Periron. He says this about his arrival in Cornwall and because he then beseiged the castle at Periron which is called Tintagel.

(107) [*Tamar*] Tamar is the river which divides Cornwall and Devon.

(108) [*Brentigia*] Brentigia is a certain wilderness in Cornwall and in our language it is called the Down of the Tree, in the language of the Saxons, Fowey Moor.

(111) [*Ventorum*] The which evil Merlin calls rough wind, that is rough wind and it is widely accepted as whatever cruelty it is possible to name.

(119) [*Fatal castle*] The fatal castle is a town in our area which in English is called Ashbury, in the British tongue the Fortress of Beli, or as it pleases some, the Castle of the High Wood.

(133) [*German reptiles*] German reptiles, that is, the white dragon, stands for the Saxons, as the red one stands for the Britons.

73 *From* **The Romance of Tristan by Béroul (c.1150)**

> They were in the forest of Moresk;
> That night they lay on a hill.
> Now Tristan is as safe
> as if he were in a castle with a wall.
>   Tristan was a good archer,
> He knew how to use a bow very well.
> Governal had taken one
> from a forester who owned it;

and two arrows feathered
and tipped he had taken.
Tristan took the bow, and went into the wood;
He saw a deer, fitted an arrow and shot,
and fiercely struck the right flank:
It cried out, leapt high and sank down.
Tristan took it and came back with it.
He made a shelter: with the sword that he held
he cut the branches, made a bower;
and strew flowers on the ground inside.
Tristan sat down with the Queen.
Governal knew how to cook:
With dry wood, he made a good fire.
Cooks have much to do!
They had neither milk nor salt
at that time in their lodging.
The Queen was very tired
because of the ordeal that she had gone through;
slumber took her, she wished to sleep,
she wanted to sleep on her lover.
My Lords, they remained for a long time
deep in the forest;
they were a long time in that wilderness.

Yseult had not delayed:
Through Perinis she reminded Tristran
of all the pain and all the anguish
that she had borne for him that year.
Now the merit would be recompensed to her!
If he willed it, she would be able to live in peace:
'Tell him that he knows the marsh well,
at the end of the plank-bridge at Malpas:
There, I muddied my clothes a little.
On the mound, at the end of the plank-bridge,
and a little this side of the Lande Blanche,
let him be, dressed in the clothes of a leper;
let him carry a wooden cup,
let him have a flask beneath
tied on with a strap;
in the other hand, let him carry a stick.
This is the strategem he must keep in mind.
At the appointed time let him be seated on the ground:
Let his face be very pock-marked.
Let him carry the cup in front of his face:
to those who pass by him
let him simply ask for alms:
they will give him gold and silver;

let him keep the silver for me, until I see him
privately, in a quiet room.'
Perinis said: 'Lady, in faith,
I shall certainly tell him all this.'

74   *From* **A Letter to certain Cardinals by John de Grandisson, Bishop of Exeter (c.1328)**

Linguam eciam, in extremis Cornubie non Anglicis sed Britonibus extat nota
[However, in the uttermost parts of Cornwall the language is familiar not to the English but to the Britons].

75   *From* **The Translation of Ranulf Higden's Polychronicon by John Trevisa (c.1385)**

Johan Cornwall, a mayster of gramer, chayngede the lore in gramer-scole, and construccion of Freynsch into Englysh; and Richard Pencrych lurnede that manere teching of hym, and other men of Pencrych, so that now, the yere of our Lord a thousand, three foure score and fyve ... in all the grammar-scoles of England children leaveth Frensch and construeth and lurneth ye Englysch and habbeth thereby advantage in on syde and desvayntage yn another. Their avauntage ys that they lurneth gramer in lesse tyme than children were i-woned to doo; desavauntage ys that now children of grammar-scole canneth na more Frensche then can thir lift heale, and that is harme for them an they schulle passe the see and travaille in straunge landes.

76   **Some Accounts for Cornish Drama (1469–1539)**

Bodmin,1469:
Item, of the player yn the Church Hay, Wm. Mason and his fellowis....5s.

Launceston, 1531:
Player of the Lord the King [and the] Queen of Gall.

Bodmin, 1539:
iii Jesus cotes ii red worsted & one of red bocrom.
iii torment towers cotes of satyn... yelo and blue.
ii. cappes of sylck toe develes cotes wherof one ys newe.
a crown of black.

77   *From* **Utopia by Thomas More (1516)**
You will not get away with that, I said. For we shall leave out those whose limbs are injured in wars whether overseas or closer to home,

263

and who return home disabled as recently from the battle with the Cornish and not long ago from the battle with the French who lose their limbs for the good of the commonwealth

78   *From* Itinerary by John Leland (c.1540)

Launston, otherwys cawlled Lostephen, yn olde tyme cawlled Dunevet, stondith ii. myles beyownd Powlston Bridge on Tamar westward. The sayde town Dunevet, otherwise Lawnston, is a walled towne ny yn cumpas a myle, but now ruinus. On the north side of the towne a castel stonding on a hye hill withyn the sayd towne, hath iii. rownde wardes. Part of the castel stonding north-west, ys parcel of the walle of the town. Ther be withun this town iii. gates and a postern; also a gate to go owt of the castel ynto the old parke. Sum gentlemen of Cornewal hold ther landes by castel-gard, that ys to say for reperation of this castel and towne, and withyn this castel ys a chapel, and a hawle for syses and sessions, for a commune gayle for al Cornwayle is yn this castel. Within this towne is a market, a mayre and burgesses, with a chapel of Mary Magdalen to theyre uses.

From Wade Bridge to Padstow a good quik fischer toun but onclenly kepte, a 4 miles. This toun is ancient bearing the name of Lodenek in Cornische, and un Englische after the trew and old writings of Adelstow Latine Athelstani Locas. And the toune there takith King Adelstaine for the chief giver of privileges onto it.

Markesju, a great long toun, burnid 3 aut 4 anno. Henr. 8 a Gallis. The paroch chirch a mile of. A pere by the Mount. Markjue and the Mount be both S. Hillaries paroche. There was found of late years syns spere heddes, axis for warre, and swerds of copper, wrappid up in lynin perishid nere the Mount in S. Hillaries paroch in tynne works ...

From Lanant by the North se to S.Just, alias Justini, beyng the very West Poynt of al Cornwayle, and wher ys no thing but a Paroch Chyrch of divers sparkeled Howses, the North Part ys Montaynes and Baren Growne, but plenteful of Tynne. The very West Poynt, as yt ys cawled now yn Cornysch, ys Penwolase, id est, infinitum caput.

From Mr. Godolcan to Pembro, wher the paroch chirch is [i.e. appertains] to Mr. Godolcan. The personage impropriate to Heyles in Gloucestreshir. The south se is about a mile from Pembro. From Mr. Godolcan to Lannate a 4 miles. Passage at ebbe over a great strond, and then over Heyle river. No greater tynne workes yn al Cornwall than be on Sir Wylliam Godolcan's ground. Heyle Haven shoken [choked] with land of tynne works.

79 *From* **The Fyrst Book of the Introduction of Knowledge: The Apendix to the Fyrst Chapter, Treatinge of Cornewall, and Cornyshe Men by Andrew Boorde (1547)**

Iche cham a Cornyshe man, al[e] che can brew;
It wyll make one to kacke, also to spew;
It is dycke and smoky, and also it is dyn;
It is lyke wash, as pygges had wrestled dryn.
Iche cannot brew, nor dresse Fleshe, nor vyshe;
Many volke do segge, I mar many a good dyshe.
Dup the dore, gos! iche hab some dyng to seg,
'When olde knaues be dead, yonge knaues be fleg.'
Iche chaym yll afyngred, iche swere by my fay
Iche nys not eate no soole sens yester daye;
Iche wolde fayne taale ons myd the cup;
Nym me a quart of ale, that iche may if of sup.
A, good gosse, iche hab a toome, vyshe, and also tyn;
Drynke, gosse, to me, or els iche chyl begyn.
God! watysh great colde, and fynger iche do abyd!
Wyl your bedauer, gosse, come home at the next tyde.
Iche pray to God to coun him wel to vare,
That, whan he comit home, myd me he do not starre
For putting a straw dorow his great net.
Another pot of ale, good gosse, now me fet;
For my bedauer wyl to London, to try the law,
To sew Tre poll pen, for waggyng of a straw.
Now, gosse, farewell! yche can no lenger abydge;
Iche must ouer to the ale howse at the yender syde;
And now come myd me, gosse, I thee pray,
And let vs make merry, as long as we may.

Cornwal is a pore and very barren countrey of al maner thing except Tyn and Fyssche. There meate and theyr bread and dryncke is marde and spylt for lacke of good ordering and dressynge. Fyrres and turues is their chief fewel; there ale is starke nought, lokinge whyte and ropye and neuer a good sope; in moste places it is worse and worse, pitie it is, them to curse, for wagginge of a straw they will go to law, and al not worth a hawe, playinge so the dawe. In Cornwal is two speches; the one is naughty Englyshe and the other is Cornyshe speche. And there be many men and women the whiche cannot speake one worde of Englyshe, but all Cornyshe. Who so wyll speake any Cornyshe, Englyshe and Cornyshe doth follow:–

One. two. thre. foure. fyue. six. seuen.
ouyn. dow. tray. peswar. pimp. whe. syth.

Eyght. nyne. ten. alewyn. twelve. thertene.

eth. naw. dec. unec. dowec. tredeec.

Fortene. fyften. syxtene. seuentine. eyghtyne.
perwerdeec. pympdeec. whedeec. sythdeec. ethdeec.

Nyntyne. twenty. one and twenty. two and twenty.
nawdeec. Igous. onyn war igous. dow war igous.

Three and twenty. fouer and twenty, &c.
tray war ygous. peswarygous, and so forth tyl you come to thyrty.

    No Cornyshman dothe number above XXX, and is named Deec warnegous. And whan they haue told thyrty they do begyn agagn, one, two and three, And so forth, and whan they haue recounted to a hondred they saye Kans, And if they number to a thousand, than they say Myle.

1 *God morow to you, syr.*
    Dar day dew a why, serra.
2 *God spede you, mayde.*
    Dar zona de why, math tath.
3 *You be welcome, good wyfe.*
    Welcom a whe, gwra da.
4 *I do thanke you, syr.*
    Dar dala de why, syra.
5 *How do you fare?*
    Vata lew genar why?
6 *Well, God thank you, good master.*
    Da, dar dala de why, master da.
7 *Hostes, have you any good meate?*
    Hostes, eus bones de why?
8 *Yes, syr, I haue enowghe.*
    Eus, sarra, grace a dew.
9 *Give me some meate, good hostes.*
    Rewh bones de vy, hostes da.
10 *Mayde, give me bread and drinke.*
    Mathtath, eus me barow ha dewas.
11 *Wyfe, bringe me a quarte of wine.*
    Gwrac drewh quart gwin de vy.
12 *Woman, bringe me some fishe.*
    Beuen, drewh pyscos de vi.
13 *Mayde, brynge me egges and butter.*
    Mathtath, drewgh me eyo hag a manyn de vi.
14 *Syr, much good do it you.*
    Syrra, betha why lowe weny cke.
15 *Hostes, what shal I paye?*
    Hostes, pendra we pay?
16 *Syr, your reckenyng is .v. pens.*

      Syrra, iges rechen eu pymp in ar.
17 *How many myles is it to London?*
      Pes myll eus a lemma de Londres?
18 *Syr, it is thre houndred myle.*
      Syrra, tray kans myle dere.
19 *God be with you, good hostes.*
      Bena tewgana a why, hostes da.
20 *God gyue you a good night.*
      Dew rebera vos da de why.
21 *God send you wel to fare.*
      Dew reth euenna thee why fare eta.
22 *God be wyth you.*
      Dew gena why.
23 *I pray you, commend me to all good felowes.*
      Meesdesyer why, commende me tha olde matas da.
24 *Syr, I wyl do your commaundement.*
      Syrra, me euyden gewel ages commaundement why.
25 *God be with you.*
      Dew gena why.

80   *From* **The Articles of the Rebels (1549)**

Item we wil not receyue the new seruyce because it is but lyke a Christmas game, but we wull haue oure olde seruice of Mattens, masse, Euensong and procession in Latten, as it was before. And so we the Cornyshe men (whereof certen of vs vnderstande no Englysh) vtterly refuse thys newe Englysh.
                By vs
                      Humphrey Arundell
                      Thomas Underhyll
                      John Sloman
                      William Segar *Chief Captaynes*
                      John Tompson *Pryeste*
                      Henry Bray *Maior of Bodma*
                      Henry Lee *Maior of Torrinton*
                      Roger Barret *Prieste*

81   *From* **The Reply to the Rebels by Edward Seymour, Duke of Somerset (1549)**

And where ye saie certain Cornishmen be offended because they haue not their s'uice in Cornish for somuch as thei vnderstand no Englysh. Whie shulde they nowe be offended more when they vnderstand it not in Englysh then when thye had it in Latin and vnderstand it not? And whie shulde not yo all the rest be gladde and well pleased that it haue it in Englysh, that ye do vnderstand.

82 *From* **The Image of Idleness by Oliver Oldwanton (c.1565–70)**

A lyttle treatyse called the Image of Idlenesse conteynunge certeyne matters moued between Walter Wedlocke and Bawdin Bachelor. Translated out of the Troyance or Cornysche tounge by Olyuer Oldwanton and dedicated to the Lady Lust. Imprinted at London by William Seres dwellynge in Powles Church Yard at the signe of the Hedge Hogg.

Olyuer: "'Tyll at length this Pigmalion died and then was his wife turned agayne into an image of alabaster which to this day so remayneth and is accompted throughout all Greece theyr best and chiefest Pylgremage for to remove or expell the passion and paynes of ielousy. The Princes of Tarent (but after some bookes, of Ottronto) finding' by unmissable proof that her husband had been behaving badly towards her 'being warned by a vision to repayre unto this blessed image for helpe, did avowe her Pylgrymage thyther and receaved the Oracle, *Marsoye thees duan Guisca ancorne Rog hatre arta* [If there is to thee grief to wear the horn, give it home again], being expounded by the prestes of that Temple to this effect in Englyshe. If to weare the horne thou fynde thy selfe agreed. Gyve hym back agayne and thou shalt sone be eased.'"

83 *From* **The Bishops' Consistory Court Depositions at Exeter (1572 and 1595)**

1572. Wm. Fytteck, of Lelant, tynner, resident from birth, aged 26, says he was in the parish church of Lelant on All Hallow day in the forenoon and at the time when the priest was at service, Agnes, wife of Moryce David and Cicely James came into the church, one after another, and were multiplying of words together and among their talk when that Cicely James was come almost to the mydle of the church she called Agnes whore and whore bitch, and Agnes went in her pew and said nothing and there were a great many of the parish there that did hear the words. Wm Hawysche, of Lelant, tynner, from birth resident, aged 40, sayeth that upon Dew Whallan Gwa Metten in Eglos De Lalant, viz. upon all hallow day late paste about the mydds of the service in the parish church of Lalant Moryshe David's wife and Cicely James came into the church of Lalant together and in chiding with words together Cycely called Agnes Davey whore and whore bitch in English and not in Cornowok.

1595: St. Ewe. Eliz. Trevathack v. Edw. John and Petronella John "in quadam causa deffamationis." Two of the witnesses called were talking together both in "Cornishe and Englishe."

84   St Ives Accounts for Cornish Drama (1573–84)

St Ives, 1573:
receiued of John Clarke for ye interlude, C^{ii} xj^d
receiuyed of William Trinwith for sixe score and three foote of elme bords in ye playing place, vj^d.

St Ives, 1575:
Itm receiued the first day of the playe		xij^s	
Itm receiued the seconde day wch amounteth to	1^{ii}	xij^s	ij^d
Itm receiued the thirde day wch amounteth to	iiij^{ii}	x^s	xj^d
Itm receiued the fourth day wch amounteth to	1^{ii}	xix^s	vj^d
Itm receiued the 5 daye wch amounteth to	iij^{ii}	ij^s	
Itm receiued the sixth day wch amounteth to	iij^{ii}		j^d
more receiued for drincke monye wch amounteth to	j^s	ij^d	
Itm receiuyed for drink monye after the playe	ij^s	viij^d	

Item payed to John Williams for things which he delivered about the laste playe –
[Incomplete]
Item payed for things for the playe   iii^s
Spent upon the carpenters yit made hevin   iiij^d

St Ives, 1584
Item paid to the players of Germal which gathered for yer Church. ij^s

85   *From* **A Topographical and Historical Description of Cornwall by John Norden (c.1584)**

The Cornish people, for the most parte, are descended of the British stocke, thowgh muche entermixed since with the Saxon and Norman bloude; but vntil of late yeares retayned, the British speache corrupted, as their is of Wales; for the south Wales man vunderstandeth not perfectlye the north Wales man, and the north Wales man litle of the Cornische, the south muche. The pronunciation of the tounge differs in all, but the Cornishe tounge is farr the easieste to be pronounced; for they strayne not their wordes so tediouslye throwgh the throate, and so harshlye throwgh and from the Roofe of the mouth; as in pronouncing Rhin, they fetch it with R^h-Rhin, and LL with a kinde of reflecting the tounge. The Welsche doe drown the true sounde of manie letters and sillables by a kinde of asperation, contrarie to moste Languages; but of late the Cornishe men haue muche conformed themselves to the vse of the Englishe tounge, and their Englishe is equall to the beste, especially in the easterne partes; euen from Truro eastwarde it is in manner wholy Englishe. In the weste parte of the Countrye, as in the hundreds of Penwith and Kerrier, the Cornishe tounge in moste in vse amongst the inhabitantes, and yet (whiche is to be marueyled) thowgh the husband and wife, parentes and children, Masters and Seruantes, doe mutually communicate in their native language, yet ther is none of them in manner but able to conuers with a Straunger in the Englishe tongue, vnless it be some obscure people, that seldome conferr with the better sorte: But it seemeth that in few yeares the Cornishe Language wil be by litle and litle abandoned ... and as they are amonge themselues litigious so seeme they yet to retayne a kinde of conceyled enuye agaynste the Englishe, whome they yet affecte with a desire of reuenge for their fathers sakes, by whome their fathers recuyued the repulse.

86 *From* **The Green Book of St. Columb Major (1589–95)**

1589: Rec. for the lont of the Robbyn hoodes clothes   xvij^d
1595: Deb'. Ryc beard oweth to be payed at or ladye daye in lent x^s of Robin hoodes monyes.

Deb' Robert Calwaye oweth for ye same	ij^s	viij^d
ffrancis Bennye owethe	x^s	
John lae owethe	iij^s	
Deb'. wylyam Tryscot owethe	vj^s	ij^d
John Pers owethe		xij^d

87 *From* **Relation of the visit of the Catholic Kings by Don Antonio Ortes (1600)**

La Lengua Cornaica: The Cornish Language
'His honour is great in thy salvation: glory and great worship shalt thou lay upon him.' Verse 5.
There spoke in this language a student, a native of that Province of England, whose language is distinct from English, as is in Spain the Biscayan from the Castilian; and it has some ways and manner of speaking, with that rapidity of the Basques: and it is the part of England which looks directly towards Biscay and in his manner he spoke it excellently.

Interprete: Translation
Said the Cornishman: that all men aim at honour and glory, but few find it, because they do not seek it where it is; they seek it in vanity and deceitful splendour of the world and they find themselves deceived and vain: because it is only found in virtue in which the Catholic Kings seek it, and therefore the true honour follows them as the shadows follow the body.

88 *From* **The Survey of Cornwall by Richard Carew (1602)**

Most of them begin with Tre, Pol, or Pen, which signify a town, a top, and a head: whence grew the common by-word:

By Tre, Pol, and Pen,
You shall know the Cornishmen.

Neither do they want some signification, as Godolfin, alias Godolghan, a white eagle: Chiwarton, the green castle on the hill: which gentlemen give such arms, Reskimer, the great dog's race, who beareth a wolf passant. Carnsew, alias Carndew, a black rock, his house Bokelly, which soundeth the lost goat, and a goat he beareth for his coat. Carminow, a little city, Cosowarth, the high grove, &c.

And as the Cornish names hold an affinity with the Welsh, so is their language deduced from the same source, and differeth only in the dialect. But the Cornish is more easy to be pronounced, and not so unpleasing in sound, with throat letters, as the Welsh.

A friend of mine, one Master Thomas Williams, discoursed once with me that the Cornish tongue was derived from, or at least had some acquaintance with the Greek, and besides divers reasons which he produced to prove the same, he vouched many words of one sense in both, as for example:

Greek	*Cornish*	*English*
Teino	Tedna	Draw
Mamma	Mamm	Mother
Episcopos	Escoppe	Bishop
Klyo	Klowo	Hear
Didaskein	Dathisky	To teach
Kyon	Kye	Dog
Kentron	Kentron	Spur
Methyo	Methow	Drink
Scaphe	Schapth	Boat
Ronchos	Ronchie	Snorting, &c.

This language is stored with sufficient plenty to express the conceits of a good wit, both in prose and rhyme; yet can they no more give a Cornish word for *tie*, than the Greeks for *ineptus*, the French for *stand*, the English for *emulus*, or the Irish for *knave*.

Oaths they have not past two or three natural, but are fain to borrow of the English; marry this want is relieved with a flood of most bitter curses and spiteful nicknames.

They place the adjective after the substantive, like the Grecians and Latins, as *paz agan*, father ours, *march guidden*, horse white, &c.

In numbering they say, Wonnen 1, Deaw 2, Tre 3, Pidder 4, Pimp 5, Whey 6, Zith 7, Eath 8, Naw 9, Deag 10, Ednack 11, Dowthack 12, Tarnack 13, Puzwarthack 14, Punthack 15, Wheytack 16, Zitack 17, Itack 18, Naunzack 19, Eygganz 20, Deaw Eigganz 40, Cans 100, Mille 1000, Molla 10,000.

Durdatha why, is Good morrow to you. *Ternestatha*, Good night. *Fatlugan a why?*, How do you do? *Da durdalatha why*, Well, I thank you. *Betha why lawannack*, Be you merry. *Benetugana*, Farewell. A sister they call *whoore*: a whore, *whorra*: a priest, *coggaz*: a partridge, *grigear*: a mare, *cazock*. *Relauta*, By my troth. *Warra fey*, By my faith. *Molla tuenda laaz*, Ten thousand mischiefs in thy guts. *Mille vengeance warna thy*, A thousand vengeances take thee. *Pedn joll*, Stinking head, and so *in infinitum*. Which terms notwithstanding, though they witness their spite on the one side, yet retain they are great a proof of their devotion on the other; for the Lord's Prayer, the Apostles' Creed, and the Ten Commandments have been used in Cornish beyond all remembrance. But the principal love and knowledge of this language lived in Dr. Kenall the civilian and with him lieth buried, for the English speech doth still encroach upon it and hath driven the same into the uttermost skirts of the shire. Most of the inhabitants can speak no word of Cornish, but very few are ignorant of the English; and yet some so affect their own as to a stranger they will not speak it, for if meeting them by chance you inquire the way or any such matter, your answer shall be, *Meea navidna cowza sawzneck*, 'I can speak no Saxonage'. The English which they speak is good and pure, as receiving it from the best hands of their own gentry and the eastern merchants, but they disgrace it in part with a broad and rude accent, somewhat like the Somersetshire men, especially in pronouncing the names, as, Thomas, they call *Tummas* and *Tubby*; Matthew, *Mathaw*; Nicholas, *Nichlaaz*; Reginald, *Reinol*; David, *Daavi*; Mary, *Maari*; Frauncis, *Frowncis*; James, *Jammez*; Walter, *Watty*; Robert, *Dobby*; Rafe, *Raw*; Clemence, *Clemmowe* &c. holding herein a contrary course of extension to the Italians' abridgement, who term Francis, *Cecco*; Dominick, *Beco*; Lawrence, *Renzo*: as also to the Turks, who name Constantinople, *Stampoli*; Adrianople, *Adrina*; an Olifant, *Fil*; and the Sicilians, who curtail Nicholas to *Cola*.

Besides these, they have taken up certain peculiar phrases which require a special dictionary for their interpretation, of which kind are: 'Tis not *bezib'd* (that is, *fortuned*) to me; Thou has no *road* (aim); He will never *scrip* (escape) it; He is nothing *pridy* (handsome): as also boobish (lubberly), dule (comfort), lidden (by-word), shun (strange), thew (threaten), skew (shun), hoase (forbear).

The gwary miracle, in English, a miracle play, is a kind of interlude, compiled in Cornish out of some scripture history, with that grossness which accompanied the Romans' vetus comedia. For representing it, they raise an earthen amphitheatre in some open field, having the diameter of his enclosed plain some forty or fifty foot. The country people flock from all sides, many miles off, to hear and see it, for they have therein devils and devices to delight as well the eye as the ear. The players con not their parts without book, but are prompted by one called the ordinary, who followeth at their back with the book in his hand, and telleth them softly what they must pronounce aloud. Which manner once gave occasion to a pleasant conceited gentleman of practising a merry prank; for he undertaking (perhaps of set purpose) an actor's room, was accordingly lessoned (beforehand) by the ordinary, that he must say after him. His turn came: quoth the ordinary, 'Go forth man, and show thyself.' The gentleman steps out upon the stage, and like a bad clerk in scripture matters, cleaving more to the letter than the sense, pronounced these words aloud. 'Oh (says the fellow softly in his ear) you mar all the play.' And with this his passion the actor makes the audience in like sort acquainted. Hereon the prompter falls to flat railing and cursing in the bitterest terms he could devise; which the gentleman with a set gesture and countenance still soberly related, until the ordinary, driven at last into mad rage, was fain to give over all; which trousse, though it break off the interlude, yet defrauded not the beholders, but dismissed them with a great deal more sport and laughter than twenty such gwaries could have afforded.

89 *From* **The Lives of the Saints by Nicholas Roscarrock (c.1620)**

Sainct Columba was the daughter of King Lodan & Queen Maingild, both Pagans, became in her hart a Christian, after which the holie Ghoste appeared vnto her in the likenes of a Doue, which perhaps was the cause of her name, assuring her of his Blessing & love, wherevpon shee vowed virginitie. And forbearing to goe with her Parents to there Idolatrous Temple, withdrew herself into a private place to praye, where she had a vewe of the Blessed Trinitye; her parents, perceiving her forbearing, cald for her to goe with them, which she refusing & professing herself a Christian it greived her Parentes so greatlie as they vsed all means, first by kinde vsage to remove her; And they saw that would not serve, fell to threaten her & caused her to be whipt & tormented. All which she indured with great patience; still praying Christ to give her grace to persever, whose prayers prevailed so farr as shee was much incouradged. And as hee comitted her to prison into a dark Dungion, it pleased God there to comfort her with an Angell whoe delivered her out of that prison and guided her into a Desert farr distant from that place; where when shee came, being destitute of all relief & bodilie foode, shee fell to prayer & having help from God whoe provided in such sort for her as shee founde convenient sustaynance. At last, a great enemie of Christian religion, dwelling hard by & hearing of her, sent certaine to apprehend her, whoe finding her on her knees prayeing toke her & carryed her to ther Master, whoe seing her beautie & modest behaviour was sodainlie surprised with it & offered to Marrye her to his sonn & make her the Mistris of all that he had, so as she would forsake her faith. For which, rendring great thankes, signified she could not accept of them, having vowed chastitie, wherewith the Tyrant caused her to be tyed to a wheele to be tormented, at which time the Angell of God did soe protect her as she received no harme. Then was she dragged at a horse taylle & brought to a Gallows where, being hanged a long time, she lived still & being cutt downe shee stoode on her feet. Then being committed to prison, Twoe ruffinlye fellowes were sent to deflowre her, whoe coulde not effect it, the Angell of God protecting & conducting her out of the prison, And directed her to goe towards the Sea coaste & take the first shipp that she did meete withal; & so shee did, being come to the depth the holie Ghoste appeared againe vnto her in the form of a Dove on the Topp of the shipp, with which being comforted she at last arrived at a place in Cornwall called Treuelgry, where the Tyrant having intelligence of it pursued her & at a place called Ruthwas overtoke her, & refusing to renownce Christian Religion, chopt of her head. At which place there is a Well at this daie which beareth her name; The Water of which being taken out (as I haue bene informed) of the Well will not seeth, whereas all the Towne of St Columbe dresseth there meat with the water take vpp without the Well, which boyleth there meat & anye thing they put in it verie well. There is also a church dedicated vnto her, called the higher Sainct Columb, which argueth there is a lower and consequently twoe, & her Feast is ever observed in the higher St Columb in Cornwall the Thursdaye following All Hallowes daye.

This I haue takenout of an olde Cornish Rymthe containing her Legend, translated by one Mr Williams, a Physion [physician] there, but howe Autentick it is I dare not saye, being loath to comptrowle that which I cannot correct.

[Sct Piran] was one of the first 12 bishoppes which Sct Patrick appointed to prech Christe in Ireland, he made good of evell, friendes of enemyes, he was very riddy to pardon such as would seeke it with sorrow, he was full of mercy, piety and charity to his neighboures; he gat the releefe of these that were with him and of others with the laboures of his owne handes' he chastised himselfe with all manner of good disciplines, and performed all the workes of charity and hospitality &c. And when he perceiued that the day of his death drew neere, he called his brethren together and towld them it was the pleasure of god that he showld go from Ireland to Cornewall in great Britain, and therefore did will them to edefie one another with good life and examples, foretelling them that mortality and warres showld follow after his death, that churches showld be distroyed and forsaken, and verity turned into iniquity, that fath should not appear in good workes, that pastors showld respecte themselues more than ther floke, and so requested them to pray for him that he might after his life finde god mercifull to him, tooke his leaue and departed from them into Cornwall, signifying that it was the will of god that he showlde dye and be buried ther. And when he came to Cornwall buylded him a mansion ther, and wher it pleased god to manifest many miracles by him. And when he perceiued himselfe weake and likly to dye, called his disciples vnto him, preached many thinges vnto them of the ioyes of heaven, and then causinge a grett caue or graue to be made for him entered into it the 5 of March, at which tyme his soule pierced the heavens with exceding brightnesse and lyeth buryed in Cornwall one the Severne sea 15 miles from Petrokesstow and 25 from Mousehole, sayth Capgraue, whom I have specially followed, who reporteth many strange thinges of him as that his mother having conceiued him imagined one night that she saw a star more cleerer then the rest fall into her mouth, and others more admirable, in discourse whereof he is much longer, He will stand with my pretended brevity to insert here, which I do rather omit for that as I haue often noted he is as I hear translated into English lately, many yeer since I began this worke, and is likly to be devoulgedc to whom such as desyre to be more fully informed may haue accesse, and will add some thinges which concerne in such sorte this our saint, which ar as follow. Geffry Mounmouth, and after him Floriligus, a. 522 Jonsonne in Hist. Eccl., writeth that Sct Piran was the chaplyne of king Arthur who made him the 8 Archb. of Yorke after Sct Sampson flying from thence to Dole in little Brittan to avoyde persequution about the year 520, for when the king coming to Yorke to keepe his Christenmasse, hee found the Archb. fledd, churches defaced and all confounded, which he indevoured to repare and remedy and made Sct Piran Archb. there. After king Arthur's death Sct Piran liued a solitary life, giuing over his Archbishoprike about the yeere 503, at a place in Cornwall wher ther was a church or chapple erected to him and bearing his name and wher he was buryed, being called Sct Pirans in the sand, which chapple hath bene overblowne with the sand though ther standeth one at his day dedicated vnto him neere that place since the other hath been drowned or overblowne (as we sayd) with sand.

90   *From* **The Probate Documents of Francis John Trevallacke of Wendron by His Testator (1622)**

[The testator,] who understood English well but could not perfectly pronounce it.

91   *From* **The Northern Lasse by Richard Brome (1632)**

Act V, Scene 8

Bullfinch: Alasse what shall we doe then? Gentlemen, have any of you any Spanish to help me understand this strange stranger?
[*They all disclaim knowledge*]
Bullfinch: What shiere of our Nation is next to Spain? Perhaps he may understand that shiere English.
Tridewell: Devonshire or Cornwall, sire.

Nonsense: Never credit me but I will spurt some Cornish at him.
Pedn bras vidne whee bis creegas.

92 *From* **Diary of the Marches of the Royal Army during the Great Civil War by Richard Symonds (1644)**

This language is spoken altogether at Goonhilly and about Pendennis, and at Land's End they speak no English. All beyond Truro they speak the Cornish language.

93 *From* **Itinerary by John Ray (1662 and 1667)**

Mr. Dickan Gwyn lives not far off, in St. Just Parish, who is the only man we could hear of that can now write the Cornish language. We met with none here but what could speak English; few of the children could speak Cornish, so that the language is like, in a short time, to be quite lost.

He is esteemed the most skilful man of any now living in the Cornish language, but being no good grammarian, we found him very deficient. Another there is, Pendarvis by name, who is said to be a scholar, who doubtless must needs have better skill in the tongue.

94 *From* **The Dutchesse of Cornwall's progresse to see the Land's end & to visit the mount by Nicholas Boson (c.1665)**

It was order'd that all Jornalls of considerable passages should be referred to be taken at return, and the end of the land to be the beginning of their observations.

Having performed their mattens devotion at the chappel of Pensance, they intended their evenson at the chappell of Carnbre, where attended Harry the Hermitt in his state and gravity: there was no little gazing at the rarity of that structure, the duchesse herself admiring the biformity therof consisting of two curious vaults the one over the other in the top of the mountain being the first English land that appears in course unto the discovery of all ships sailing from the Aquitane, mediterranean, Attlantick & Indian Oceans. The common people flock'd about her some of which understanding little other than the Cornish language, yet such was their ayre & meene that some of the courtiers who had been travellers assured her Highness that amongst all the vulgar people of all parts they had ever travell'd, they never observed any that had naturally so little of Boorishness and peasantry as they observ'd in these vulgar Cornish; one of them expressing it thus.

> Teste Britannorum veterum jam stirpe videmus
> hos habuisse animum quos non habuisse putemus.

These offspring of the ancient Brittains have A spirit & grace, the best that nature gave.

The dutchesse smiling at his rustick simplicity required some memorable instance of his language. The Hermitt like an ancient bard extempore pronounced this Cornish Distick:

> Nages travith dale talues an bees
> Bus gen dieu benegas do gweel gan crees.

And as readily deliver'd it thus in English:

> This world hath nothing worth our love
> But to make peace with God above.

That Michell his Monk was indeed a man studious & curious of antiquities, known in History, & endued with a faculty of predicting events.

The prospect of Silly was the next divertisement which offer'd itself very clear & conspicuous insomuch that the sands could be discerned as well as the Land.

The Government of the Island was not then establish'd in the honourable house of Godolphin untill afterwards the Dukedom came to be united to the Crown.

They fell upon this facetious project having the Dean of Burrian of their faction who drew up a cornish petition against Harry the Hermitt representing unto her Highness what grounds they had to suspect him to be witch, wherof so much was found in an old Tinnen box amidst the ruins of King Arthur's castle in old Brittish characters, hardly preserved from the Injury of the moths. Here followeth.

> Rag an Arlothas an wolas Kernow.
>
> Dreth gwz Kibmias Benigas, Why ra Cavas dreeu an gwas Harry ma Poddrack broas.
>
> 1 Kensa, vrt an hagar auall iggeva gweell do derevoll warneny Keniffer termen drerany moas durt pedden an wolas do sillan &c.
>
> 2 Nessa, vrt an skauoll Crackan codna iggeva setha war en crees an aules ewhall heb drogi veeth.
>
> 3 Tregyra, vrt an Gurroll iggeva gweell gen askern skooth davas, &c.

> To the Dutchess of the Dominion of Cornwall.
>
> By your sacred leave your Highness shall find this fellow Harry is a great witch.
>
> 1 Because of the many dangerous storms he hath risen upon us betwixt Silly & Land's end for no other reason but because (as he pretends) our wives would not pay him their tyth egges, although it is to be suspected he hath more from them than is his due, the tyth belonging to the Dean of Burrian.
>
> 2 That almost all the day long he sits in a cliff of a Rock called there Harry an Pader, in an inaccessible stupendious cliff, where it is impossible for any to come but himself without breaking

their necks.

3 That they had many times seen him come foorth out of his cave called Toll pedden penwith, into the open ocean upon a bone of shoulder of mutton untill they had warn'd all the inhabitants of those parts to pierce a hole in that bone as soon as the fleash was eaten off &c.

On one of the outmost rocks they espy'd a huge beast which they perceived to be a sea horse.

Afar off they beheld a meermaid, & upon the right hand a Triton sounding his Trumpett attended with a great many Dolphins.

Thence she came to Newlyn and to Michel's mount.

The countrey had cut up the sea horse to pieces.

The road for ships by Newlyn is call'd Gwavas Lake.

That ominous rock in the sea, call'd the Armed Knight, which your Highness so admired is indeed of admirable regard not only because of its magnitude & stateliness with the resemblance of a helmett on his head bidding defiance to the Ocean, and protection to the nation. But because it is a type of a great monarch of this realm (which hasteneth its subjection under one sole potentate of another line, with a series of uninterrupted succession of Kings of England from generation to generation &c.).

And had your Highness had but the leisure then you might have seen two ancient circles of high stones (called Daunce mine) set up in two distant places for memorialls of the great battles there obtained against the Danes by the unconquered Cornish as on the rocky cliff doth plainly appear the ancient ruines of their impregnable castle, by the double walls, & draw-bridges yet to be discerned: called Castoll Trerine as our Language sutes much with the original tongues by giving derivative and significant names unto most persons & things. Tre signifyeth a Town, village, or place and Rine the current, stream or tide, The place of this castle being incompass'd , both by a running stream at Land, & a strong tide at sea, Penrin on ffalmouth [.....] importing the same, also the seats of those stones have their derivations the one call'd Boscawen from Bos Antwnty a wood and scawen an elder tree, as it were a wood of elders, the opennesse of the country not so much favouring other plants as those sorts of trees. The other stones in Rosmoddres from Ros the commons. But I am loth to grate your Highness eares &c. – much of our corn. Gentry deriving their names from their places.

Madam as to rock we were upon, Tradition calls it Carrack Looes en Cooes, a hoary or ven[erable] rock in the wood of fforest; but we have not record extant when the furious inundation made wonderfull changes upon this part, (yet there is a Tradition in the house of Trevillian that their ancestor inhabiting the city of Lyoness betwixt Silly and Land's end only escaped the suddenesse of the flood by the help of his horse that swimmed him over) That bodyes & roots of trees lye along the sand betwixt this & Newlyn the opposite village is very evident in winter &c. I have likewise seen the form of various

leaves in the washed earth as of oak, nutt, elm, willow & holm; etc.
Eue Rateera war mean Merlin
Ra leske pawl, pensans, ha Newlyn.

There shall land on the Stone Merlin
Shall burn Pawl, pensans, & Newlyn

– registred that from that time forward the Annual summe, on Marhasion should be found fourty six shillings and eight pence, Pensance 12 shillings, Newlyn twenty shillings, and Mousehole one hundred shillings in proportion according to their usual fishery to be paid yearly unto the Havener of the Dutchie's deputy &c.

Marhasion so call'd from a market held by the Sea shore or nigh the breach of the Sea which it aptly signifies: Pensance (as some offer) from St. John Baptist's Head, their town arms, (others) from the Head of the creeks, it being the inmost town of the Bay, & not from the former, because their chappell was dedicated to St. Mary, & not to St. J. Bapt^t., Newlyn so call'd from their good saint & chappell &c. &c. &c. Moushole called Porthennis because of the shutting out of the both hills of merlin & Pelle confining it between their antiquity, Their traffique, their quondam grandure when their magistrates wore scarlett gowns is testified as yet by the Reliques of many chappels & magnificent buildings.

The common proverb (By west the mount, By west good manners).

The Brittains fled over to Britain in France in the days of Augustulus being beaten by the Angles.

[Pensans chappel is a chappel of ease depending upon Maddern, in a remote part of which lyeth and old chappel call'd Maddern Well chappel, unto which much people do resort; some will have it to be devotion, others account it superstition, whatever was the cause of it's first reputation, this is a known truth, & I have known the cripple, that was thus being made whole, being a poore boy of the church town, and having unhappily a blow on the back, became a cripple for 20 years time going on his hands and feet; but dreaming at length once & again that washing at the chapple he should sleep on the green bed of turf adjoying to the alter, & so be restored which having performed by the help of a neighbour, he found his joynts loosen'd, & very much ease. and getting 2 crooches he did it the 2d time, & then he returns with the help of one only; After the 3d Essay and was perfectly whole continuing sound ever after to his death. The healing of this cripple some account a miracle (our physitians concluding the water to be neither mineral nor sanative) but our learned Bishop hath resolv'd it to be non miraculum sed mirum.

As Pensans on the East, so Morva on the west sea is a dependent upon Maddern, where a good woman of discretion hath told me of certain, that sitting up late in her Father's house she often sawe the Faires (neat little creatures) who familiarly talked with her, & gave her

279

many groats untill she bewrayed this converse against their charge & order.]

Peth Prawnter. A priest's goods or estate. –
Newlyn so call'd from the cornish word Newl signifying mist.

The cornish teinners strongly fancy that Noah's flood upon withdrawing so shak'd the surface of the earth that the looser stones they call'd shoads were then rolled from the standing mines that they call the Loads.–

> Rag gun Arlothas da
> Ny en gweel gun moyha;
>
> For our most excellent Dutchesse Right
> Unto the utmost we will fight.

Hurling the particular game of this western part of the county –
meanamber a remarkable stone, Truro by the ancient cornish Treyou quasi Treluou The town of Ashes, but the modern have refin'd it Truro quasi Tre-our i.e. a Town of Gold.

pendennis looks out stoutly fortifyed in a true cornish dress: quasis head of the promontory.

The Dutchesse presented them with a golden Ball with this engraved on't.
> Theram Ry do why an Bele ma
> do gware gen bonogath da;

I do bestow on you this Ball in good will for to play withall.

Cornish from an Old Romance of Mr. Boson's of Newlyn call'd the Dutchess of Cornwall's progress to the Land's end & the Mount.
a Device said to be worn by the Cornish men on Ribbons upon their laps.

| Rag gun Arlothaze da | Four our good Duchesse |
| Ny en gweel gun moya | We will fight (or do) our best. |

Motto on a hurling ball said to be given by the Duchess.

| Theram ky do why an Belema | I do bestow on you this Ball |
| Do guave gen Bonogath da | In good will for to play withall. |

At the Elevation of a Maypole the Cornish at Newlyn are said to have us'd this Cantation.

Haile an Taw, and Golly Rumbelaw

Mr. Carew has an expression pa. 22 wch. has some thing of this "& so with Har & Tue pursue (the Fox) to death".

95 Antiquities Cornuontanic: The Causes of Cornish Speech's Decay by William Scawen (1680)

1   The first and great cause of the decay of the Cornish speech was their want of a character, which not only contributed to the decay of the tongue, but to the vanquishing of the nation of Britons, they being thereby disabled upon emergent occasions to write or communicate with one another against their invaders, and so *"dum pugnabant singuli vincuntur universi,"* as Tacitus says; and he also observes, *"non aliud adversus validissimas gentes pro Romanis utilius quàm quod in commune non consulebant."*

What would have become of the Roman tongue, when the Goths and Vandals broke in upon Rome and all Italy, mixing the Roman tongue with their Runa-Gothica, if there had not been learned men (amounting to 160 elegant classical authors in Augustus his time) who preserved the tongue in their works?

I know it hath been and yet is the judgment of learned men, that the old Britons never had any character, yet I hope they will give me the liberty of declaring the reasons of my dissenting. It hath always been supposed that Ireland had a character; now Ireland was always accounted a British Island, however; yet I cannot positively affirm that the character which the Bishop of Tuam sets forth as British be really so, there seeming to be little difference between that and the old Saxon; neither can I consent to what he saith, that the Saxons, whom he calls their neighbours, learned their very characters from Ireland.

2   Though we may depend on Cæsar's authority, that *Druidum doctrina non fuit literis mandata, sed mermoriæ fuit, ne aut in vulgus proficiscentur, aut juventus qui eam perdiscebant negligentia aut in curia remitterent*, which reasons, in my judgment, rather demonstrate that they had a character to communicate their doctrines by, if they had pleased to use it. The great use made of the Roman tongue, the laws of their conquest extending to letters and speech, as well as to territory; and where there is delight, there are things best retained. *Linguam Britanni non abnuebant, ut eloquentium concupisserent. Tacit.*

   Fertur habere meos, si vera est fama, libellos
      Inter declicias puchra Vienna suas.
   Dicitur et nostros cantare Britannia versus.
            Martial.

   Afri, Galli, Hispani avido arripuerunt et inducto novo paulatim obliturerunt veterum sermonem. Lips.

3   The great loss of Armorica, near unto us, by friendship, by cognition, by interest, by correspondence. Cornwall has received princes from thence, and they from us. We had heretofore mutual interchanges of private families, but as to our speech we are alike careless. We can understand words of one another, but have not the benefit of conferences with one another in our ancient tongue.

I have met some Friars born and bred there, who, one would think, should be able to discourse of their own pristine tongue, and of their own birthplaces, yet found them, though not totally ignorant that such things had been, yet insensible and careless of their former condition. They could tell me that my name Scawen, was in their tongue Elders, as here it is; that there are those that bear the same name, and one of them a bishop; but when he writ it he changed it to Sambucus, shewing thereby a mind declared to a new, rather than an inclination to his old name, and relation to his country speech.

4   But, least the tender lamentations of those losses should be thought to put us out of memory of the loss of our tongue, the matter which we have in hand, we are here to mention a fourth case, and that which most concerns this Peninsula of Cornwall, which is the giving over of the Guirremears, which were used at the great conventions of the people, at which they had famous interludes celebrated with great preparations, and not without shews of devotion in them; solemnized in open and spacious downs of great capacity, encompassed about with earthen banks, and in some part stone work of largeness to contain thousands, the shapes of which remain in many places at this day, though the use of them long since gone. These were frequently used in most parts of the county, at the conveniency of the people, for their meeting together, in which they represented it, by grave actings, scriptural histories, personating patriarchs, princes, and other persons; and with great oratory pronounced their harangue, framed by art, and composed with heroic stile, such as have been known to be of old in other nations, as Gualterius, an ancient father, hath been mentioned to be. This was a great means to keep in use the tongue with delight and admiration, and it continued also friendship and good correspondency in the people. They had recitations in them poetical and divine, one of which I may suppose this small relique of antiquity to be, in which the passion of our Saviour, and his resurrection, is described. They also had their Carols at several times, especially at Christmas, which they solemnly sung, and sometimes used, as I have heard, in their churches after prayers, the burden of which songs, "Nowell, Nowell, good news, good news of the Gospel," by which means they kept use of the tongue the better.

5   I cannot find that the British have boasted of many miracles done among them; if any such antiently there were, they were deprived of the memory of them by the Romans. I cannot affirm with so much reason (as some of our neighbours have done with confidence) who say, that at the last digging on the Haw for the foundation of the citadel of Plymouth, the great jaws and teeth therein found, were those of Gogmagog who was there said to be thrown down by Corineus, whom some will have to be the founder of the Cornish; nor am I able to assert, that some great instru-

ments of war in brass, and huge limbs and portraitures of persons long ago, as some say that have been in some of the western parishes, were parts of giants, or other great men, who had formerly had their being there. But we may rather think those to be imaginary things or devices of old bards said to be there, though we have no certain memory of them neither. Nor may we think it strange that such things may be spoken of, since we may well credit some good historians, that write that Alexander, after that he had returned from his journey to India, caused a great representation to be made on the ground on the western side of the river Indus, of a huge campaign almost immeasurable, with tents, cabins, and platforms, and arms also, for horses, racks, and mangers, of such height as were not to be reached at; and that there were also scattered about the ground bits and bridles for horses, of extraordinary length and bigness, and that all this "ut de magnis majora loquantur," and to make men think upon him and his miraculous acts with the more admiration.

6   The sixth cause is, the loss of the ancient records, not of the Duchy or the Earldom of Cornwall, (which some affirm were burnt, and other lost in the ancient ruins of the castles of Rostormell, and other such,) but of those of whole Cornwall, whilst one of the four dynasties of this island, (or, as Pancirollus,) one of the five.

7   The seventh cause is desuetude, or want of a continued use; and it is no wonder, if, after so many losses, the true use of the tongue vanished away or grew not into contempt. Speeches are compounded of words, and both of them of one nature, and continued according to their use, and of one of them it may be said as of the other

*Multa recensentur quæ nunc cecidere, cadentque
Quæ nunc sunt in honore vocabula, si volet usus.*

Words many and tongues we recount,
Which being fallen do oft remount,
And those that are now priz'd by us,
May fall to ground for want of use.

8   A general stupidity may be observed to be in the whole county. As to other matters monumental, there is little mention made of our antient stately fabrics amongst us, now ruinated; as to the founders of them, castles, battles fought, and other things: and as to churches (though we have abundance of fair ones for so small a county, where there is no city nor any great town in it) excellent foundations, but who the builders were we have no intelligence, only a great many false tutelaries of them we hear of. Little of the monasteries hath been said by those that have written copiously of others elsewhere. Scarcely anything of the ancient bishops here, or of the bishop's see; only we know it to be said antiently, that it was removed from Bodmyn to St. German's, and that it was about

anno 1000, Danorum turbine, from a country more open, to a place more woodland. The cathedral indeed might have been better memorized by Godwin in his Catalogue of Bishops, and enumeration of all the bishopricks; yet little is said of it or the four several chapels in several distinct places of the parish thereto belonging; and as for the monastery nothing at all. It is strange too that Mr. Camden should say, *"Germani viculum nihil aliud est hodie, quam piscatorum casulæ:"* whereas, there are no such things belonging to such a trade there seen, but instead thereof a cathedral, maintained at the great cost of the inhabitants, (though a great part, by an accident, about one hundred years since fell down,) a good monastical house yet undemolished, and hospitably inhabited, to the relief of poor people. The bishop's seat and house are yet eminently extant in a Cornish name. The borough of St. German's enjoys still the privilege of sending burgesses to Parliament by prescription. Pity it is that St German, who came hither to suppress the Pelagian heresy, should have so bad a going off; for an old fable remains yet in report, that St German being ill used fled away, leaving a sad curse behind him, to the cliffs at Rame near the head; where bewailing his misfortunes, the compassionating rocks in the cliffs shed tears with him, at a place ever since called St German's Well. True it is, such a spring there is, but the occasion of it cannot be more truly affirmed than the other part of the story that follows, viz. That he should be carried thence into remote countries by angels in a fiery chariot, the tract of whose wheels were said to be seen those cliffs, but they are invisible. Thus much for the site of the place. As to the person of St German, who perhaps never saw the place, I need not turn over old fabulous legends, not a better sort who have written his life heretofore, but I may have liberty to relate what I have from the better hands of learned persons. That besides his disputation and confutation of Pelagius at Verulam, and thereby freeing the church and nation from those heresies by a public edict from the Emperor Valentinian, whereby they were no more troubled with them afterwards, he the said St. German did other great works for his land, viz. 1st. the institution of schools of learning among the Britons; Dubritius and *Iltutus* being both of them his disciples. Dubritius was made Archbishop of Carlehon; *Iltutus* sent to Lan *Iltut*, a church bearing his name to this day; and one Daniell, made Bishop of Bangor; from these famous men the monastery of Bangor, and other monasteries in this land, were so well furnished with learned men, at the coming in of St. Austin from the Pope, they stood upon discreet and honourable terms.

The introduction of the Gallican Liturgy into use in the churches of Brittany, which was ever different from the Romans, and thereby a happy mean to have kept this nation from so much acquaintance with the Pope, as they had with him afterwards, to their great trouble. It is also said that St. Patrick, who carried over into Ireland the education monastic, and good principles therewith, and is held to be the Apostle of Ireland, spent many years under the discipline of St. German, when he came hither: who, after he had been employed in the embassy to the Emperor at Ravenna, died there one year before the Saxons' arrival.

All this time we are left in the dark concerning the fabric of the Monastery of St. German's, which could not be built till two or three hundred years perhaps after the Saxons got a perfect dominion here over the land, but we may believe that that and the cathedral might be dedicated to his memory afterwards, in respect of the many good works he had done elsewhere.

9   As we have had an ill registry of monumental matters, so for five or six centuries past (before the two last), I doubt we had but few learned men here, which induces me to put that to the ninth cause of the decay of the Cornish tongue. After the suppression of the Druids, and that Christianity was received, yet learning decayed some while amongst the people, the best of them being carried abroad by the Romans and never returned; and then the supposed Saints coming in after them, made no reparation thereof, but by their supposed miracles, with which they entertained the people. So they had very few learned men amongst them, places of breeding and obtaining learning being remote, scarcely approachable, and the nation in continual troubles and dangers; and for latter times such learned men as came to us, seeing our own neglect of our tongue, have thought it not fit to take the pains to inquire into it, as a thing obscure and not fit to be studied by them, and so suffered to decay insensibly by them and the inhabitants.

10   The Cornish tongue hath mostly resided for some ages past in the names of the people, the gentry chiefly, and in the names of places, observed to be significant mostly as to the site, &c. or for some things eminent about them. Concerning both these, I must take liberty to shew how the speech had been invaded, and eaten up by intrusion, much of which hath been about churches and their sites, as well as by neglectful inobservation; for those Saxon saints have hungrily eaten up the antient names, which, when they could not well digest for hardness of the words, many catched up others from those whom they feigned to be the tutelaries of those places, churches, and fountains, and supposed miracles wrought thereabouts, at St. Kaine, St. Gurrion, St. Tudy, St. Ive, St. Endellion, St. Kue, Landulph, St. Ust, St. Just, St. Marthren, &c. Of St. Mardren's Well, (which is a parish west to the Mount) a fresh true story of two persons, both of them lame and decrepit, thus recovered from their infirmity. These two persons, after they had applied themselves to divers physicians and chirurgeons for cure, and finding no success by them, they resorted to St. Mardren's Well, and according to the ancient custom, which they had heard of, the same which was once in a year, to wit, on

Corpus Christi evening, to lay some small offering on the altar there, and to lie on the ground all night, drink of the water there, and in the morning after, to take a goodly draught more, and to take and carry away some of the water, each of them in a bottle, at their departure. This course these two men followed, and within three weeks they found the effect of it, and by degrees their strength increasing, were able to move themselves on crutches. The year following they take the same course again, after which they were able to go with the help of a stick; and at length one of them, John Thomas, being a fisherman, was, and is able at this day, to follow his fishing craft. The other, whose name was William Cork, was a soldier under the command of my kinsman, Colonel William Godolphin, (as he has often told me) was able to perform his duty, and died in the service of his majesty King Charles I. But here with take also this: one Mr. Hutchens, a person well known in those parts, and now lately dead, being parson of Ludgvan, a near neighbouring parish to St. Mardren's Well, he observing that many of his parishioners often frequented this well superstitiously, for which he reproved them privately, and sometimes publicly in his sermons; but afterwards, he the said Mr. Hutchens, meeting with a woman coming from the well with a bottle in her hand, desired her earnestly that he might drink thereof, being then troubled with cholical pains, which accordingly he did, and was eased of his infirmity. The latter story is a full confutation of the former, for if the taking the water accidentally thus prevailed upon the party to his cure, as it is likely it did, then the miracle which was intended to be the ceremony of lying on the ground and offering, is wholly fled, and it leaves the virtue of the water to be the true cause of the cure. And we have here, as in many places of the land, great variety of salutary springs, which have diversity of operations, which by natural reason have been found to be productive of good effects, and not by miracle, as the vain fancies of monks and friars have been exercised in heretofore.

Howbeit, there are some old names yet remaining of places of prayers or oratories, and the ruins shewing them to be such, as V. Gr. Paderda, which is prayers good, (of which many places are so named); Eglarose, the church in the vale, supposed antienter than the names of their churches. Their sites are eminent and ancient, standing towards the east, though no mention made how they came to be in decay, but supposed to be after the Saxon churches came to be erected, and miracles supposed to be wrought by those whose names they bear. Churches' sites took new names, whereas the old Cornish names remain in all other places of the parishes generally; yet the names of the four old castles remain, and of manors also for the most part, and some other things in the Cornish, and do so continue the better, by reason of men's particular interest in them: and so are the eminent hills likewise, especially towards the sea, and the hundred or hamlet names of the country remain so chiefly in the western parts; those on the eastern, standing towards the borders, have their names wrested away by neighbourhood, as are other things by like accidents in the eastern parts of the county; other names have been encroached upon by fantastical or vainglorious builders calling their houses after their own names, and other upon vain toys; but these are not many. Moreover, concerning the loss of our speech, and the names of families, I must here (but tenderly though) blame the incuriosity of some of our gentry; who, forsaking the etymologies of their own speech, have studied out new derivations of their names, endeavouring to make themselves as it were descended from French or Norman originals, in adopting or adapting their names thereunto; whereas, their own names in the Cornish are more honourable, genuine, and true; from the Conquest, forsooth, those would have their descent, (no illustrious thing in itself) whereas the ancestry of many of them have been here long before. How finely many have cozened themselves thereby, might be shewn, if it would not be offensively taken, by taking up of coat armour as from French originals. The art of heraldry hath been drawn out to us in French terms and trickings, mostly begun when our kings had most to do in those parts, and so from thence it hath continued ever since; and our Cornish gentry, finding the English so much addicted thereunto, have followed in that tract the same mode, and would fain have themselves understood such, when they were much better before than those French or Latin terms could make them, in which many of the English may be blamed as well as we; for the herald's art hath many mysteries in it under their French and Latin terms, and many mistakes may be thereby to us and others who are not well acquainted with them, but in those that concern our own tongue, it is evident many have wronged themselves, and more may do so if not well heeded.

The grounds of two mistakes are very obvious. 1st. Upon the Tre or Ter. 2dly. Upon the Ross or Rose. Tre or Ter is Cornish commonly signifies a town, or rather place, and it has always an adjunct with it. Tri is the number. 3. Those men willingly mistake one for another; and so in French heraldry terms, they use to fancy and contrive those with any such three things as may be like or cohere with, or may be adapted to any thing or things in their surnames; whether very handsome or not, is not much stood upon. Another usual mistake is upon Ross, which, as they seem to fancy, should be a rose; but Ross in Cornish is a vale or valley. Now for this their French-Latin tutors, when they go into the field of Mars, put them in their coat armour prettily to smell out a rose or flower (a fading honour instead of a durable one); so any three such things, agreeable perhaps a little to their names, are taken up and retained from abroad, when their own at home have a much better scent and more lasting.

Some, however, amongst us, have kept themselves better to the antiquities of their Cornish names in their coat armour, as that honourable family Godolphin, in keeping still displayed abroad his white eagle, from the Cornish Gothulgon. Richard, king of the Romans, Emperor elect, supplied his Cornish border with silver (perhaps tin) plates, deducing them from the antient earls of Cornwall, as borne by them before the Norman Conquest, and, in honour to them and himself, still bearing the same afterwards. Chiverton, whose name in Cornish is a house on a green place or hill, he beareth a coat thereunto accordant, a castle with a green field under it; which may be well thought on as to the name in Cornish, though, in the heraldry it had been more complete. V. a castle A, as I apprehend; Scaberius, which is sweepers or sweeping, A. 3 broom besoms V.; Gavergan, a goat; Keverel, a he-goat, or he-goats; that creature taking most delight, as it is observed, in the cliffs thereabout. These are better significations taken from home, than the other that are foreign; and yet the assumption of a coat from any particular act of a man's own, is better than such as have reference barely to names, without some special signification therewith.

I had thoughts formerly, and made preparation to give many more instances, where many amongst us have been mistaken in those two particulars; but since it is a hard thing to convince men of old errors, and a harder to make a question against any concerning their gentelicions and the old forms thereof, though intended more for their honour, I shall forbear the further prosecution thereof; but in this, however, I shall do them right, that they, i.e. their ancestors, in this way thus trodden, have walked generally as antiently as any other gentry of this nation, and to my seeming, it had been better if they had stood still super vias antiquas avorum suorum, since most of those ancient families who have strayed abroad as aforesaid, have yet some of them, and many more had, lands and places of their own names in their possession long enjoyed; and nearer passage it had been to their journey's end, viz. their honour, if they had not adventured abroad: a testimony whereof we have in that great contention which happened in the time of King Edward III. between Carminow of this county (a family to which most of the ancient gentry here have relation) and a great person of the nation [Lord Scroope], for bearing of one and the same coat armour, Azure, a bend Or. After many heats about it, a reference was made of it by the king to the most eminent Knights of that time, of which John of Gaunt, King of Castille, was one, before whom Carminow proved his right by the continual hearing thereof, and that before the Conquest, which was not disapproved nor disallowed, but applauded: yet, because the other contendant was a baron of the realm, Carminow was adjudged to bear the same coat still, but a file in chief for distinction sake. The decision was no way dishonourable, and the remembrance of the contention continued to the glory of his posterity, to which his motto in Cornish seems to have an allusion – in English, "A Straw for Whifflers or Dissemblers;" or as some have said to be, "A Fig Cala Rag Whetlow;" but we may take the same better, I think, from the very name of Carminow being in Cornish a rock immoveable, as a sign of his resolution, from thence, or formerly taken up.

Having gone through this passage, which I know not how it may be taken by my countrymen, let me make this observation, that since the gentry here have thought fit, or endeavoured by mistake, to forsake the antiquity of their Cornish names, and thereby their greatest interest, might perhaps prognosticate that their language, which was their ancient glory, should in revenge forsake them, as now it hath almost done; and I shall proceed to assign some other causes of the decay thereof.

11   The vicinity, or near neighbourhood with Devon. I may say that vicinity only with the Devonians, we having none else, which next to the corruption of tongues by time and superstition to saints, hath most devoured the names of places, especially on the borders of Cornwall with Devon; and there is the worst language commonly spoken, and spoken rudely too, which corrupts not only their own country tongue but ours also, in the places that are nearest to them, and those infect others nearest to them. The names of the places are thereby also much altered in the Cornish, which antiently they had generally, and the particulars that do yet appear, do stand as marks only to shew that what were formerly had are now much eaten away, on the borders especially. 'Tis observed also elsewhere in the county furthest west, where the Cornish hath been most spoken, that the English thereabouts is much better than the same is in Devon, or the places bordering on them, by being most remote from thence from whence the corruption proceeds.

12   Our gentry, and others, antiently kept themselves in their matches unmixt, commonly at home in their own country, both sons and daughters desiring much to do so, whereby they preserved their names here, and races the better; and when their names changed, it hath been observed to be to the places of their abode, sometimes unwillingly, sometimes by accident. So it hath continued the Cornish names to the places, and consequently the tongue. But indeed of late our gentry have frequently sought out foreign marriages in other counties, whereby, though it may be confessed they have brought in much wealth, and have goodly inheritances abroad, yet their offsprings have been dissipated, and their affection less intire to the county, the country-men, and country-speech; yet it is to be observed, that not many of them have been very prosperous or of long continuance in other counties, where they cannot muster up very many of our names of gentry, Prideaux, Trevilian, Tregonwell, Penruddock, and a few others excepted, which shews that our Cornish are like those trees that

thrive best and live longest in their own peculiar soil and air, which yet is fruitful and durable to those that come in amongst us. Not only gentry, which are very many, that have great inheritance by their matches here with Cornish families, but many others also, which seldom leave this country when they have been planted here.

13 The coming-in of strangers of all sorts upon us, artificers, traders, home-born and foreigners, whom our great commodities of tin (more profitable to others than ourselves) and fishing, have invited to us to converse with, and often to stay with us; these all, as they could not easily learn our tongue for which they could not find any guide or direction, especially in these latter days, nor the same generally spoken or affected amongst ourselves, so they were more apt and ready to let loose their own tongues to be commixed with ours, and such, for the novelty sake thereof, people were more ready to receive than to communicate ours to any improvement to them. But ministers in particular have much decreased the speech; this country being far from academies, strangers from other parts of the kingdom have sought, as they still do, and have had their promotions here, where benefices are observed to be very good, and those have left their progenies, and thereby their names, remaining behind them, whereby the Cornish names have been diminished, as the tongue also: so that, as the reputed saints heretofore where they seated themselves, have robbed the places where their churches now stand for the most part of the Cornish names they had before, so the ministers since those times coming from other places, and other strangers, have filled up in many places the inhabitants and places here with their new names and titles brought amongst us, to the loss of many of the old. Here too we may add what wrong another sort of strangers have done to us, especially in the civil wars, and in particular by destroying of Mincamber, a famous monument, being a rock of infinite weight, which, as a burden, was laid upon other great stones, and yet so equally thereon poised up by nature only, as a little child could instantly move it, but no one man or many remove it. This natural monument all travellers that came that way desired to behold; but in the time of Oliver's usurpation, when all monumental things became despicable, one Shrubsall, one of Oliver's heroes, then governor of Pendennes, by labour and much ado caused to be undermined and thrown down, to the great grief of the country, but to his own great glory as he thought, doing it as he said, with a small cane in his hand. I myself have heard him to boast of this act, being a prisoner then under him.

14 Another cause I shall mention as a great loss of the tongue, though it be a great and wonderful advantage to the people otherwise: the orders of the church and state, commanding all the people young to learn the Lord's Prayer, Belief, &c. in the vulgar tongue, supposing that to be intended the English, if a mother,

surely a stepmother to us. Younglings take in that most, and retain longest, wherewith they are seasoned and bred up in their education.

Herein we must complain also of another new neglect to our speech, that the like care was not taken for us as for our brethren in Wales, in the making of the late act of Parliament for the uniformity of the Common Prayer, by which the five Bishops for Wales were commanded to see the Service Book to be printed in the Welch tongue. If it had been so here it had been a good counterpoise for the loss formerly mentioned concerning young people; this might also perhaps have saved us some labour in this our undertaking, and it would have been of good use for some our old folks also, for we have some among these few that do speak Cornish, who do not understand a word of English, as well as those in Wales, and those may be many in some of the western parts, to whom Mr. Francis Robinson, parson of Landawednack told me, he had preached a sermon not long since in the Cornish tongue, only well understood by his auditory. This should have been taken into consideration by our gentlemen burgesses in that and other Parliaments, and by our bishops also; but better it had been if our ancient bishops when they fled hither from their invaders, had brought with them a character of their ancient speech, or left books written therein; or, in defect thereof, they or any other had done for us as Ulphius the bishop did for the Goths when they came to be seated in Italy, who there invented new Gothic letters for his people, and translated the Holy Scriptures into that language for them. This indeed had deserved our greatest thanks from our bishops, as no doubt they had them from those persons who received so great a benefit by their former and latter kindness therein; nor let that good old bishop Ulphius be censured (as he seems to be) for doing a superfluous work, because he might perhaps know that the then service of the church was celebrated in the Greek and Latin tongues, but rather let him be commended for his zeal in religion, and his love to his country and to his country people then with him, dwelling with strangers in another land, that continued so mindful of them and their speech, as we have been neglectful of ours. He by that means continued that tongue in use; we by his example might have regained ours, if the like care had been taken; but our people, as I have heard, in Queen Elizabeth's time, desired that the Common Liturgy should be in the English tongue, to which they were then for novelty's sake affected, not out of true judgement desired it. But, besides negligence, fatality is to be considered; fatality is a boundary beyond which nothing can pass; it hath been eminent in kingdoms and states, and those have had commonly fatal periods, as to a time determined five hundred years commonly. But more usual it is, that upon such mutations of kingdoms, there have happened losses and mutations of tongues; it may therefore be the more wondered at, that this of the British, being none of the learned tongues to which the Lord had intrusted the writing of his Sacred Scriptures, should have here lasted so long through so many mutations, and that there is yet such a record thereof, as our old manuscript imports, with the purity of the doctrine therein contained, and some other small things in the Bodleian Library,

15 The little or no help, rather discouragement, which the gentry and other people of our own have given in these latter days, who have lived in those parts where the tongue hath been in some use. In the time of the late unhappy civil war, we began to make some use of it upon the runnagates that went from us to the contrary part from our opposite works, and more we should have done if the enemy had not been jealous of them, and prevented us. This may be fit to be improved into somewhat, if the like occasion happen, for it may be talked freely and aloud to advantage, to which no other tongue hath reference. The poorest sort at this day, when they speak it as they come abroad, are laughed at by the rich that understand it not, which is by their own fault in not endeavouring after it.

16 The want of writing it is the great cause of its decay; for, though there wanted a proper character for it, yet we might have written it in the character now in use, but I never saw a letter written in it from one gentleman to another, or by any scholar; which is to be wondered at, and blamed as a thing unbecoming such as ought to be studious in every thing that is ancient: but since I began to set about this work, I prevailed upon those that translated it to write me several letters, which they at first found very hard to be done; but after some practice it seemed easier.

Here I cannot but lament the want of such persons, books, records and papers, which were late in being, and not now to be had, and my misfortune in not having translated them, that most unhappily escaped me; one was the manuscript of Anguin, who had translated out of Cornish into English .... his relations, after his decease, (having suits before me as Vice-Warden of the Stanneries for tin bounds) promised me the favour of those translations, but before their return to their houses, their people tearing up all about for their controverted goods, had torn to pieces all those papers. In another place I was promised the sight of a Cornish Accidence; but that by another such-like accident was totally spoiled by children before it could be brought me. I have heard also that a Matins in Cornish was amongst the books of Dr. Joseph Maynard, but I could never attain to it. But besides the no helps by which I lie in this labyrinth, I have likewise had discouragements amongst ourselves at home. I have been often told that, besides the difficulty of the attempt, it would be thought ridiculous for one to go about the restoring of that tongue which he himself could not speak nor understand when truly spoken, to which I have made answer with these two following instances: one is of a countryman of ours, Langford by name; who being blind was yet able to teach others the noble science of defence, only he desired to know still the length of the weapon of his fellow combatant, with a guess of his posture, and this he practised with good success. The other is one Grizling, of whom Mr. Camden says, that he being deaf could see words; that is, that notwithstanding his deafness he could answer any man's question that set at table with him by the motion of his lips. This man I have seen also, and he would complain of such men as in those days wore great munchadoes, as they then called them, i.e. nourishing of much hair, by which he was hindered somewhat of the observation of their lips.

I may place these two men, one blind, the other deaf, for these qualities among the observable things of the county, knowing them to be true, – if the mentioning these examples in their comparison do not excuse me from being laughed at by those men that have censured me for my attempt.

96 *From* **The First English Translation of William Camden's Britannia by Edmund Gibson (1695)**

Their language, too, is English; and (which is something surprising) observed by travellers to be the most pure and refined than that of their neighbours Devonshire and Somersetshire. The most probable reason whereof seems to be this, that English is to them introduced, not an original, language, and those who brought it in were the gentry and merchants, who imitated the dialect of the Court, which is most nice and accurate. Their neat way of living and housewifery, upon which they justly value themselves above their neighbours, does possibly proceed from the same cause.

The old Cornish is almost driven out of the county being spoken only by the vulgar in two or three parishes at the Land's End and they too understand English. 'Tis a good while since, that only two men could write it, and one of them being no scholar or grammarian and then blind with age.

97 *From* **Letters written to Thomas Tonkin by Edward Lhuyd (1700–08)**

Honoured Sir,

You will receive by the bearer (Mr. Jones) Mr. Carew's Survey of Cornwall, together with what else I borrow'd, with my most humble thanks. I once designed to have waited on you myself long ere this; but now it so happens, that I take the South coast, and leave the North to the bearer, to copy such old inscriptions as shall occur, and to take what account he can of the geography of the parishes. I know you will be pleased to favour and assist him in your neighbourhood; but where we have no acquaintance, we find the people more suspicious and jealous (not withstanding we have my Lord Bishop's approbation of the undertaking) than in any country we have travelled. And upon that account, I beg the trouble of you, when he leaves your neighbourhood, to give him two or three letters to any of your acquaintance more eastward. Mr. Pennick not being at home, we have been strictly examined in several places, and I am told by the people, not withstanding our long continuance here, have not yet removed their jealousy. I was forced, for their satisfaction, to open your letter to Mr. Pennick, and that proving to be just such an account of me, as I had given, we were immediately dismissed.

The monument at Burien, in the last edition of Camden, is somewhat erroneous, as you will find by the draught I here send you. The true reading is *Clarice la Femme Cheffrei De Bolleit Giticy: Deu de L'alme eit mercy; E ke pur le alme punt, di ior de pardun averund*. Clarice the wife of Geffrey de Bolleit lies here: God on her soul have mercy: And whoever shall pray for her soul, shall have ten days pardon. The other inscription is on a large moor-stone in a common, called Gwn mên Screpha, in Maddern parish. The reading is – *Rialobran Cunoval Fil*. In British, Rhiwalhvran map kynwal, names not uncommon in our old Welsh pedigrees. – I take it to be about a thousand years standing, and do not much question but the neighbouring parish of Gulval is denominated from this Kynwal, because I have found many such instances in Wales. I am, Honoured Sir, Your much obliged humble servant.

Edw. Lhuyd.
St. Ives, Oct,15, 1700.

Honoured Sir,

I take this opportunity of returning my most humble thanks for your late kindness to my fellow traveller; who is, I suppose, by this time got safe to Oxford. For my own part, I am desirous to spend two or three months in Brittany, before I return to my charge; and am here waiting for a passage, having failed getting one at Looe and Foy: – Since my coming hither, I understand your father-in-law corresponds at Morlaix, which is the port I am bound for. His letter of recommendation thither might do me a singular kindness; which if you please to request of him, I desire you would send him two or three lines, inclosed and directed to me at Mr. Swanson's in this town, and I'll wait on him with it. Mr. Hicks of Trevithick promised me his letter to him, but it happened that when I called there, he was very much indisposed, and so I would not trouble him, altho' he offered to write nevertheless. – I desire the purport of Mr. Kemp's letter may be, to acquaint his friend of my place at Oxford, and that I am engaged in composing a Dictionary of the British Language; and that this is the main reason of my journey into that country, in regard the British of Wales and Cornwall, and that of their country, are but so many dialects of one and the same language: Requesting his favour therefore, in getting me recommended to some scholar well acquainted with the British language, and antiquities; and then I hope to shift for myself. —I have already letters to two Abbots; the one from Dr. Lister, and the other from Mr. Moyle; but these live at Paris, and I am as yet unprovided for Bretagne.

I had lately a letter from our old friend, Mr. Tanner, with the inclosed in it; upon presumption, I suppose, that I had not waited on you since my coming to the country. He has been searching all the libraries and studies of note in England, for materials towards his edition of *Leland de Scriptoribus Brit*. He tells me Mr. Gibson is upon his year of grace, having got a good living in Essex. Mr. Maundril (he says) has a Treatise in the press, containing some account of his travels: This gentleman is Fellow of Exeter, and Chaplain to the factory of Aleppo. He adds, that Dr. Hicks's Saxon and Francic Grammar is above half done; and that it will contain 200 sheets in folio, being rather a Thesaurus of Northern Learning, than a Grammar.

I hear trouble you with the oldest inscription we have met with, additional to the two I formerly sent you. The first Figure is of a Cross, by the almshouse at St. Blasey; but the inscription I do not at all understand. The second is the Half-stone, which doubtless must be read as Mr. Camden hath it, tho' his letters are erroneous. The third was once the tomb-stone of a Briton whose name was Kynadav 'ap Ichdinow, but is now a foot bridge at Gulval near Penzans. The fourth is the tomb-stone of another Briton, which is known by the name of The Long-Stone, within a mile of Foy, (this is probably fifth or sixth century) his name in British was Kiris ap Kynvor; and in all probability, Polkiris, within half a mile of the stone, is denominated from him. – The fifth and sixth Figures are two Iron Plates of that form and size whereof several horse-loads were found about six years since. – Quere. Whether there may not be the British money mentioned by Cæsar, in these words – *Nummo utuntur parvo & areo, aut ferreis laminis pro nummo*. Fearing to lose the opportunity of sending this, I add no more than that I am, &c.

Ewd. Lhuyd
Falmouth, Nov, 29, 1700.

Honoured Sir,

I take this opportunity (which I must confess is a very late one) of beging your pardon for not writing to you, neither out of France, nor since my return; which, as you have heard I suppose long since, was five or six weeks after landing; whereas, when I went thither, I proposed not to return in seven or eight months. I am very sensible, and shall always continue so, of your singular civility, both in Cornwall, and in procuring and giving us letters of recommendation thither; where we found a kind reception from all we conversed with, excepting the Indendant of Brest; who, having a little before received a check from Court for some negligence, was pleased, by the way of making amends, to exercise his double diligence on me, and several other English then in this neighbourhood.

Sir, Mr. Ankerstein, the gentleman that brings you this, is come into England, purely to improve his experience as to mines; and having been already at the (reputed) silver mines of Cardiganshire, he comes now to see your tin works of Cornwall. His father and himself (as I take it) have some considerable places in the King of Sweden's copper works: and in order the better to qualify himself, he has already seen most of the celebrated mines of Europe. Finding, by experience, that strangers, when they come to the remote parts of any country, are often suspected, at least by the common people, I have presumed to recommend him to your favour, as a very honest gentleman; and very knowing in that study he had applied himself to; which is all at present from, Worthy Sir, Your's, &c.

Edw. Lhuyd.
Oxford, Oct. 1. 1702.

Honoured Sir,

It was but three days since that Mr. Thomson shewed me your letter about the Cornish MSS. &c. Those two I formerly gave him an account of, are all the books here in that language. – One of them (which is the more valuable) is a small folio, written on parchment, in court hand, about 200 years since. This has formerly been copied and Mr. Anstis has (I suppose) the only copy that ever was taken from it. Having compared Mr. Anstis's copy (which he was pleased to lend me) with the original, I find it has several small errata. The Bishop (Sir Jonat. Trelawney) was pleased to communicate to me Mr. Keigwyn's translation, and transcript of Mr Anstis's copy, which I have also transcribed for my own use; but comparing this book of Mr. Keigwyns's with the Bodley original, I find the old gentleman did not always keep to his text, but varied sometimes as could make sense. 'Tis therefore, as you truly conclude, the best course to transcribe from the originals. – Mr. Thomson tells me he can get the Taberders to transcribe by turns: and one Griffith of our College (who has transcribed mine, and is well acquainted with the hand, and partly understands the language) offers his service to copy both, at six-pence a sheet: so be pleased to write to either of us your orders, and they shall be observed. This book consists of three plays; and the other which is on paper, written about 100 years since by one W. Jordan, contains I think but one. If you are for Mr. Keigwyn's translation, it shall be also transcribed; but I must acquaint Mr Anstis with it: or if you would have the English in a book apart, with the same figures, number of lines in a page that the Cornish hath, &c. it may be done without mentioning, though for ought I know, you and Mr. Anstis are intimate friends. – Four-pence a sheet will be enough for transcribing the English, but the Cornish you know will be twice as tedious.

Sir, I am sorry the Swedish gentleman neglected to leave my letter behind him, wherein I begged your pardon (as I now heartily do) for not returning my thanks at our coming from France. My Cornish verses have I doubt so many Wallicisms, that they are not worth your enquiring after. I sent the printed copy by the Swede to Mr. Moor; and 'twas left with his widow: and it had been sent them before in writing, with a translation of them. Those few things that occurred to me in Cornwall, which are chiefly Inscriptions, and a Vocabulary as copious as I can make it, I design to insert (God willing) in my Archæologia Britannica; which I hope to print some time this next summer. I am, &c.

Edw. Lhuyd.
Oxford, Feb, 8, 1702–3.

P.S. The parchment MS. consists of 41 leaves, and was given to the Bodleian Library by one James Button of Worcestershire, Esq. anno 1615. I am heartily glad to find you curious (amongst your other studies) in your own country language and antiquities; and must recommend to you the taking in of the Armorick antiquities and language, which will much illustrate your own.

Honoured Sir,

The Cornish Verses (since you must have them) are here sent you; though they are not worth the trouble of reading, much less the sending so far. I aimed at imitating the Book Cornish, rather than the Cornish now spoken; for, as you'll find when you receive your manuscripts, it has been much corrupted this last age or two. Mr. Thomson tells me you were pleased to acquaint him in one of your letters, that you have an old man in your neighbourhood, that understands the present Cornish; if so, I should be glad of any such riddles, or rhimes, you can pick up from him, as also to know how much he understands of these of mine.

This sort of verse was, for what I can yet find, the oldest, if not the only verse amongst the ancient Briton: for 'tis the oldest in our Welsh books, and I have heard an old fellow repeat one of them in the Highlands of Scotland; and had another from the Clerk of St. Just, viz.

An Lavar koth yw lavar gwîr,
Na boz nevra dôz vâz an tavaz re hîr;
Bez dên heb davaz a gollaz i dîr.

The old saying is a true saying,
A tongue too long never did good:
But he that had no tongue, lost his land.

Amongst our old British Elegies whereof a good number are still preserved in parchment MSS. (though I was refused access to the two studies where they chiefly are) I find one on Gereint ab Erbyn in the same kind of verse, which I design to print with some others in my Archæologia. This Gereint ab Erbyn, according to our account, was a Prince of your country, and co-temporary with King Arthur: and I observed that you have places called yet Gerens, and Trev Erbyn, denominated for ought we know from this Gereint, and his Father. The Elegy celebrates his valour at the battle of Lhongborth, where he was slain. Camden tells us London was called Longport, by an old British bard; but I am apt to think that place meant here, must have been somewhere in the West.

Mr. Thomson has already got Jordan's MS. copied for you, by the Taberders; which being a late plain hand, they have done I hope well enough: but he did not design to set them upon the other, because it is a large task, and an old court hand; so I'll put either Griffith, or Parry, about that, and the other writings, as you desire. Be pleased in your next to inform us, whether you would have Keigwyn's English translation written on the opposite pages, or these pages left blank for your own Latin or English translation hereafter; and have Keigwyn's translation by itself. The reason I propose this is, because Keigwyn's English makes the Cornish poems appear very ridiculous to strangers; in regard he has been scrupulous in placing his English words according to the Cornish, throughout all his work. Be pleased to favour us with two lines at your first leisure, and it shall be done as you order; and sent you as you shall direct, either in loose sheets, or bound.

The subscriptions I took were towards my travels, which are now over. I have had but few subscribers; but all I have, excepting some few of our country (who were brought in by example) are gentlemen of learning, and curiosity. All the return I can make them, will be copies of what I shall print, and the mentioning in the title page, that 'twas done at their command and expences, &c. with a catalogue of the subscribers, and the book dedicated to them in general. They have subscribed according to their quality, some more, some less, from twenty to fifty shillings; but some only have made punctual payments. I have only four from Cornwall, viz. my Lord Bishop, Sir Joseph Tredenham, Mr. Moyle, and Mr. Hicks, of Trevithig. Mr. John Tredenham has also subscribed, but amongst our countrymen. I would by no means put you to unnecessary charges, but if it be your pleasure, let the sum before hand be as small as you please, and 'twill be gratefully accepted by, &c.

Edw. Lhuyd.
Oxford, March, 16, 1702–3.

[Honoured Sir,]

I know not whether I mentioned in my former letter, that I had sent Mr. Moor a copy of an old Cornish Glossary, which Will. Jones met with in the Cotton Library. Be pleased to get some friend to procure it of his executor, if possible; for it is a valuable curiosity; the Cotton MS. being probably six or seven hundred years old. If you cannot procure it, you shall have a copy of mine: whether you will alphabetically, or in the order of the Cotton MS. which is in continued lines, but with some regard to natural order. I recommend to you by all means the improving your acquaintance with Mr. Anstis, who is, I believe, the best acquainted of any living with the Offices and Libraries about London; and a very hearty good friend as may be. I have formerly heard my Lord of Exeter say, he hoped he would undertake some kind of History of Cornwall; but I presume he is full of business. — I have lately had a loss of poor Will. Jones, whom you are pleased to remember. He died in Shropshire, at a small living the Bishop of Hereford had given him. I am, &c.

Edw. Lhuyd.
[place and date not recorded]

Honoured Sir,

Your Cornish MS. is at last transcribed; and your copy is the only true one that I presume was ever taken, for Mr. Anstis's transcriber, being wholly a stranger to the language and the hand, has committed innumerable mistakes, and then never collated it with the original, which Mr. Griffith has done, but his hand is not so good as could be wished, though legible enough. Mr. Keigwyn finding it erroneous, transcribed it himself, so as to make his sense of it; but neither of them agree with the original: so I believe Mr. Keigwyn must sometimes have mistaken his author. – The English is not yet all written, but will be finished about a fortnight hence. The writing of the English and Cornish, at the rate I mentioned (which I think enough, and not too much) comes to thirty shillings; for the note I had taken of the size of the book, proved a mistake, it being much larger.

You need not at all despair of learning the sense of the Cornish names of places: but for the better avoiding mistakes therein, I recommend to you the making a catalogue of all the Christian names you find in the oldest Cornish pedigrees, if you have any very ancient; if not, you may be supplied out of our Welsh books. But as for that part, if you please at your leisure to send me a catalogue of such names, as you are desirous should be interpreted, (out of deeds, or other ancient records) I can promise you a translation of many of them, without the least straining: formost of our British names of places, are as intelligible to us, as any other part of our language. And for such as appear obscure, I shall take care to distinguish the doubt, or leave them alone. – Almost every word that follows – Tre – is a man's name, once proprietor of the place; which not being adverted by Mr. Carew and others, has put them on several mistakes.

The word – Pol – signifies not, a head, in Cornish, or any other dialect of the British; but, a pit, or hole, and, sometimes, a pool.

I have just now given your service to Mr. Tanner, who is married to the Bishop of Norwich's daughter, and is Chancellor of that diocese.

As you have leisure and opportunity, I would desire you to collect and procure all the variety you can hear of, of the tin ores: for though I thought I was tolerably well furnished, yet I find by the Swede, who was last winter in your county, that I have but a poor collection. I am in no haste at all for them; but willing to make use of all occasions of improving my collection of English fossils, since the Museum is so proper a place to reposit them in. We met with no fossil shells, or other marine bodies in Cornwall; but if you should hear of any, they would be no less acceptable to, Your humble Servant,

Edw. Lhuyd.
Oxford, May, 4, 1703.

Honoured Sir,

I received the former of your's, of June the 19th, and thought then to have had the MSS. ready to be sent you by this time. The copies of the two Cornish books have been ready since the time mentioned in my last, but it falls out, that my own copy of Jordan is lost, so that we cannot add the English here; but that you may as well get done in the country, where there are several copies of it. As for the old MS. (or Ordinale) I find that Keigwyn, when he translated it, altered it as he pleased where he did not like it, or understand it, and then transcribed it: on which account his translation does but sometimes agree with the old copy. I have therefore ordered it to be written by itself; and so the alternate pages are left vacant, where perhaps you may in time insert a Latin translation of your own. I shall send the two Cornish MSS. the first opportunity, which I hope will be soon: perhaps by Mr. Paget of Truro, if he be not already set out. The English of the Ordinalia is not yet finished; the person first employed having left us on a sudden: when 'tis all writ, which will be about a month hence, I'll take care to send it the first occasion, and as for all charges, 'twill be but just what I mentioned in my last.

Sir, I make bold to trouble you with a paper of proposals, towards the printing the first volume of my Archæologia Britannica, which I desire you to communicate to such friends, as you shall guess likeliest to further this design; and in case any shall subscribe, to return their names, some time before the 10th of September, to, &c.

Ewd. Lhuyd.
Oxford, July, 26, 1703.

Mr. Thomson gives you his most humble service. One Mr. Moor comes down shortly to your county, to collect plants, insects, &c. He was recommended to me by our friend Mr. Tanner, and I have made bold to give him a letter to yourself, and another to Mr. Moyle.

Honoured Sir,

The manuscripts had been sent by Mr. Paget, but upon enquiry, one of Pembroke College told me he was gone out of town, which, as I guess by your's, was a mistake. I have, since my last, met with Keigwyn's translation of Jordan's play, which I then told you I had lost; and Mr. Thomson has got it transcribed for you' and will send it you the first conveniency. The translation of the old plays is writ out: but I must desire to keep these old plays, and their translation, a little longer, because it is a much truer copy than mine, and I am now upon the Cornish Vocabulary promised in the proposals. I thank you for your own subscription, and the other two gentlemen's you mention: I was sensible the subjects were too singular to have many subscribers; however, I hope to have a good number yet out of your county, seeing the Bishop of Carlisle has returned twenty out of Cumberland.

Our latest news here is the death of Dr. Wallis, who is succeeded in the place of keeper of the Archives, by Dr. Gardiner, the Warden of All-Souls: and 'tis discoursed, the place of Savilian Professor will be offered to Mr. Hally. Dr. Hicks's *Thesaurus Linguarum Septentrionalium*, will be published about the Christmas holy-days. I am in no haste for the ores; so I desire you would keep them, till you have what variety you suppose the country may afford: and then send them by water to London, directed to be left with Mr. Griffith Davies, next door to the Golden Ball, in Monmouth-street, St. Giles in the Fields, and he'll take care to send them to, &c.

Edw. Lhuyd.
Oxford, Dec, 8, 1703.

Honoured Sir,

The reason I did not sooner return my most humble thanks for your generous contribution, was because Mr. Thomson and I could not agree on a time, for the consumption of the remainder of the five pounds (which was seven shillings) according to your orders. We have now lately drank you health, together with Mr. Thwaites, and one or two more of the fellows of Queen's. The transcript of Dooms-Day Book, as also of the *Taxatio Beneficiorum Angliæ, 20 Edw.* 1. has been done ever since your first orders, being but a small business. The old Cornish Glossary is also copied a month since; and I have now done with the old plays I desired the use of in my last: so that I only wait for your orders how I shall send them, whether by the Devonshire carrier? and if so, where they shall be left for you? the Cornish MS. in the Publick Library, Arch B.31, is only Wm. Jordan's play, which is one of the books transcribed for you; but there is not a word therein of the glass-windows of St. Neot's: so that Mr. Gibson (or whoever sent him that note) must mean, that the customs of the Jews are well described in that MS. which if omitted had been no great loss to the reader. I am, &c.

Edw. Lhuyd.
Oxford, March, 3, 1703–4.

Honoured Sir,

I ordered the books (Archæologia Britannica) to be sent from London, according to your directions, to Mr. Bishop of Exeter, and I hope you have long since received them .... The same friend (whose name is Mr. Philip Williams, of Diffryn near Neath) acquaints me, that one of the said Ithel, Prince of Gwent's seats, was called

Penkarn, whence the name of Karn: and if Le was ever prefixed to it, 'twas done in the imitation of the Normans, among whom they lived. The word Karn, Kairn, or Karned, signifies a heap of stones, and there are hundreds of places so named in Wales, Scotland, and Ireland: there are not a few in Cornwall likewise. A continuance of your obliging correspondence, would always be esteemed as one of the greatest happiness of the remainder of his days, by, &c.

Edw. Lhuyd.
Oxford, March, 7, 1707–8.

Honoured Sir,

This hopes to find you in perfect health and prosperity, though not so much at leisure for correspondence as formerly. The four books were sent immediately to be left with Mr. Philip Bishop, bookseller, at Exeter: (I received soon after three of them, and no more) But having not received any letter from you since, I begin to question whether he took care to forward them, as you then acquainted me you had writ to him .... I hope your friend, if living, has by this time finished his Cornish Latimar; which was what I hinted at in the English preface. It is a thing I would much rejoice to see, either in manuscript, or print. You were pleased several years since to acquaint me, that you had got together a considerable collection of ores, stones, &c. which I should be very glad, at your leisure, to hear some further news of – This place affords but little worth sending. Exeter College flourishes so well, that they are about another building, having received as I am told a thousand pounds from the Lord Primate. Mr. Thwaites of Queen's, you have heard, I suppose, is our Greek Professor; and has had lately a grant of that 100l. per annum, which of late years, was usually conferred on the Proctors. I am, &c.

Edw. Lhuyd.
Oxford, Sept, 1, 1708.

Honoured Sir,

You may be always assured, that whenever your leters come to my hands, I am as glad to see them as any I ever receive. That of October the 28th had the misfortune to come a little too late to London, to find Mr. Pugh there, whence (after a considerable delay, I suppose) it was sent into North Wales, and from thence it came to my hands just now. – I was here when the books were sent from London, and gave orders for four books; but whether my man, who is also now here, blundered, I cannot say. – I am very glad the Cornish Latimar goes on, however, and should be very glad of a copy of one letter, or else of two sheets, for specimen. He ought to exemplify all the uncommon words, or at least all that are not common, in those few Cornish writings remaining; and also now and then to confirm and illustrate their signification, by the help of our dialect. If the specimen be inclosed for me to the Honourable Sir Jeffrey Jeffrys, M.P. at his house in St. Mary Axe, London, it will save postage; and in regard he lives generally in London, if you please to direct your's so hereafter, they will be likelier to come in due time. When you favour me with you next letter, I should be glad to know whether old Keigwyn be yet living, and if so, whether either he himself, or your neighbour, can make a shift to understand the preface to the Cornish Grammar. There are some words in it, I own, that I have not read in the Cornish, and were therefore borrowed out of the Welsh, but they are very few; and if they please to send me a catalogue of all that are not understood, I will readily explain them. – I am encouraged to stand for the place of Divinity Beadle, which is represented to be somewhat better than 100l. per annum. – If yourself of friends could favour me with a speedy recommendation to Mr. Verman, it mights perhaps prove very serviceable to, Your's, &c.

Edw. Lhuyd.
Oxford, Dec, 22, 1708.

P.S. If any one write to Mr. Verman, I would gladly deliver it myself.

98   *From* **The Exmoor Scolding by Andrew Brice (1727)**

As it's natural and full of Honour to love one's Country so it's so natural (and why not as praiseworthy?) to love its language. And I hear of a Gentleman in Cornwall (in Antique Renowned for Love to Saints and Shipwrecks!) who has taken noble mighty pains in translating the Bible to Cornish or Cornubian Welch.

99   *From* **The Compleat History of Cornwall by William Hals (c.1736)**

Boyton: And here it may not be impertinent to show, that our Ancestors, the Britons of Cornwall, received and took the Blessed Sacrament in the same sence as Agnes Prest did, viz, by Faith only, contrary to the Doctrine of Transubstantiation, as is evident from Mount Calvary, a Manuscript in Verse of the Cornish Tongue, written about 500 years since, a copy of which is now in my own Custody, which containeth the History and Incarnation and Passion of Christ according to St. John's Gospels.

Tintagel: This History [of King Arthur and Genevour] for Substance is collected out of Gilfridus and other Chronologers, 1150, John Trevisa's Book of the Acts of King Arthur, temp. Henry IV. John Lydyate, a Monk at St. Edmondsbury, who write a Tract of a King Arthur's Round Table, Anno Dom 1470, William Caxton, Author of that Chronicle called *Fructus Temporum*, who also writ the History of K. Arthur, 1484; Nicholas Upton, Canon of the Cathedral Church of Wells, 1440; and others.

Feock: The Cornish Tongue was so retain'd in this Parish by the old Inhabitants thereof, 'till about the Year 1640 that Mr Wan Jackman then Vicar thereof, Chaplain of Pendenis Castle, at the Siege thereof of the Parliament Army, Son-in-Law to the Former Governor Sir Nich. Hals, Brother to John Jackman, Vicar of Kenwyn and Keye, was forced for divers Years to administer the Sacrament to the Communicants in the Cornish Tongue, because the Aged People did not well understand the English, as he often told me.

100 *From* **Archæologia Cornu-Britannica by Thomas Tonkin (c.1707–36)**

As for the Cornish and the Armoric [Breton], the difference is so very wide betwixt their manuscripts of the later centuries and ours, that tho' one were well-skilled in Welsh, it would yet require about a months time to understand a Book written in either of those Dialects, but if there be any writings extant therein, so old as the 7th, 8th, 9th or 10th centuries, I presume they are scarce distinguishable as to Grammar from Welsh, and may be known only by some words, peculiar to those countries; wherein the curious may in some measure satisfy themselves from their respective vocabularies.

That [the englyn] is ancient enough to have been the verse used by the Druids is manifest from there being some traditional remains of it this day, in Wales, Cornwall and Scotland, tho' it be immemorial when any such were last made and that it really was used by them, seems also highly probable in that a great number of the Welsh englyns of this sort have always some Doctrine, divine or moral, in the Conclusion; the rest being often insignificant, and serving only as Meeter thereinto.

101 *From* **Antiquities Historical and Monumental of the County of Cornwall by William Borlase (1754)**

Mr. Lhuyd observes, in his Preface to his Cornish Grammar, "That to preserve any old Language in Print is, without all Doubt, a most pleasant and obliging Thing to Scholars and Gentlemen, and altogether necessary in the Studies of Antiquity."

It was in Hopes of throwing some Lights upon the History of my native Country, that I undertook the Task of inspecting the few Things that remain in the Cornish Language, and forming out of them, as far as my Time and Reading could reach, the little Vocabulary that follows.

I am sensible that it is not so compleat as I could wish, the Reason of which may be partly owing to the Authour, and partly to the Subject, and partly to the Materials. If the Authour had no other points of Antiquity to divide and share his Attention, he would be more inexcusable that it is not more correct. Had not the Subject been difused among People of Literature for so many Ages, it would have been easier compassed; and if the Materials have been in greater Plenty, there would have been more Choice, and the Work might have been better executed. But the Materials were not only few, but they were much dispersed, and so many as fell into my Hands might not probably have come to the Share of another, and the Helps for such a Work were still growing fewer by Time and Accident; it being with Languages as with Buildings, when they are in a State of Decay, the Ruins become every Day less distinct, and the sooner the Remains are traced and copied out, the more visible both the Plan and the Superstructure will appear.

The sooner therefore such a Work was undertaken, the greater Likelihood there was that more of the Language might be preserved, than if the Attempt was deferred; and as some who had a Regard for their Country lamented, that is should utterly lose its ancient Language, and those who were curious had a mind to understand something of it, I found the Work was much desired; and I was willing to do something towards restoring the Cornish Language, though I might not be able to do all the fewer Avocations would have permitted.

As incompleat as the following Vocabulary is, I am persuaded, that it will be of some Use. In the present Language of my Countrymen, there are many Words which are neither English, nor derived from the Learned Languages, and therefore thought Improprieties by Strangers, and ridiculed as if they had no Meaning; but they are indeed the Remnants of their antient Language, esteemed equal in Purity and Age to any Language in Europe.

The technical Names belonging to the Arts of Mining, Husbandry, Fishing, and Building, are all in Cornish, and much oftener used than the English Terms for the same Things. The Names of Houses and Manors, Promontories, Lakes, Rivers, Mountains, Towns, and Castles in Cornwall (especially in the Western Parts), are all in ancient Cornish. Many Families retain still their Cornish Names. To those, therefore, who are earnest to know the Meaning of what they hear and see every Day, I cannot but think that the present Vocabulary, imperfect as it is (and as all Vocabularies, perhaps, are at first), will be of some Satisfaction.

102 *From* **The Natural History of Cornwall by William Borlase (1758)**

The most material singularities in this tongue are, that the substantive is placed generally before the adjective, the preposition comes sometimes after the case governed, the nominative, and governed case, and pronouns, one oftentimes incorporated with the verb; letters are changed in the beginning, middle, or end of a word, or syllable, some omitted, some inserted; and (much to the commendation of this tongue) of several words one is compounded (as in the Greek) for the sake of brevity, sound and expression.

103   On the Expiration of the Cornish Language by Daines Barrington (1776)

I myself made a very complete tour of Cornwall in 1768, and recollecting what I had heard from my brother, I mentioned to several persons of that country, that I did not think it impossible I might meet with some remains of the language who, however, considered it entirely lost. I set out from Penzance, however, with the landlord of the principal inn for my guide, towards Sennan, or most western point; and when I approached the village, I said, that there must probably be some remains of the language in those parts, if anywhere, as the village was in the road to no place whatsoever; and the only alehouse announced itself to be the last in England. My guide, however, told me that I should be disappointed, but that if I would ride ten miles about in my return to Penzance he would carry me to a village called Mousehole, on the western side of Mount's Bay, where there was an old woman called Dolly Pentreath, who could speak Cornish very fluently. Whilst we were travelling together towards Mousehole, I enquired how he knew that this woman spoke Cornish; when he informed me that he frequently went from Penzance to Mousehole to buy fish, which was sold by her, and that when he did not offer a price which was satisfactory, she grumbled to some other old women in an unknown tongue which he concluded therefore to be the Cornish. When we reached Mousehole I desired to be introduced as a person who had laid a wager that there was no one who could converse in Cornish, upon which Dolly Pentreath spoke in an angry tone of voice for two or three minutes, and in a language which sounded very much like Welsh. The hut in which she lived was in a narrow lane, opposite to two rather better cottages at the doors of which two other women stood, who were advanced in years, and who, I observed, were laughing at what Dolly Pentreath said to me. Upon this, I asked them whether she had not been abusing me, to which they answered 'Very heartily and because I had supposed she could not speak Cornish'. I then said that they must be able to talk the language: to which they answered, that they could not speak it readily, but understood it, being only 10 or 12 years younger than Dolly Pentreath.

I continued nine or ten days in Cornwall after this, but found that my friends, whom I had left to eastwards, continued as incredulous almost as they were before, about these last remains of the Cornish language, because (amongst other reasons) Dr. Borlase had supposed, in his Natural History of Cornwall, that it had entirely ceased to be spoken. It was also urged, that as he lived within four or five miles of the old woman at Mousehole, he consequently must have heard of no singular a thing as her continuing to use the vernacular tongue. I had scarcely said or thought anything more on the matter, till last summer having mentioned it to some Cornish people I found they could not credit that any person had existed within these five years who could speak their native language; and therefore, though I imagined there was but a small chance of Dolly Pentreath continuing to live, yet I wrote to the President, then in Devonshire, to desire that he would make some enquiry with regard to her: and he was so obliging as to procure me information from a gentleman whose house was within three miles of Mousehole, a considerable part of whose letter I shall subjoin.

'Dolly Pentreath is short of stature, and bends very much with old age, being in her eighty seventh year, so lusty, however, as to walk hither (viz. Castle Horneck) above three miles in bad weather, in the morning, and back again. She is somewhat deaf, but her intellect seemingly unimpaired, has a good memory, so good that she remembers perfectly well that about four or five years ago, at Mousehole, where she lives, she was sent for a gentleman, who, being a stranger had a curiosity to hear the Cornish language, which she was famed for retaining and speaking fluently, and that the inn keeper, where the gentleman came from, attended him.'

This gentleman was myself, however, I did not presume to send for her, but waited upon her.

'She does indeed, at this time, talk Cornish as readily as others do English, being bred up from a child to know no other language; nor could she (if we may believe her) talk a word of English before she was twenty years of age; as her father being a fisherman, she was sent with fish to Penzance at twelve years old, and sold them in the Cornish language, which the inhabitants in general (even the gentry) did then well understand. She is positive, however, that there is neither in Mousehole, nor in any part of the country, any person who knows anything of it, or at least can converse in it. She is poor and maintained mostly by the parish, and partly by fortune telling and gabbling Cornish.'

I have thus thought it right to lay before the Society this account of the last spoken Cornish tongue, and cannot but think, that a linguist (who understands Welsh) might still pick up a more complete vocabulary of the Cornish than any we are as yet possessed of, especially as the two neighbours of this old woman, whom I have had occasion to mention, are not above 77 or 78 years of age, and were very healthy when I saw them; so that the whole does not depend on the life of this Cornish Sybil, as she is willing to insinuate. If it is said, that I have stated that they cannot converse so readily in it as she does, because I mentioned that they comprehend her abuse upon me, which implies a certain knowledge of the Cornish tongue. Thus, the most learned men of this country cannot speak Latin fluently, for want of practise, yet it would be very easy to form a Latin vocabulary from them. It is also much to be wished, that such a linguist would go into the Isle of Man and report to the Society in what state that expiring language may be at present. As for the Welsh, I do not see the least probability of its being lost in the more mountainous parts; for as there are no valuable mines in several of the parishes thus situated, I do not conceive, that it is possible to introduce the use of English. The present inhabitants, therefore, will continue to speak their native language in those districts, for the Welsh cannot settle in England because they cannot speak our tongue, nor will English servants for husbandry live with the Welsh because they would not understand their masters. I am, dear sir, your faithful humble servant.

Daines Barrington.

104 *From* **An Explanation of the Cornu-Technical Terms and Idioms of Tinners in Mineralogia Cornubiensis by William Pryce (1778)**

Astel: A board or a plank. (Lhuyd). – Still – An arch or ceiling of boards over the mens heads in a Mine, to save them from the falling stones, rocks, or scales of the Lode or its walls. To "throw the Dead to Stulls", is to throw the refuse part of the Mine on these arches or Stalls, both to save the trouble of bringing it up to grass, and because this helps to make the Mine more secure.

Cuare: (Cornish) A quarry of stones.

Dol: Pronounced Doll, is Cornish for a valley or dale. Dol-côth, the old field or meadow. Dol-côth, the old valley or dale. The name of a great mine in Cornwall.

Elvan: (Elven, in Cornish, an element, a spark of fire). A very hard close grained stone, thought to be a bastard limestone, but I do not find that it has any calcarious quality. A very unpromising Stratum for Copper Ore.

Gad: (Gedn is Cornish for a wedge, Gad an iron wedge, Gad is Armoric for a Hare). A Gad is a an iron wedge to drive between the joints of rocks, in order to loosen the ground for the pickaxe.

Guag: (Hunger, emptiness; ac idem, Leary, Cornish). Tinners holeing into a place which has been wrought before, call it "Holeing the Guag".

Huel: A work, a Mine, as Huel Stean, a Tin Mine: Huel Kalish, the hard work.

Kal: (See Cal and Gal). Kal. A Phallus, Membrum Virile. (Lhuyd). Kalish, hard.

Kernou: Cornwall. Kernuack. Cornish.

Pryan: (from Pryi, Clay, Cornish). Pryan Ore, Pryan Tin, Pryan Lode, that which is productive of Copper Ore or Tin, but does not break in large solid stones, only in gross pebbles, or sandy with a mixture of clay.

Stannary: Laws, Stannaries, and Stannary-Courts, are Laws, Precincts, Customs, and Courts peculiar only to Tinners and Tin Mines.

Zigher: (Slow, Cornish) When a very small flow stream of water issues through a cranny under-ground, is said to Zighyr or sigger.

105 *From* **Universal Magazine by Peter Pindar (1785)**

Hail Mousehole! birth place of old Doll Pentreath
   the last who gabber'd Cornish – so says Daines
Who bat-like haunted ruins, lane and heath,
   With Will o' Wisp to brighten up his brains
Daines! who a thousand miles unweary trots
For bones, brass farthings, ashes and old pots
To prove that folks of old, like us were made,
With head, eyes, hand and toes, to drive a trade.

106 *From* **Archæologia Cornu-Britannica by William Pryce (1790)**

I have heard from a very old man, now living in Mousehole, near Penzance, who I believe is, at this time, the only person capable of holding half an hour's conversation on common subjects in the Cornish tongue. He tells me that above three score years ago, being at Morlaix on board a smuggling cutter and the only time he was ever there, he was ordered on shore, with another young man, to buy some greens, not knowing a word of French, as he thought, he was much surprised to find that he understood a great part of the conversation of some boys at play in the street, and upon further enquiry, he found he could make known all his wants in Cornish, and be better understood than he could be at home, when he used that dialect.

107 *From* **To the Courteous and Noble Inhabitants of Cornwall .... by Edward Lhuyd as found in Archæologia Cornu-Britannica by William Pryce (1790)**

'To the Courteous and Noble Inhabitants of the County of Cornwall, Honour, Wealth, and Happiness Everlasting.'

The way that I took to get some knowledge of the Cornish Language, was partly by writing some down from the mouths of the people in the West of Cornwall, in particular in the parish of St. Just; and partly, by the like help of some Gentlemen, who wrote out for me many Cornish words, in particular, Mr. John Keigwyn of the lower house in Mousehole, Mr. Eustick in the aforesaid parish of St. Just, Mr. James Jenkyns of Alverton, by Penzance, and Mr. Nicholas Boson of Newlyn in the parish of Paul. But I got the best part of my learning from three Manuscript books, put into my hands by the most Reverend and most worshipful Father in God Sir Jonathan Trelawney, Bishop of Exeter; and the most knowing and most learned gentleman, John Anstis, Esq. one of the senators of the county of Cornwall, in London, and the aforesaid Mr. Keigwyn, who, by the request of the before named Bishop, translated the said books into Englysh and who is without any comparison, the most skilfull judge of our age in the Cornish language.

What number of Britons are now in Cornwall no man knows; for that there are no books (according to my knowledge) neither in Cornish, nor yet in English, old and of authority sufficient for the discovery of this thing. I know very well there are some old writers, or antiquaries, who think there are not many (if there be any) of the Cornish gentlemen of our age descended from the Britons. For my own part I cannot believe that it is a thing of much value from what people a gentleman is descended; for I consider,

> That learning, which good lives do grace,
> Is better than the noblest race.

And therefore I would never contend, whether a gentleman may better be said to be a Saxon, a Dane, or a Norman, than to be a Briton. But if one generation be more honourable than another, wherefore should it be less esteemed, at least by the people inhabiting this island, to be many ages since descended from such a Roman, under Julius Caesar? And (though I have not yet seen any old writings, concerning those two counties) yet I make no great doubt, but that there are thousand in Cornwall and many in Devon, descended from the first inhabitants of the west parts of this Kingdom.

108 *From* Ancient Cathedral of Cornwall and Supplement to the First and Second Books of Polwhele's History of Cornwall by John Whitaker (1804)

English too was not desired by the Cornish, as vulgar history says and as Dr. Borlase avers, but, as the case shows itself plainly to be, forced upon Cornwall by the tyranny of England at a time when the English language was yet unknown in Cornwall. This act of tyranny was at once gross barbarity to the Cornish people and a death blow to the language.

I have heard in my visit to the west of two persons still alive that could speak the Cornish language. On my offer of English money for Cornish words to the men at Land's End they referred me to an old man living about three miles off towards the south at St. Levan (I think) a second chapelry with St. Sennan in the parish of St. Buryan; and intimated that I might have as many words as I would choose to purchase.

109 *From* **The History of Cornwall by Richard Polwhele (1806)**

The origin and genius of the Cornish language, and its affinity with the Welch and Armorican, have been sufficiently illustrated in the ancient history. Little else remains, but to notice its extent; and observe it gradually contracting its limits, till we see it reduced to a mere point, though not sure of its extinction.

The Cornish language was current in a part of the South-hams, (which I have called East-Cornwall) in the time of Edward the First; and long after, in all the vicinities of the Tamar. In Cornwall, it was universally spoken. Those of superior rank and education could have supported no sort of intercourse with the lower classes, if they had totally abandoned it. That the gentlemen of Cornwall were not unacquainted with the Cornish language at the time of the Reformation, I infer from the following circumstance: When the Liturgy was appointed by authority to take place of the Mass, they desired that "it might not be enjoined them in Cornish;" not pleading their ignorance of the Cornish, but preferring the English, for the sake of their mercantile and other connexions. At the same time we should presume, that the common people understood a little English; as the legislature would scarcely have forced the Liturgy upon them in a tongue utterly unknown.

110 *From* **Magna Britannia: Cornwall by Daniel Lysons and Samuel Lysons (1812)**

By its royal privileges, and retention of its ancient language, Cornwall still continued nevertheless to retain some semblance of a distinct sovereignty. The Language, which was a dialect of the ancient British, was generally spoken till the reign of Henry VIII., when the introduction of the English liturgy paved the way towards its gradual disuse.

It is said to have been at the desire of the Cornish, that the English service was enjoined in preference to that of their native tongue; whilst in Wales, a contrary system, which has proved the preservation of their language, was adopted. Dr. Moreman, the learned vicar of Menheniot, is said to have been the first in those days (speaking of the kingdom at large), who "taught his parishioners and people to say the Lord's prayer, the belief, and the commandments, in the English tongue, and did teach and catechize them therein."...

... Hals tells us that in the reign of Charles the First, some of the aged people in the neighbourhood of Penryn were quite ignorant of the English language, and that the Rev. Mr. Jackman, vicar of St. Feock, was obliged to administer the sacrament to them in the Cornish. Ray found only one person who could write the language in 1663, but we are told by Mr. Scawen, that not long before the year 1678, a sermon was preached in it by the Rev. Mr. Robinson, rector of Landewednack. In the early part of the last century, as Dr. Borlase informs us, it was still generally spoken by the fishermen and market-women in the extreme southern part of the peninsula; in his Natural History, published in 1758 he speaks of the language as having altogether ceased, so, as not to be spoken anywhere in conversation. Some aged people however retained it rather later; Mr. Daines Barrington gives an account of an old fish-woman of Mousehole, the only person he could find or hear of, who spoke the Cornish language, when he made the tour of Cornwall in 1768, as related in a communication to the Society of Antiquaries. In 1776, in a further communication on the same subject to the society, it is stated on the authority of a fisherman of Mousehole, that there were then four or five persons beside himself who could converse in Cornish.

Dr. Pryce of Redruth, in his preface to his Archeologia Cornu-Britannica, published in 1790, speaks of a very old man then living at Mousehole, as the only person, to the best of his knowledge, who was capable of holding half an hour's conversation on common subjects in the Cornish tongue. He afterwards says, that there were a few other ancient persons who pretended to jabber it, but they were very illiterate, and their speech very much corrupted, although their pronunciation was generally correct. Mr. Whitaker, in his tour to the Land's End, in 1799, heard of two persons who even then spoke it, but he had not an opportunity of ascertaining the fact. We find, upon inquiry, that there is no person now who can converse in the language, though some old people are acquainted with many words of it, which they have learned from those of the last generation.

111 Two Cornish Poems by Robert Stephen Hawker (c.1825)

The Song of the Western Men (Trelawny)

A good sword and a trusty hand!
  A merry heart and true!
King James's men shall understand
  What Cornish lads can do.

And have they fixed the where and when?
  And shall Trelawny die?
Here's twenty thousand Cornish men
  Will know the reason why!

Out spake their captain brave and bold,
  A merry wight was he:
'If London Tower were Michael's hold,
  We'll set Trelawny free!'

'We'll cross the Tamar, land to land,
  The Severn is no stay,
With 'one and all', and hand in hand,

And who shall bid us nay?'

'And when we come to London Wall,
   A pleasant sight to view,
Come forth! come forth, ye cowards all,
   Here's men as good as you!'

'Trelawny he's in the keep and hold,
   Trelawny he may die,
But here's twenty thousand Cornish bold,
   Will know the reason why!'

Modryb Marya – Aunt Mary

Now of all the trees by the king's highway,
   Which do you love the best?
O! the one that is green upon Christmas Day,
   The bush with the bleeding breast.
Now the holly with her drops of blood for me:
For that is our dear Aunt Mary's tree.

Its leaves are sweet with our Saviour's Name,
   'Tis a plant that loves the poor:
Summer and winter it shines the same,
   Beside the cottage door.
O! the holly with her drops of blood for me:
For that is our kind Aunt Mary's tree.

'Tis a bush that the birds will never leave:
   They sing in it all day long;
But sweetest of all upon Christmas Eve,
   Is to hear the robin's song.
'Tis the merriest sound upon earth and sea:
For it comes from our own Aunt Mary's tree.

So, of all that grows by the king's highway,
   I love that tree the best;
'Tis a bower for the birds upon Christmas Day,
   The bush of the bleeding breast.
O! the holly with her drops of blood for me:
For that is our sweet Aunt Mary's tree.

112 *From* Mount Calvary, edited by Davies Gilbert (1826)

No one more sincerely rejoices, than does the Editor of this ancient mystery, that the Cornish dialect of the Celtic or Gaelic language has ceased altogether from being used by the inhabitants of Cornwall;

whatever may have been its degree of intrinsic excellence: experience amply demonstrating, that no infliction on a province is equally severe, or irremediable, as the separation by distinct speech from a great and enlightened Nation, of which it forms a part. A separation closing against it most of the avenues to knowledge, and wholly intercepting that course of rapid improvement which eminently distinguishes the present age from all other periods in the history of man ...

... The history of the Celtic nation and language seems sufficiently obvious, when it is divested of mythological fancies, and cleared from the sorites heaped about it, by authors repeating one after another, the idle tales invented by their predecessors, till these legends acquired from such accumulated authority, the semblance, or at least the currency, of truth.

Rude and aboriginal inhabitants of the whole Western and South portions of Europe, they, like the natives of America in modern times, were driven by more intelligent or more warlike invaders from the open country; into remote, barren, or mountainous districts; into Cornwall, Wales, Ireland, Scotland, Brittany: where secluded in these fastnesses, from all intercourse with each other, during many centuries, and unacquainted with the arts, which have imparted steadiness even to the most flitting sounds, the various portions of this ancient people naturally fell into the use of as many dialects. Of these dialects, the Armoric (or Bas Britain), is said to approach more nearly than any other to the Cornish; and the Irish to be most remote: perhaps the alleged emigration of Celts from the West of Britain to Armorica may be so far true, that finding themselves more and more harassed by the victorious Saxons, great numbers fled for protection to their kindred tribes in that country: and this comparatively late admixture, may account for the similarity of speech between two districts, not apparently more intimately connected than several others.

If an opinion entertained by many learned persons, both in England and France, is entitled to weight, the Celtic language, *venerabilis mater linguarum*, may demand the homage of every one aspiring to accuracy in classic learning.

They contend, that the South-eastern branches of the great aboriginal family, instead of the slavery, extermination, or banishment, of their Western brethreren, experienced the milder fate of uniting with various Asiatic colonies, which settled peaceably on their coasts, bringing with them the Sanscrit in different degrees of purity; and that "this language of perfection", retaining its original structure of conjugations and declensions, but adopting words and idioms from its new associate, grew up into the tongues of Greece and Rome.

With this view of the subject, etymology changes the entire direction of its course. The numerous Cornish words almost identified with Greek, are no longer referred to the accidental resort of merchants in pursuit of tin; but, traced in the other cognate dialects, the Celtic scholar investigates their origin on the principle of *Reges de nobis, non nos de regibus.*

113 Cornish Cantata by Edward Collins Giddy (1828)

Chorus: An Lap-yeor Tom from Ball-a-noon did hie,
He saw Shalal-a-Shackets passing by;
With Jallow Clathing Lap-yeor's lambs were grac'd,
Shalal a Petticoat had round his waist;
Tom did rejoice, and as he walked along
Sweet as a Jaypie - sung a Cornish song.

Verses: Vel-an-drukya Cracka Cudna
Tuzemenhall Chun Crowzenwhrah,
Banns Burnuhal Brance Bosfrancan,
Treeve Trewhidden Try Trembah.

Carn Kenidgiac Castle-Skudiac,
Beagle-Tuben Amalvear,
Amalibria Amal-whidden,
Skilliwadden Trink Polpeor.

Pellalith Pellalla-wortha,
Buzza-vean Chyponds Boswase,
Venton-gimps Boskestal Raftra,
Hendra Grancan Treen Bostraze.

Tregenebbris Embla Bridgia,
Menadarva Treveneage,
Tregaminion Fouge Trevidgia.
Gwarnick Trewey Reskajeage.

Luggans Vellan-vrance Treglisson,
Gear Noon-gumpus Helan-gove,
Carnequidden Brea Bojoucan,
Drym Chykembra Dowran Trove.

Menagwithers Castle-gotha,
Carnon-grease Trevespan-vean,
Praze-an-beeble Men Trebarva,
Bone Trengwainton Lethargwean.

Stable-hobba Bal-as-whidden,
Tringy Trannack Try Trenear,
Fraddam Crowles Gwallan Cranken,
Drift Bojedna Cayle Trebear.

Haltergantic Carnaliezy,
Gumford Brunion Nancekeage,
Reen Trevasken Mevagizzy,
Killiow Carbus Carn Tretheage.

114 From **Rambles Beyond Railways by Wilkie Collins (1851)**

You follow your long road, visible miles on before you, winding white and serpent-like over the dark ground, until you suddenly observe in the distance an object which rises strangely above the level prospect. You approach nearer, and behold a circular turf embankment; a wide, lonesome, desolate enclosure, looking like a witches' dancing-ring that has sprung up in the midst of the open moor. This is Piran Round. Here, the old inhabitants of Cornwall assembled to form the audience of the drama of former days.

A level area of grassy ground, one hundred and thirty feet in diameter, is enclosed by the embankment. There are two entrances to this area cut through the boundary circle of turf and earth, which rises to a height of nine or ten feet, and narrows towards the top, where it is seven feet wide. All round the inside of the embankment steps were formerly cut; but their traces are now almost obliterated by the growth of the grass. They were originally seven in number; the spectators stood on them in rows, one above another – a closely packed multitude, all looking down at the dramatic performances taking place on the wide circumference of the plain. When it was well-filled, the amphitheatre must have contained upwards of two thousand people ...

... And now let us close the book, look forth over this lonesome country and lonesome amphitheatre, and imagine what a scene both must have presented, when a play was to be acted on a fine summer's morning in the year 1611.

Fancy, at the outset, the arrival of the audience – people dressed in the picturesque holiday costume of the time, which varied with each varying task, hurrying to their daylight play from miles off; all visible in every direction on the surface of the open moor, and all converging from every point of the compass to the one common centre of Piran Round. Then, imagine the assembling in the amphitheatre; the running round the outer circle of the embankment to get at the entrances; the tumbling and rushing up the steps inside; the racing of hot-headed youngsters to get to the top places; the sly deliberation of the elders in selecting the lower and safer positions; the quarrelling when a tall man chanced to stand before a short one; the giggling and blushing of buxom peasant wenches when the gallant young bachelors of the district happened to be placed behind them; the universal speculations on the weather; the universal shouting for pots of ale – and finally, as the time of the performance drew near and the minstrels appeared with their pipes, the gradual hush and stillness among the multitude; the combined stare of the whole circular mass of spectators on one point in the plain of the amphitheatre, where all knew that the actors lay hidden in a pit, properly covered in from observation – the mysterious "green-room" of the strolling players of old Cornwall!

The end of the play, too – how picturesque, how striking all the circumstances attending it must have been! Oh that we could hear again the merry old English tune piped by the minstrels, and see the merry old English dancing of the audience to the music! Then, think of the separation and the return home of the populace, at sunset; the fishing people strolling off towards the seashore, the miners walking away farther inland; the agricultural labourers spreading in all directions, wherever cottages and farmhouses were visible in the far distance over the moor. And then the darkness coming on, and the moon rising over the amphitheatre, so silent and empty, save at one corner, where the poor worn-out actors are bivouacking gipsy-like in their tents, cooking supper over the fire that flames up red in the moonlight, and talking languidly over the fatigues and triumphs of the play. What a moral and what a beauty in the quiet night-view of the old amphitheatre, after the sight that it must have presented during the noise, the bustle, and the magnificence of the day!

115 *From* **Netherton's Cornish Almanac (1854)**

Metten dah tha whey. – A good morning to you.
Elo why clapier Kernuack? – Can you speak Cornish?
Me ellam. – I can.
Tatla ello why giel? po tatla gan a why? – How do you do? or how is it with you?
Dah, durdalatha why. – Well, I thank you.
Etho ve por loan tha gwellas why a metten ma. – I am very glad to see you this morning.
Pan a priz rag Hearne? – What price for pilchards?
Priz dah. – A good price.
Betha why lawanneck. – Be you merry.
Bene tu gana. – Farewell.
Tho ve guz gavaz izal. – I am your humble servant.
Gwag o ve. re ve gawas haunsell? – I am hungry, shall I have breakfast?
Ry tha stêner deck pens en blethan. – Give to the tinner ten pound a year.
Cariah an stuff stena tha an stampes. – Carry the tin stuff to the stamping-mill.
Cariah an stean tha an foge. – Carry the tin to the blowing-house.
Danen rag teese tha trehe gorra. – Send for men to cut hay.
Menjam. – I will.
Stean San Agnes an gwella stean en Kernow. – St. Agnes tin is the best tin in Cornwall.

116 Two Notes about Cornish Speakers by John Bodinar and Matthias Wallis (1856–1859)

I John Bodinar, the Grandson of William Bodinar, am now 85 years of

age. I remember him well and also seeing Gentlemen at his house to hear him talk and see him write Cornish and I have been afishing with him and it is about 72 years since he is dead and also remember a Dorithy Pentreath.
    Witness by my hand 27 May 1856.
        John Bodinar, Mousehole.

I Matthias Wallis do certify that my Grandmother Ann Wallis have spoke in my hearing the Cornish language well. She died about fifteen years ago – and she was in her ninetieth year of her age. Jane Barnicoate died two years ago and she could speak Cornish too.
    St Buryan August 14th 1859.
        Matthias Wallis.

117 The Memorial to Dolly Pentreath at Paul (1860)

Here lieth interred Dorothy Pentreath, who died in 1777, said to have been the last person who conversed in the ancient Cornish, the peculiar language of this country from the earliest records till it expired in the eighteenth century, in this parish of St. Paul. This stone is erected by the Prince Louis Lucien Bonaparte in union with the Rev. John Garret vicar of Paul, June 1860.
    Honour thy father and thy mother, that thy days may be long in the land which the Lord thy God giveth thee. Exod. xx. 12.
    Gwra pethi de taz ha de mam: mal de Dythiow bethenz hyr war an tyr neb an arleth de dew ryes dees. Exod. xx. 12.

118 *From* On the Cornish Language by John Bellow (1861)

It may perhaps be said that as Cornish is no longer spoken and contains no literature worth mention, there is no sufficient inducement to learn it. This is true. So far as regards its use as a medium of communication. But there is another aspect in which a language may have claim on our attention, besides this, viz., the aid it is capable of affording in tracing the roots of words in other tongues – the light it may cast on the relationship of some of those tongues to each other. Even a dead language will thus furnish us at times with links in a chain that must otherwise remain imperfect. In this, then, lies the present value of Cornish to us; and if the language is suffered to disappear entirely the science of philology will sustain some loss by its doing so.

The ancient Cornish language likes like a buried city under our feet – we pass to and fro above it, but heed not in the hustle of everyday life. Yet in its words there is as much reality as ever there was in sculptural obelisks of Egypt or marble slabs of Nineveh, for they hide treasures of history, never recorded by pen, but not the less true or accessible to diligent research. It is for Cornishmen to say whether this search shall be made or not: and it is but reasonable to hope that a language, which has proved so interesting to a foreign prince, as to bring him to our shores for the purpose of investigating it, may also excite some interest among the descendants of the men who spoke it.

119 *From* **The Gentleman's Magazine by J. H. Nancekivell (1865)**

When wandering by the lovely shores of the Mount's Bay one may often hear the fisher boys shouting to each other 'Jack, where did you get your breel?' (Mackerel) and on board the mackerel boat when the nets are taken up, the men exclaim: 'Breel! mata! idn! deaw, try, pedwar, pymp, whea, all scawd!' (A mackerel! His fellow, 1, 2, 3, 4, 5, 6 all the shoal!) A few years ago the hearth or fireplace used in these boats was a piece of granite hollowed out, and it was called 'myn olla'; the same kind of simple hearth is still used by the Breton fishermen and they call it by the same name 'myn olla'... It is not much, but I believe that there is more to be found. The greatest district of the Lizard or Meneage peninsula had not yet been searched, but there are several workers in the field, and before long we shall perhaps know for certain how much tradition remains.

120 *From* **Popular Romances of the West of England: The Drolls, Traditions, and Superstitions of Old Cornwall by Robert Hunt (1865)**

The wandering minstrel, story-teller, and newsmonger appears to have been an old institution amongst the Cornish. Indeed Carew, in his "Survey of Cornwall," tells us that "the last of the Wideslades, whose estates were forfeited in the Rebellion, was called Sir Tristram. He led a walking life with his harp to gentlemen's houses." As the newspaper gradually found its way into this western county (the first one circulated in Cornwall being the *Sherborne Mercury*), the occupation of this representative of the bards was taken away; but he has only become extinct within the last twenty years. These old men wandered constantly from house to house, finding a hearty welcome at all. Board and bed were readily found [for] them, their only payment being a song or a droll (story)...

...These wanderers perpetuated the traditions of the old inhabitants; but they modified the stories, according to the activity of their fancy, to please the auditors. Not merely this: they without doubt introduced the names of people remembered by the villagers; and when they knew that a man had incurred the hatred of his neighbours, they made him do duty as a demon, or placed him in no very enviable relation to with the devil. The legends of Tregeagle are illustrations of this. The man who has gained the notoriety of being attached to a tale as old as that of Orestes, – was a magistrate in Cornwall two hundred years since. The story of the murderess of Ludgvan and her lover is another, and a very modern, example of the process by which recent events are interwoven with very ancient superstitions.

When the task of arranging my romances was commenced, I found that the traditions of Devonshire, as far east as Exeter – the tract of country which was known as "Danmonium", or even more recently as "Old Cornwall" – had a striking family resemblance. My collection then received the name it bears, as embracing the district ordinarily known as the West of England. Although I have avoided repeating any of the traditions which are to be found in Mrs Bray's books; I have not altered my title; for the examples of folklore given in these volumes belong strictly to "Old Cornwall." ...

... One word on the subject of arrangement. In the First Series are arranged all such stories as appear to belong to the most ancient inhabitants of these islands. It is true that many of them, as they are now told, assume a mediæval, or even a modern character. This is the natural result of the passage of a tradition or myth from one generation to another. The customs of the age in which the story is told are interpolated for the purposes are rendering them intelligible to the listeners, and thus they are constantly changing in their exterior form. I am, however, disposed to believe that the spirit of the romances included in this series shows them to have originated before the Christian era. The romances of the Second Series belong certainly to this historic period, though the dates of many of them are exceedingly problematical.

All the stories given in these volumes are the genuine household tales of the people. The only liberties which have been taken with them has been to alter them from the vernacular – in which they were for the most part related – into modern language. This applies to every romance but one. "The Mermaid's Vengeance" is a combination of three stories, having no doubt a common origin, but varying considerably in their details. They were too much alike to bear repeating; consequently it was thought best to throw them into one tale, which should preserve the peculiarities of all. This has been done with much care; and even the songs given preserve lines which are said by the fisherman – from whom the stories were obtained – to have been sung by the mermaids.

The traditions which are told, the superstitions which are spoken of, and the customs which are described in these volumes, may be regarded as true types of the ancient Cornish mythology, and genuine examples of the manners and customs of a people who will not readily deviate from the rules taught them by their fathers.

Romances such as these have floated down to us as wreck upon the ocean. We gather a fragment here and a fragment there, and at length, it may be, we learn something of the name and character of the vessel when it was freighted with life, and obtain a shadowy image of the people who have perished.

121 From **Stories and Folk-Lore of West Cornwall by William Bottrell (1873)**

We know that miracle plays continued to be performed in the western parishes during Queen Elizabeth's reign, and probably much later. A short time ago, William Sandys Esq., F.S.A., published his learned paper, entitled the "Cornish Drama," in the "Journal of the Royal Institution of Cornwall," an extract from a MS. volume, entitled, "A Book declaring the Royalties of which Sir John Arundell, of Lanhern, and his ancestors, have had within the Hundred of Penwith," &c. which sayeth that –

"Ao. 10, E. John Veal of Boraine, gentleman, of the age of 78. Sworn at a Court holden at Penzance the 20th day of June, Ano decimo E. by William Gilbert, under Steward of the Hundred Court of Penwyth, being upon his oath examined touching the liberties of Connerton, and the Hundred of Penwyth appendant unto the same manor, said that when he was a Boy of good remembrance his grandfath. and his Father both dwelling then at Sancras, within the hundred of Penwyth, did see one Sr. John Trwrye (or Trevrye) knight, a sanctuary man at St. Borains, which had committed some great offence then against the King, and thereupon committed to the Tower, and by means of a servant which he had, broke prison and came into Cornwall to St. Borian, and claimed priviledge of the Sanctuary. It fortuned within a while after there was a mirable (sic) Play at Sanckras Parish. Divers men came to the play amongst whom came a servant of this Mr. Trevrye, named Quenall and (in the place before the play began) the said Quenall fell at variance with one Richard James Veane, and so both went out of the Play and fought together, the said Quenall had a sword and a buckler, and the other had a single sword, the said Quenall was a very tall man in his Fight, the other gave back and fell over a mole Hill, and ere he could recover himself the said Quenall thrust his sword through him and so he immediately dyed, and Quenall taken and bound to the end of Play and before the Play was done his Mastr. hearing thereof came to the Place with other Sanctuary men and by force would have taken him away from his said Grandfather, Mr. Veal and others, but he was not able so to do, but with a sufficient Guard he was carried to Conertone Gaol where he was after hanged on the Gallows in Conerton Down, and so was more in his time, for there was no prisoner then carried to Launston Gaol."

Mr Sandys, in the work from which we have largely quoted, also gives us the following interesting bit of information:–

"In 1428, a sum of four pounds was given to Jakke Trevail and his companions, for making various plays and interludes before the king at Christmas."

Surely Jackie and his comrades went up from St. Just or Sancras to show King Henry VI what a Cornish guise-dance was like.

122 A Letter to Henry Jenner by W. Lach-Szyrma (c.1875)

>Newlyn
>Feb 5

Dear Jenner,

I was thinking relative to our subject how would it be to encourage the study of old Cornish by giving prizes – 3 or 4 (1st, 2nd, 3rd) for acquaintance with it in connection with our Newlyn Institute. The people certainly take an interest in it, their only objection is that Methodists think it "carnal" and wicked (which does not affect our old fashioned church people) and that "it does not pay". 2 or 3 pounds in prizes would just secure the memory of what remains and the restoration of a good deal more for a generation. A Cornish exam would draw better than a Spelling Bee.

The difficulty is a manual. Have you yours ready? I suspect the lingering affection for the old tongue is stronger in Newlyn than is supposed. The Archæological Society are due here in '76.

How did your paper go off? I shall be glad to hear. Will you publish it anywhere besides in the Transactions. I think in the county it would be valued. The curious thing about old Cornish is that the Upper Middle Class do not care for it half as much as the better artisan class (of the Kelynack or Victor status) [and has] to be very plain to make these men understand a statement.

If you wish your paper locally noticed I think I can get it, or a resumé of it in any Cornish or Plymouth papers.

A plain sort of school manual of Cornish illustrating existing words and terms and giving the main principles of the old language is what is required.

>Yours faithfully,
>W. Lach-Szyrma

123 A Letter to Henry Jenner by William Copeland Borlase (1878)

>Laregan, Penzance.
>May 24 1878

My dear Jenner,

I am going to say at the Meeting of the R.I.C. on Friday the 31st that we must give up for the present, if not altogether the MSS Society. I feel it is so long since the idea was started that (from what I hear) we should not get the additional support we require. I think it will be the best way. Don't you? Let me hear your opinion, however, first. You are engaged in other work just now, and I think your future volume on the language, to which we look forward, would answer better by itself. We have hardly enough money to begin, even, if you were ready.

    Kind regard to your wife.
        Yours sincerely,
          W. C. B.

124 *From* **Last Relics of the Cornish Language by W. Lach-Szyrma (c.1879)**

After Dolly Pentreath there may have been a few persons who could express a few ideas in Cornish, as to this day, there are to be found two or three old people who recollect a sentence or two in the old tongue, or can count up to twenty, or who use Cornish words for certain things, not knowing what the proper name of that thing is. As an instance, I give a case – "John, hand me the buzza," said a woman recently in my presence. "What is a buzza?" I asked. The woman had no English word to express the idea, but told John to show what the "buzza" was. She was using Cornish with English words.

This sentence was, of course, mingled Cornish and English, as not a few sentences used by Cornish miners and fishing-folk still are. "Going to bal," is not pure English but is Anglo-Cornish. The "going" and "to" may be Saxon, but the "bal" is Celtic.

Thus the language of the people, to a certain degree, is still, so to speak, Anglo-Celtic. The accent especially shows vitality, for that which makes the existing Cornish dialect of the miners and fishermen so difficult to comprehend, is not so much the number of provincial words, as the peculiar foreign accent with which the sentences composed of words, mostly really of good ordinary English, are pronounced. The tendency to speak syllabically, with a prolonged stress at the final syllable of each sentence, somewhat after the French mode, is the reason why the Cornish dialect is so difficult for a stranger to understand.

The real point of interest, however, about the Cornish is not whether a certain old woman at Mousehole was the last to speak the language or not; but, how does an Aryan language in a civilised country die out? What is the diagnosis of the last struggle for existence of a European tongue? The diagnosis of the final struggle of old Cornish can be discovered with fair accuracy; and, if we compare it with the symptoms of decay in other declining Aryan languages, it would seem that general laws are at work here also.

I. The first point that is curious about the decay of Cornish is that it lingered in the small towns and villages after it had expired in the country districts. For traditions of Cornish, one should not go to

Zennor, or Morvah, but to small towns like Mousehole and Newlyn, where history affirms the language was used in the vernacular after it had been given up by the rural population. Although this is not such as *a priori* one would expect, yet it may be accounted for. The rural population of most parts of Europe are somewhat migratory – i.e., from their farmsteads or villages into the towns on market days. To the Cornish rustics, from an early date, probably from the age of Elizabeth, English must have been essential, and Cornish a mere luxury. As rustics are generally economical in ideas and expression, the luxury of the Cornish tongue was soon given up and the necessary English was retained. In the small towns or large villages (as one chooses to define them) of Mousehole, Newlyn, and S. Just, there lingered until the early part of last century, or the end of the seventeenth century, a small Cornish-speaking population; just as in Kirk Arbory, or Kirk Braddon, in the Isle of Man, there now is a Manx-speaking population, though from Mr. Jenner's account, in the Isle of Man there would seem to be still as many Manx-speaking people as West Cornwall had persons who talked Cornish in the age of the later Stuarts.

Is the vitality of a declining language in large villages a law, or only a Cornish exception to the rule? In Luzatian it possibly applies. The vitality of the Slavonic amidst the German-speaking population is probably due mainly to the fact that the Luzatians are village-dwellers. So we may say of the other minor Slavonic tongues, which have seemed to be in danger, but which are now intrenched in their village strongholds, and occasionally bud forth into gushes of literary effort.

The inhabitants of small towns or villages can live to themselves, but this is impossible to scattered populations. A coterie may be formed of peasant families who love old ways, old customs, and even the old language, where that is in danger from the foreigner. As the Luzatian peasant in the village community surrounded by Germans clings nowadays to his old Slav, so once the Cornish peasant in Mousehole, or Newlyn, clung to the old Cornish; and probably, had it lingered to the present day, an age of literary revival would have caught it up, as it had caught the Luzatian-Sorb, and saved it from extinction. The village-dweller is generally less nomadic than the scattered agriculturist. National spirit and national language are more ingrained in the dwellers of large villages in Eastern as well as Western Europe than in lonely, scattered populations, where one would expect (at first sight) to find most old-fashioned ideas. The moorsman of England nowadays is often a semi-townsman, half jockey, half grazier and cattle dealer. The moorsmen of Cornwall, a century or two ago, was more Anglicised than the village-dwellers of the western coasts.

II. Another point is that a language survives in jest when it has ceased to be used seriously; in other words, that its last stage is that of a local slang, supposed to have a rather comical effect. Probably

Welsh may be so used in some parts of the English border, and Irish among some Irishmen, who really cannot speak their ancient Celtic tongue, but quote an Irish sentence or a word now and then to point a joke.

To a philologist there is nothing comical in the sound of an expiring language; but not so to the peasant. Everything strange to him is ridiculous; and the only use to which he can put an ancient, expiring language is either to keep a secret understanding with his comrades – as the Manx do now – or else to point a joke. This desire for a second language for such purposes is really one of the causes of the formation of slang. But in an ancient language the elements of a local slang are ready at hand. So the old Cornish, though dead as a language, may have long survived, and still almost survives as a slang dialect. This is one of the difficulties which surround the tracing of its remains in common speech; for Cornish words are thought vulgar or naughty; and the young especially are inclined to laugh when asked about them, as if there was something particularly comical in the old Celtic speech – which is now considered as an old-fashioned slang. Religious motives and scrupulosity, I believe, in some cases, have hindered their use.

III. Proverbs are the most vital parts of a language – i.e., except its isolated words and its accents, both of which may be handed on to a dialect. An illustration of this fact is to be found in the collection of Cornish proverbs which seem to have lingered till the middle of the last century. Some of these in the so-called Pryce's Grammar were probably extinct a long time before the publication of that book. But there is no doubt that the Cornish proverbs and sayings had a long vitality. Deu gena why – God be with you – which is said still to be remembered; the words (almost the same) pedn-a-mean, or game of heads and tails; the fishing cry, Breal meta truja, peswartha, pempthes wethes – "All is scrawed" are perhaps all that are really remembered, if we except Mr. Bernard Victor's sayings, which he seems to have recollected from childhood.

The reasons why proverbs should survive the true languages of which they form a part, are manifest:–

1. Ordinary people, and especially peasants, regard language from a standpoint of utility. If the old language is of little practical use, they cease to employ it. But proverbs have a sort of traditional value. They are the sayings of the ancients, and do not bear translation into a new tongue. So men retain the proverb when they have ceased to speak the language.

2. Another reason may be that old people who cannot express themselves any longer in the dying language, still like to retain some relics of it, and recite by rote the "old saws" which they learnt in childhood. Those who cannot express even a common want in a language, may still learn and utter proverbs in it. We see this in Latin. How many thousands of Englishmen there are who this day could not write a line of decent Latin prose, and still less hold a conversation in

Latin, but who yet like to "lug in" a Latin quotation whenever it is appropriate, and sometimes when it is not. What Latin is to the learned of Europe to-day, that Cornish was to a few aged Cornishmen a century or so ago – a language to be quoted, but not to be generally used.

IV. The last stage of decay of a language which may be said to follow its actual death – as words without grammar are the mere bones of speech – is the survival of words into the patois of the country where the dead language once lived. In Cornwall, these linguistic bones may be picked up here and there, like the remains of mortality in an overcrowded churchyard. They exist as actual words in common use, supposed by the people to be English, but really quite foreign to the English language. This vitality of words is more manifest in nouns than in verbs; but every part of speech, except the preposition, is affected by the old Celtic in some cases. The fact is, the English language is rich in verbs, and there was scarcely an action or state which English did not provide for. Still the Cornishmen could not give up his expressive verb, to clunk, to swallow; or to laggen, to splash; and English has not perhaps any simple verb for to jowdy, or wade with the boots on.

Trade terms have great vitality. The English trade term is not known, or is not exactly equivalent, and so the Cornish word lingers in common speech. The names of animals and plants also are often retained when the English name is not known.

The present conditions of the old Cornish may be best recognised by the Glossaries connnected with the Essays on the language by Messrs. Victor and Pentreath. Many Saxon terms, of course, found entrance into those Glossaries, but they give, on a whole, a fair idea of the still lingering relics of the old language.

Such are the main points noticeable in the decay of the Old Cornish, which, with the Old Prussian, may be said to be the only important European language that has actually died out in modern times. How far the laws of decay which I have noticed in Cornish are applicable to Prussian (which my readers will remember was a tongue akin to the Lithuanian, nearer to Sanscrit than most of our European languages) I cannot say; but it seems to me that both with regard to Manx and to Wendish some of these rule apply. The whole subject is one of the deepest interest, both from an historical and a philological standpoint.

125 From **Stories and Folk-Lore of West Cornwall by William Bottrell (1880)**

The Ancient Cornish Language in the Colonies: Cornishmen's propensities are well-known and are most apparent when they meet in foreign lands. At the gold-fields of Australia, as elsewhere, they stand by and support each other "through thick and thin." Cornishmen are also preferred for many kinds of work which require some degree of engineering skill, and they seldom undertake any employment for which they are incompetent. Consequently, many persons from other shires who have never been west of the Tamar try to pass themselves off as Cornishmen, and sometimes succeed in being received into the fellowship of "One and All". If, however, the stranger is suspected of "sailing under false colours," when they are all in familiar chat about nothing in particular, "Cousin Jackey" will take occasion to say to the new chum "My dear, ded he ever see a duck klunk a gay?" If the stranger be up to the intent of the question he will probably reply, "Learn thy granny to lap ashes," which is the West Country equivalent for teaching the venerable dame to such eggs; but if ignorant of what the questions means, he is given to understand that they regard him as an interloper and will be no more deceived by him than a duck can be made to klunk (swallow) a gay (fragment of broken crockery.)

The proverbial saying of "nobody ever saw a duck klunk a gay" – meaning that no one will be deceived beyond a certain point – may be puzzling to some Cornish readers as well as to strangers; those, however, who are country-born and bred remember that when children they often left the table with their meals unfinished and ran out with their morsels in their hands and their "gays" in their pockets, eager to join their playmates in the town-place; and how the village ducks – knowing the children's custom – gathered around them to pick up the crumbs, or to snatch the food from the childrens' hands, and the urchins often tossed them a "gay," which the greedy fowl gobble up and drop, one after the other, but never swallow. It is a comical sight to see how the ducks, on having discovered the cheat, look askaunt at the "didjan" of broken clome, shaking their tails and quacking in anger or scorn the while.

The Gileadites' Shibboleth served much the same purpose in the times of the Judges of Israel as the old prover does to-day among Cornishmen abroad. (Judges xii chap., 5 and 6 verses.)

The usual test above-mentioned fails sometimes, chiefly from young Cornishmen making comrades of strangers, as they are apt to do for short spells, in which case they have other tests for the next opportunity, but all turn on the same idea – that of using words only understood by themselves. One more will serve as an example.

A Cornishmen will come behind the stranger who wishes to pass for a genuine Cornubian and say, quite natural-like, "Mate! there's a green myryan on thy nudack." The venomous bite or sting of a green myryan (ant) being much dreaded, a Cornishman would either put his hand to the nape of his neck, to brush it off, or show in some way that he understood the meaning – looking "as dazed as a duck against (on hearing) thunder" the while.

Old Cornish Words: Strangers are often puzzled to know what we Cornish people mean by some of our words. Let us take some old Cornish words still in common use, as skaw for the elder-tree; skaw-dower, water-elder; bannel, broom; skedgewith, privet; griglans, heath; padgy-paw (from padzar, four), the small grey lizard; muryan, the ant; quilkin, the frog (which retains its English name when in the water); pul-cronack (literally pool-toad) is the name given to a small fish with a head much like that of a toad, which is often found in the pool (pulans) left by the receding tide among the rocks along shore; visnan, the sand-lance; bul-horn, the shell-snail; dumble-dory, the black beetle (but this may be a corruption of the dor-beetle). A small, solid wheel has still the old name of drucshar. Finely pulverized soil is called grute. The roots and other light matter harrowed up on the surface of the ground for burning we call tabs. Guldaize, harvest feast. Plum means soft; quail, withered; crum, crooked; bruyans, crumbs; with a few other terms more rarely used.

Many of our ordinary expressions (often mistaken for vulgar provincialisms) are French words slightly modified, which were probably introduced into the west by the old Norman families who long resided there. For instance; a large apron to come quite round, worn for the sake of keeping the under clothing clean, is called a touser (tout serre); a game of running romps is a courant (from courir). Very rough play is a regular cow's courant. Going into a neighbour's for a spell of friendly chat is going to cursey (couser) a bit. The loins are called the cheens (old French echine). The plant sweet-leaf, a kind of St. John's wort, here called tutsen, is the French toute saine (heal all). There are some others which however, are not peculiar to the west, as kick-shaws (quelque chose), &c. We have also many inverted words, as swap for wasp, cruds for curds &c. Then again we call a fly a flea; and a flea a flay; and the smallest stream of water a river.

Ishan is a genuine old Cornish word; it is only given to such dust as comes from winnowing, the result of which process is husks, chaff &c.

Refuse, consisting of defective grains, seeds, &c., on the "tail" (leeward end) of a winnowing sheet, was, by old "winsters" called attal.

Harvest-time reminds one of our free-hearted old farmers and their bountiful goolthise, at which all comers were welcome to eat, drink and be merry. This name for an entertainment given on the principal corn-carrying day – generally the last – is preserved from our ancient language. In Scilly a harvest feast is called Nicklethise.

In addition to the above we have the following terms connected with harvest work and the preparation of corn for mill or market. Dram, a swathe of cut corn; croust, the afternoon's refreshment, generally of hot fuggans (cakes) and ale (Latin crusta).

Collebrands, defective and smutty ears, supposed to be blighted by the fine weather's lightning, called by the same name.

Pederack and brummal, arish mows. The former is conical in shape, with the ear ends of all the sheaves turned inward and upwards; the latter, which is also called a culver-house mow, is in shape much like an old-fashioned, round, stone-built pigeon house;

having the part which answers to a culver-house roof finished with the sheaves turned, ear end, downwards and outwards. A brummal mow is the best for continued moist weather, because the ears on a mow-top are less liable to sprout when reversed. An ill-shaped bulging pederack mow is said, in derision, to be "like an old culver-house," by those who don't know what the object of their comparison means.

Brummal is so much like a Gallic name for the sort of weather we call slaggy (full of misty rain), that they are, probably, offshoots from the same old root.

Colp, a short rope for carrying sheaves from a mow-hay to the barn; also a blow. Keveran, a strip of hide or leather which unites the two sticks of a "threshal" (flail) here called the "hand-staff and slash-staff". Liners, threshed wheaten sheaves. Kayer, a coarse sieve (probably a modern corruption of Cader a-Chair, e.g., Cader Michel; St. Michael's Chair on St. Michael's Mount). Layer, a winnowing-sheet. To reeve, to separate with a fine sieve, small corn, seeds, &c., from the good grain.

Most West Country folk use many other words connected with husbandry which sound very unlike English, and are unknown in the eastern part of the county, as Colpas, anything which serves as a prop, or an underset, to a crowbar, or other object when used as a lever. Visgey (mutation for Pigol), a large pick, or mattock; tubble is another name for the same. Piggal, a beat axe. Monger, a straw horse-collar, &c., &c.

126 *From* **Bibliotheca Cornubiensis by G.C. Boase and W.P. Courtney (1882)**

Sermons in Cornish and English. Preached by Rev. Joseph Sherwood at St Ives, Marazion and Penzance 1680. MSS. penes Jonathan Rashleigh, esq. Menabilly.

127 *From* **The Introduction to An English-Cornish Dictionary by Frederick W. P. Jago (1887)**

It has been, and still is, a popular belief, that there is not much of the old language left. The catalogue of remains here given goes far to prove that the popular belief is wrong. It should be remembered that besides the printed books in Cornish, there are numbers of ancient Cornish words still in use. Then, again, the names of persons and places derived from the old tongue, amount to at least 20,000 words. These may be seen in 'The Glossary of Cornish Names' by the Rev. John Bannister. Roughly counted there are about eight thousand Cornish words in Dr. Williams's Lexicon, four thousand in Pryce's Vocabulary, and about four thousand in that of Borlase.

Their numbers must not be added together. Excluding the names of persons and places, and numbering from all other sources, it may be stated that about fifteen thousand words of the Celtic language of Cornwall have been saved to us. Borlase has many words not to be found in Pryce and vice versa. There are also many words in Pryce and Borlase not to be found in Williams. Such works in Cornish as are preserved are valuable, because we find in them specimens of the language in its various stages of purity and decay. Although the books are not numerous and would occupy a small space in a library, yet the words and phrases are sufficient to express almost every form of thought.

It has been said that the husbandman expresses all his thoughts by using four or five hundred words, and Shakespeare used about 15,000 words. Thus it may be seen that the "remains" of Celtic Cornish stand far beyond the vocabulary of the rustic, and rival in their amount the words of Shakespeare.

128 *From* **Guavas the Tinner by Sabine Baring-Gould (c.1897)**

"Well – and then?" asked Guavas further.

"Dickan Rawle saith that you, the Cornishman, have cut your bounds and made your pitch just under Yealm Steps, and that at the Deluge, when the waters washed away so much of the earth, the tin was carried over the tip and spilled in the largers and purest lumps under the Steps."

"That is not true," said Guavas.

"And that his pitch is above the Steps, whence all the tin was carried away by the retreating waters. Therefore you have his tin as well as your own – ."

"Was it his tin when the Deluge swept it down, and the waters retreated from off the face of the earth?"

129 *From* **Cornish Whiddles for Teenin' Time by Mrs Frank Morris (1898)**

Rôs, flour hy hynsé

This, in the old talk, means "Rose, flower of her sex."

Rose was her name, and her admirers added the rest.

The stranger from beyond the seas who was soon to be the husband of Rose, wrote a song in her praise in his own language, and after each verse, as a refrain he sang, "Rôs, flour he hynsé."

Which showed how much he loved Rose; for he had a contempt for the Cornish tongue, and for the Cornish people, the only exceptions being Rose, and the refrain of his song in her praise – so at least Rose believed. But others thought that her farm lands, and her being the chief heiress on the banks of the Tamar, had all the admiration; and that as the owner of these, Rose had to be won.

Rose blushed each time she heard the refrain of the song, and her curling brown lashes rested on her delicately pink cheeks. Her lover looked handsome as a picture, with his curling dark looks, his bold black eyes, and his velvet attire – so handsome, that Rose may be pardoned for believing him to be as gallant as he seemed.

In vain her old godmother, who lived across the water, warned her Florion was a stranger of whom nothing was known.

Rose was as obstinate as she was silly, as silly as she was young, and as young as she was pretty. And when I tell you she was the prettiest maid in the Duchy, you will be able to judge that she was the silliest, and most obstinate.

She was also tender-hearted as she was pretty, and that makes her worthy of a story all to herself.

Hecca Hellier, the young hunter from Mount's Bay, hated the stranger; so also did Nagonan, Rose's dog. They hated Florion as much as they loved Rose; and I can't say more than that.

"Why don't you tell Rose you love her?" asked Rose's old godmother.

"I'm too rough for her to care about me, Dama Widden," answered Hecca.

Every one called the old woman Dama Widden.

"Um," grumbled the old woman, patting the ground with her ebony stick.

"Folks say, *'Too long a tongue, too short a hand, but –'*"

Here she raised her stick and shot it at Heccas, as she continued impressively –

"The man that has no tongue, loses his land."

"I don't want land," said Heccas angrily."

"You don't love Rose enough to forget that she is rich, and that you are poor."

"I should not love her if I took advantage of her love to make myself rich."

"Nonsense! You're proud, lazy, and love yourself more than any one else. Oh, I'll prove it. You're too proud, to bear to hear folks say that you married a wife for her riches. You're too lazy, to dress yourself smartly, and improve your manners, and try to amuse Rose. And you love yourself most, because you let your pride, and laziness stand between you and Rose."

The old woman paused for breath, then cried –

"What, going?"

"Yes, going away. Give this to Rose when winter comes."

Hecca flung a coat of otter skins on the cottage floor, and strode down the garden, got into his boat, pushed off, and rowed out to one of the ships in the harbour, climbed on board it, and sailed down to the open sea and away to make his fortune, and to forget Rose.

"What fools, nice men are," laughed the old woman, as she put the otter-skin cloak across her old white donkey's back, climbed up herself, and hit it with her ebony stick gently.

It went off at a gallop, swam the Tamar, and was soon along the road up the hill, that led to Rose's farm.

As the old dame entered the farmyard, her bushy eyebrows met in a frown to see Florion poking the fat sides of the pigs, as though they were already his own, whilst Rose stood unheeded by him at his side.

"If thee cussen't scheemy, theest must louster, folks say," quoted the old dame.

"Your shiner will never need to louster, Rose."

Rose looked up, startled; she had not heard the donkey's hooves.

"Dama Widden, Dama Widden, how glad I am to see you!" she exclaimed.

"What do you call her grandmother, when she is no relation to you?" asked Florion haughtily.

Rose was too astonished at her gallant lover's rude manner and words to reply. The old woman did so for her:

"Soft, and fair, Sweet sir, goes far. Everyone calls me Dama Widden; it suits my white hair."

Rose was helping her godmother to alight, and took the fur cloak off the donkey's back.

"What a lovely one!" cried the girl, rubbing her soft pink cheek against the otter skin.

"Hecca Hellier left it for me to give a girl," said Dama Widden.

Rose put it quickly back upon the donkey's back; and Dama Widden chuckled to herself as she leaned heavily on her stick.

The heart of no man would have held out against Dama Widden, whilst eating the dishes she had prepared for Rose's lover. Florion's cheecks puffed out, and his eyes shone, as his red, thick lips closed over the steaming morsels.

"You may stay and cook for me," he said amiably to the old Dame.

She tapped the hearthstone loudly with her stick as she sat by the fireside.

"Speak little, And speak well; But to speak little is best," was her reply.

"Remember that yourself, old hag," snarled Florion; turning on his heel, and stamping up the stairs to his bedroom, the door of which he slammed.

He gobbled his breakfast as quickly as he could, jumped up, kissed Rose, smiled on the serving folk, and was down the hill and off before Rose realised her had gone.

"Smiles, and no money, Are to servers, as lamb without mint,' grumbled Dama Widden.

"True, true," cried Rose's servants.

But Rose did not hear – she was running as fast as she could after her lover to bid him goodbye. But she was too late – the boat had rowed off before she reached the shore.

130 *From* **Mystère de St-Gwénnolé – The Celtic Drama Revived by R.A.H. Bickford-Smith (1899)**

It is a well-established fact that there is a nearer kinship between the inhabitants of Cornwall and Brittany than between any other pair of Celtic peoples; and the closeness of the relationship is evident not only to the man of words or letters, but quite as overwhelmingly to the student of botany, of folk-lore, of religious observances and of customs generally. Geographical proximity would have led us to expect this *a priori*, especially if any credence be attached to the tradition of the old continuity of land between the two countries, the solution of which is in a sense but another tie between them.

Among the most interesting points of contact is the possession by both branches of the family of the dramatic instinct and its somewhat peculiar specialisation into the miracle-play. More than half our little Cornish literature consists of religious dramas of this kind, and there are a good many Breton mysteries extant. One of the them, 'The Life of St. Gwénnolé', has recently been revived, and the whole Celtic world – and especially the Cornish, for it deals with the Lyonesse story – will no doubt view the experiment with sympathetic interest. This drama was probably written in the middle of the sixteenth century. It was first published, at Morlaix, in 1557, five other plays – 'Calvary', 'The Passion', 'The Holy Virgin', 'The Life of Man' and 'St. Barbe' – having preceded it. It was accordingly appropriate that Morlaix should be chosen as the scene of its reproduction. The story on which the play is based was written in Latin in the ninth century by a monk of Landévennec (our Landewednack) called Gourdisten. It is probable that the publication at Tréguier in 1499 and at Paris in 1501 of the 'Catholicon', a Breton-French-Latin dictionary, acted as a final stimulus to anonymous priestly playwrights of Armorica.

The origin of the Celtic drama is obscure. That the race was naturally prone to this species of art may be assumed, as Celts of all latitudes are religious, heroic and idealist, quick to act and not slow to speak. The first three of these characteristics make poetry a necessity, and the two others tend to give it a dramatic form. What is perhaps most surprising in the miracle-play is a distinct similarity to the early Greek tragedy, for the Greek race was the least religious of all the Aryans. Besides, such religious sincerity as the Hellenes, and notably Æschylus, possessed, does not appear to have been as profound and unshakeable as that of the Bretons. At the same time the dram must have been developed from more or less the same sources in the Britains as in Hellas (unless the later was very directly affected by the earlier), so we may take for granted that God-worship and hero-worship were its causæ causantes. It we accept the sixteenth century as the birth-period of the earliest Breton play, we may suppose that the Greco-Roman stage was largely responsible for its existence. Nevertheless it seems more probable that an indigenous Celtic drama was already in process of evolution, and was only modified (improved, no doubt) by contact with the perfected organism of Greece and Rome.

The resuscitation of the mediæval Breton theatre is only part of a plan for reinforcing the Breton element generally, for the promoters of the scheme have in view the buttressing of the already threatened language, the preservation of indigenous customs, and the practical increase of Breton influence in every sense. There is, perhaps, also a more political and more probably a vague religious motive, though politics and religion are expressly excluded from discussion. These latter subjects however do not concern us particularly.

'The Union régionaliste bretonne' opened on August 13 last at Morlaix in Finisterre (Land's end). The morning and afternoon were spent in business of a practical kind, and the evening in the reading of papers on the Breton theatre and on Breton music, with very interesting illustrations. On the following afternoon, a representation was given of one of the most thrilling of the old plays. This took place at Ploujean (village of St. John), which is about three miles from Morlaix. The drive was a pretty one: first the massive viaduct, recalling our new stone bridges, but higher and more cyclopean-looking than any of ours; then the tidal river, reminding one of Gweek; and then a mile or more beside an enclosed park, an almost exact reproduction of Clowance, for the peasants boast that the wall which completely surrounds the demesne is over five kilometres long. Ploujean itself might be anywhere is southern or western Cornwall. The open-air theatre was, I dare say, a very good imitation of its mediæval predecessor. A rude stage, painted in a no doubt intentionally primitive style, had its back to the churchyard (with a narrow screen of Cornish elms between) and its front to the village green, or rather 'place' – for unfortunately they have no plan-an-gwaré near Morlaix. There were about twelve hundred seats (from ten francs downwards), and standing-room for a thousand spectators more. The favourite places were under a triple row of shady chestnuts on the southern side of the square. All Celtic countries were represented except, I think, the Isle of Man. The Côtes du Nord had but a scanty number of delegates, but the old language is of course less spoken there than elsewhere in Brittany. Oddly enough, the scene was surmounted by the fleur-de-lys. While the crowds were assembling, the performers were good enough to submit to a great deal of kodaking, while some of them, foremost among them the hero Saint Gwénnolé, were industriously engaged in the sale of 'books of the words'. The actors (there were no actresses, in strict conformity to ancient usage) were twelve in number; four were small farmers, three shop-boys, one a road-mender, one a carter, one a stable-boy, and one (taking a girl's part) a blacksmith, while the king had himself enough trades to equip a hamlet, being farmer, baker, innkeeper, and barber.

The audience was very enthusiastic, and the orchestra, consisting of two bagpipes, had a most cordial reception. The particular instrument used in Brittany is of a rather higher-toned sort than the Scotch variety; it is called biniou, which is really only the plural of benvek, an instrument of any kind. The overture was of a weird character, which a mere Cornish Celt could not properly appreciate; but the big Breton audience undoubtedly enjoyed it. Then came a short prologue in French, and the play began.

What struck me most was the clear intonation of the actors. They could not act, of course, for they were peasants and its was their first attempt, but they could speak their Breton sonorously and rhythmically, and after a few minutes one realised the loss to our island of such a strong and musical language as Cornish had evidently been. In some words there was a certain stress, a certain sing-song even, which amusingly recalled the Land's End district. And there was always the familiar raising of the voice; and the frequently accentuated penultima was very noticeable.

The plot is as follows:–

Gralon, king of the two Brittanies, or Britains, who lives in French Brittany, hearing of sedition in his northern (English) dominions, sends his cousin Fragan to restore order there. He (Fragan) meets with a very unfavourable reception – his forces being almost annihilated – and decides to return with his family to the court of Gralon. His daughter suggests that they should pray for succour: they do so, and an angel appears; she foretells the birth of a son, Gwénnolé, who will be the friend of the Creator and will 'content his father's spirit.' Gralon receives this unsuccessful cousin kindly, and makes him governor of the town of Is. Gwénnolé when three years old, goes to the pious Budoc for instruction. He cures the broken leg of a naughty fellow-pupil instantaneously with a word of prayer, and Budoc from being his master becomes his disciple. After a further miracle the barbarians, who have invaded Brittany, are repulsed in answer to prayer. Gralon, however, renounces Christianity for the worship of Jupiter, and the town of Is is the scene of very unchristian license; the rest of his sovereignty the king hands over to Fragan and Gwénnolé. Gralon at length repents, and with Gwénnolé tried to reconvert his subjects, but in vain. The king, forewarned, escapes on horseback with Gwénnolé's aid, and the town of Is is engulfed in the sea.

The play itself is not great, nor are there many citeworthy passages; but it is undoubtedly musical. I need hardly add that it is most instructive historically, though the periods on which light is thrown are those of writers of the biography and of the drama rather than that of Gralon.

A few short passages may be of interest:–

'Na eus med Breiz-Meuris a raî chagrin d'in.' (It is only the people of Great Britain who give us trouble.)

'Danva ar zaladenn.' (Taste the salad, i.e., be killed; this seems akin to the use of 'panier à salade' for 'Black Maria,' though it is difficult to see how the connection can have arisen.)

'Aotrous Doue' (Lord God – literally, 'Mr. God,' like the Greek kyrios.)

'Bevet bepred en hennt euz ar basianted.' (Live always in the path of patience.)

'Lezenn ar fé.' (The law of faith.)

'Allas! me 'zo paoz-glaou, a bep-tu, grant'r luc'hed.' (Alas! I am quite cooked, every way, by the lightnings.)

'En pewar c'horn ar bet.' (In the four corners of the world.)

'Arruët-mad da veet.' (Welcome - literally 'be well arrived.')

'Tan-a-joa' (Feux de joie.)

'Enfin, re'd eo comer plijadur, er bed-man,
Hac tanvad a bep-mad, a-roac mont diwarnhan.'
(In fine, there's need to have pleasure in this world,
To taste everything good, before leaving it.)

'Tad ar Brodivanz.' (Father of Providence.)

'Ebars en carreojo ho devo dioueskel.' (In carriages which will have wings.)

'Reït d'in peuc'h ha chanchet a gonversation.' (Give me peace and change the conversation.)

There is quoted also a Latin line of considerable interest:

'Deus septem arivores Gratiarum.'

The angel's song has point and a certain pleasant swing:–

> Eur mab a defo da briet,
> A vezo Gwennole hanvet;
> Ar bugel ze 'vô binniguet
> Ha mignon da grouer ar bed.

> Hen cass a ri d'ann Occidant,
> D'ar studi, gant eun den savant:
> Gant Doue eo predestinet
> Ewit beza sanctifiet.

> Soufr a raï calz euz a ankenn,
> Er bed, oc'h ober pinijen;
> Anduri raï da speret,
> Euz trec'hi ann aërouant.

> Kers war ar mor d'ann Armoric
> Gwennole 'vezo da vabic;
> Contantin a raï da speret,
> Euz ann holi grasou vô carget.

Which may be roughly rendered:–

> A son thy spouse shall bear to thee,
> And Gwénnolé his name shall be;
> The child shall blest be to the end,
> Ay, more – the World-Creator's friend.

> Westwards thou shalt his footsteps turn,
> There from a wise man he shall learn;
> For fore-ordained by God is he
> Unto a life of sanctity.
>
> Suffer he must full many a pain
> In this world, penitence to gain,
> And many torments undergo,
> Ere he the Dragon overthrow.
>
> Go then by sea to Brittany.
> Thy dear son's name is Gwénnolé.
> Thy spirit's yearnings he shall sate,
> With all the graces for his freight.

The sentiments are very Biblical – and very Cornish.

131 *From* **A Book of the West by Sabine Baring-Gould (1899)**

It may seem paradoxical, but I contend that for intellectual matters it is a great loss to the Cornish to have abandoned their native tongue. To be bi-lingual is educative to the intellect in a very marked degree. In their determination not to abandon their tongue, the Welsh show great prudence. I have no hesitation in saying that a Welsh peasant is much ahead, intellectually, of the English peasant of the same social position, and I attribute this mainly to the fact of the greater agility given to his brain in having to think and speak in two languages. When he gives up one of these he abandons mental gymnastics as well as the exercise of the vocal organs in two different modes of speech.

What we do with infinite labour in the upper and middle classes is to teach our children to acquire French and German as well as English, and this is not only because these tongues open to them literary treasures, but for educative purposes to the mind, teaching to acquire other words, forms of grammar, and modulation of sounds than those the children have at home.

By God's mercy the Welsh child is so situated that from infancy it has to acquire simultaneously two tongues, and that in the lowest class of life; and this I contend is an advantage of a very high order, which is not enjoyed by children of even a class above it in England.

The West Cornish dialect is a growth of comparatively recent times. It is on the outside not more than four hundred years old. Whence was it derived? That is a problem that has yet to be studied.

132 *From* **The Literature of the Celts by Magnus Maclean (1902)**

As for Cornwall, whose dialect is now extinct, she never produced much of Celtic literature. What there is still extant is preserved in MSS. of the fifteenth century, representing possibly all the ancient literature she ever had, and dates from that or the preceding fourteenth century. These pieces consist of one poem entitled "Mount Calvary," and three drama or miracle plays, with nothing distinctly Celtic about them save the language. With the exception of these and another dramas of the seventeenth century (1611), and the Lord's Prayer translated, the obsolete and defunct Cornish dialect has no literature to show, and therefore is not concerned in the special Celtic revivals characteristic of the literature in the other dialects.

133 *From* **From a Cornish Window by Arthur Quiller Couch (1906)**

Enthusiasts beg us to make the experiment of 'reviving' these old plays in their old surroundings. But here I pause, while admitting the temptation. One would like to give life again, if only for a day to the picture which Mr Norris conjures up.

But alas! I foresee the terrible unreality which would infect the whole business. Very pretty, no doubt, and suggestive would be the picture of the audience arrayed around the turf benches – *In gradibus sedit populus de cespite factis* – but one does not want an audience to be acting; and this audience would be making-believe even more heroically than the actors – that is, if it took the trouble to be in earnest at all. For the success of the experiment would depend on our reconstructing the whole scene – the ring of entranced spectators as well as the primitive show; and the country-people would probably, and not entirely without reason, regard the business as 'a stupid old May game.' The only spectators properly impressed would be a handful of visitors and solemn antiquarians. I can see those visitors. If it has ever been your lot to witness the performance of a 'literary' play in London and cast an eye over the audience it attracts, you too, will know them and their stigmata – their ineffable attire, their strange hirsuteness, their air of combining instruction with amusement, their soft felt hats indented along the crown. No! We may, perhaps, produce new religious dramas in these ancient Rounds: decidedly we cannot revive the old ones.

Glossary

Ambrosius Merlin – the Merlin of Brythonic literature.
Armoric – Breton.
Athelstan – the King of Wessex, who in AD 927 attacked the Cornish-speaking Celts living in Exeter, forcing back across over the River Tamar, which became a boundary. According to William of Malmesbury, he described the Cornish as a 'filthy race'.
Ausonius – Decimus Magnus Ausonius (died AD 395) was a rhetorician and consul from Roman Gaul.
Beunans Meriasek – the drama of the Life of St Meriasek, a Breton and Cornish saint.
Brythonic – the Celtic language group comprising Cornish, Breton and Welsh.
Bucca – a mischievous sprite.
Carn Brea – a hill in west Cornwall.
Castle-an-dinas – a circular hill fort in mid-Cornwall associated with King Arthur.
Cornish Revival – the term applied to the revival of interest in Cornish language, politics and culture in the period 1890–1940.
Cornubian – old word for a Cornish person.
Droll – Anglo-Cornish word for a story, possibly from the Cornish *daralla*.
Englyn – a rhyming Brythonic verse form. The most common form in Cornwall is a triplet, while in Wales it is usually a quatrain.
Glasney College – the Collegiate Church of St Thomas at Glasney in Penryn in Cornwall, founded in 1265. It was Cornwall's seat of learning until the Dissolution of the Monasteries under Henry VIII, and was probably where the *Ordinalia* was written.
Gomer – the son of Japheth, the son of Noah, and mythical progenitor of the Cornish, Welsh and Bretons.
Gorseth – a ceremonial event held to celebrate Cornish identity and culture. The first Gorseth was held at Boscawen Ûn stone circle in 1928. The first Grand Bard was Henry Jenner.
Grey Rock in the Wood – *Garrack glase en Kooz*, St Michael's Mount. Mount's Bay was once wooded.
Gwavas Lake – an area of sea outside Newlyn. *Gwavas* means 'winter farm'.
Gwreans an bys – the *Creacion of the World*, a play written by William Jordan in 1611. The play's full title is 'The Creacion of the World with Noye's Flude'.
Haile an Taw – a song, more commonly known as Hal-an-tow, sung every year at Helston Flora Day.
Joseph of Arrimathea – a follower of Jesus, who made a mythical journey to Britain with the child Jesus, arriving in Cornwall. Also associated with Glastonbury in Somerset.
Kernow – Cornish language; Cornwall.
Lamech – a descendant of Cain.
Late Cornish – the period of the Cornish language and literature from 1550–1900.
Legend of the Rood – The legend tells the story of the creation of the wood for Christ's cross, and is a unifying theme of the *Ordinalia*.
Middle Cornish – the period of Cornish language and literature from 1250 to 1550.
Ordinalia – the Middle Cornish verse drama based on Biblical narrative. There are three plays: Origo Mundi, Passio Domini and Resurrexio Domini.
Old Cornish – the period of Cornish language and literature from 800 to 1250.
Origo Mundi – the first play of the extant *Ordinalia*, this tells the story of the beginning of the world.
Pascon Agan Arluth – the Cornish poem of the Passion of Christ.
Passio Christi – the second play of the *Ordinalia*, telling the story of Christ's Passion. The play

is sometimes known as Passio Domini.

Piran Round – the name of a *plen-an-gwarry* found between Perranporth and Perranzabuloe.

Plen-an-gwarry – the name given to circular 'in-the-round' theatre spaces found in Cornwall, where Cornish drama was enacted.

Polsethow – in Cornish 'mire' or 'pit'. The site of Glasney College.

Prayer Book Rebellion – the rebellion generated by the 1549 Act of Uniformity, which enforced the use of the Book of Common Prayer in English.

Polychronicon – a history of the world up to 1327.

Recusancy – refusal to recognise the Established Church after the Reformation.

Resurrexio Domini – the third and final play of the *Ordinalia*, which tells the story of Christ's resurrection.

Stannaries – the administrative divisions of the mining community in Devon and Cornwall.

Tyrconnell – Richard Talbot, first Earl of Tyrconnell, was James II's viceroy in Ireland. He tried unsuccessfully to change sides when James was defeated by William of Orange.

Commentaries

Texts in Cornish

1   *From* **Vocabularium Cornicum/The Old Cornish Vocabulary (c.1000)**

This selection is taken from a much longer Old Cornish-Latin thesaurus, probably compiled by Ælfric, the abbot of Eynsham. It classifies biblical and everyday terms for Cornish speakers learning Latin.

2   **'Golsoug ty cowez'/The Charter Endorsement (c.1380)**

The Charter Endorsement was discovered by Henry Jenner (1848–1934), the 'father' of the Cornish Revival, in 1877 on a the back of an older land charter from the parish of St Stephen-in-Brannel, dated 1340. It takes the form of advice to a young couple about to marry and is thought by some to have been part of a longer drama and by others as a wedding speech.

3   **'In Polsethow'/War Meane Merlyn/Two Cornish Prophecies (1265 and no date)**

The first prophesy refers to Polsethow, the site of the monastic institution Glasney College, later associated with the composition of the drama cycle *Ordinalia*. The second was interpreted as foretelling later events – the sacking of Paul, Penzance and Newlyn in 1595 by the Spanish.

4   **'En tas a nef y'm gylwyr'/The Creation (c. 1380)**

This extract is taken from Origo Mundi – The Beginning of the World (Origo Mundi 1–92), the first play of the *Ordinalia* (plural of the Latin Ordinale – prompt or service book), the three-day drama cycle based upon the liturgical cycle of the Christian year. The plays combine biblical and other popular narratives, such as the legend of the rood (see text 6), and may have been written by a cleric or clerics at Glasney College. The action begins with the creation of the world, based on the accounts in the accounts in Genesis 1: 1–31 and Genesis 2: 15–7.

5   **'Yt'hanwaf bugh ha tarow'/The Naming of the Animals (c. 1380)**

This passage (Origo Mundi 117–140) is based on Genesis 2: 19–20. In naming the animals Adam uses French words to describe the porpoise (*porpus*), salmon (*sowmens*) and peacock (*payon*), while the swan is given in English.

6   **'Seth pan-dra yv the nygys'/The Errand of Seth (c.1380)**

In this dramatisation of the legend of the rood (Origo Mundi 733–834), Seth, one of Adam's younger sons, goes to Paradise to look for the Oil of Mercy promised his father. He is told to take three pips from the apple of the Tree of Knowledge he finds growing there and to put them in his father's mouth when he dies. The tree will become the True Cross upon which Christ was crucified. A representation of this appears in one of the stained-glass windows of the church of St Neot near Bodmin.

7 'Damsel er the gentylys'/David and Bathsheba (c. 1380)

Based on the story of King David's seduction of Bathsheba, the wife of Uriah the Hittite (II Samuel 1), this passage (Origo Mundi 2105–2254) is a sustained clerical attack on the medieval convention of courtly love, which, like the Cornish legend of Tristan and Isolde, is essentially adulterous. The Cornish text contains Romance loan-words such as *damsel*, *gentylys*, and *chambour*. The stage direction at the end of the text has a contrite David speaking the first line of the first Psalm attributed to him, 'Blessed is the man ... '.

8 'Dun the leuerel yn scon'/Solomon and the Temple Builders (C.1380)

In building the Temple the carpenters use a timber that simply refuses to fit. Solomon orders that it be put in a place of honour, and in due course it becomes the True Cross upon which Christ was curcified. Here (Origo Mundi ll. 2579–98), the builders are given charters to places aound the Fal estuary (Bohelland, Penryn, Gwerthour, Arwennack, Tregenver, Kegyllack) in payment.

9 'Mara ieves yl dybbry'/The Temptation of Jesus (c. 1380)

This passage (Passio Christi ll. 47–172) is the first from the second play, performed on the second day of the *Ordinalia*, Passio Christi – Christ's Passion, and is based on the descriptions of the temptation of Christ in Matthew 4: 1–11, Mark 1: 12–3 and Luke 4: 1–14. The angel Michael, who ministers to Christ, is regarded along with St Piran as a patron saint of Cornwall.

10 'Newethow mere clewes'/Palm Sunday (c. 1380)

This passage (Passio Christi 229–310) is taken from the accounts of Christ's triumphant entry into Jerusalem on Palm Sunday, the Sunday before his crucifixion, in Matthew 21: 1–11, Mark 11: 1–11, Luke 19: 28–40, John 12: 12–19. The Hebrew children sing 'Blessed is he that cometh in the name of the Lord', Psalm 118, 25–6.

11 'Arluth henna yv gurys da'/Mary Magdalene (c. 1380)

This extract (Passio Christi 467–552) is based on Luke 7: 36–50 where Jesus is anointed by a woman described as a 'sinner' in the house of Simon the Pharisee. In this version the woman is identified as Mary Magdalene, while Simon is described as Simon the Leper.

12 'Sevyn yn ban'/The Arrest of Jesus (c. 1380)

The dramatisation of the arrest of Jesus (Passio Christi 1113–1200) is based on the accounts in Matthew 26: 59–66, Mark 14: 55–64, Luke 22: 47–53 and John 18: 19–24.

13 'Mar a pythe dylyfrys'/Prosecution and defence (c. 1380)

Christ is taken by Prince Annas before Pilate and Caiaphas, the High Priest (described as *epscop* – bishop in the Cornish text), where two doctors, or learned men, argue about his crucifixion (Passio Christi 2371–2475). Defending Christ, the First Doctor uses the image of the duality of the mermaid, half fish, half woman, to explain the dual nature of Christ, God and man. The implication of Christ's silence, so infuriating to the prosecution, was that a man might not be compelled to testify against himself. The biblical accounts of the judgement of Pilate are at Matthew 26: 57–66, Mark 14: 53–64, Luke 22: 54 and John 18: 12–31.

14 'Ellas a cryst'/The Lament of Mary (c. 1380)

In Luke 23:73 we are told that when Jesus was taken to be crucified he was followed by women wailing. The dramatist, following a widespread tradition, has identified one of these women with Jesus' mother and composed a lament for her to sing when she receives her son's body (Passio Christi 2591–2614, 3162–3195).

15 'Why pryncys a'n dewolow'/The Harrowing of Hell (c. 1380)
This text (Resurrexio Domini 97–124) is from the third play of the *Ordinalia*, Resurrexio Domini – The Resurrection of Our Lord, and describes Christ's descent into Hell. Woven into the text are the words from Psalm 24, 'Who is the King of Glory?'

16 'Lowene thy's syr pilat'/Pilate and the Sepulchre Guards (c. 1380)
In this reworking of the descriptions of the disappearance of Christ's body from the tomb (Matthew 28: 4), the guards tell the enraged Pilate to look for the body with Joseph of Arimathea and Nicodemus, two followers of Jesus, in this version lately imprisoned. But they too are missing. When the guards themselves admit that Christ has risen from the dead, Pilate buys their silence with with the gift of Penryn and Helston, both near Glasney College. (Resurrexio Domini 60–78).

17 'Nep a wruk nef'/Mary Magdalene and Jesus (c. 1380)
According to John 20: 14–18, when Mary Magdalene first saw the risen Jesus, she mistook him for a gardener (Resurrexio Domini 835–892).

18 'Ow dewolow duegh gynef'/Pilate taken to Hell (c. 1380)
According to legend, Pilate took his own life and both land and sea refused to accept his body. In the final verse the dramatist may be poking fun at the new fashions in church music (Resurrexio Domini 2307–60).

19 'Tays ha mab han speris sans'/Father and Son and Holy Ghost (c. 1450)
This is the first text from *Pascon agan Arluth* –The Passion of Our Lord. Only one original manuscript survives, though there are several later copies. The language and other features of the text indicate that the poem may have been written about the middle of the fifteenth century, but there is still much debate surrounding the issue. It is possible that this text in fact predates the *Ordinalia* and may have provided some of its central material. The seven-syllabled lines are woven into eight-line stanzas with alternating rhymes (Pascon agan Arluth 1–72).

20 'Dew zen crist a zanvonas'/The Last Supper (c. 1450)
This passage (Pascon agan Arluth 353–498) is based on the narratives in Matthew 26, Mark 14, Luke 22 and John 13, and has much in common with lines 832–927 of Passio Christi.

21 'Han zewna pan vons squyth'/The Scourging of Christ (c. 1450)
This passage (Pascon agan Arluth 1057–1112), based on the narratives in Matthew 27, Mark 15, and John 13, vividly describes the suffering of Christ before his crucifixion. It has much in common with lines 2127–2150 of Passio Christi.

22 'Rag porrys rys o zozo'/The Death of Christ (c. 1450)
This passage is based on Matthew 27: 51 and Mark 15: 33, where at the time of Christ's death there was an eclipse and an earthquake, graves opened and the bodies of the saints rose (Pascon agan Arluth 1657–1961).

23 'Mam Ihesus Marya wyn'/The Price of Sin (c. 1450)
The sufferings of Christ, carefully enumerated, offer redemption for mankind (Pascon agan Arluth 1769–1824).

24 'A das ha mam ov megyans'/The Education of Meriasek (1504)
This extract is the first from *Beunans Meriasek,* an exuberant weaving together of historical and legendary characters from different centuries, with strong undertones of contemporary Cornish politics. It was written by a clergyman, probably called Radulphus Ton. St Meriasek lived in Brittany in the seventh century, and is one of the patron saints of Camborne. In the text, the name of his father is given as Duke Conan, the actual name of the ruler of Brittany at the time of the drama's composition, the Duke of Brittany being his real title. In this episode Meriasek is sent to school with a benevolent if bibulous teacher with a degree from a dubious university (Bonnilapper). But Meriasek's mind is already set on rejecting worldly comforts (Beunans Meriasek 25–141).

25 'Marners dorsona dywy'/Meriasek comes to Cornwall (1504)
Having with difficulty persuaded his parents to let him forsake worldly ambition, Meriasek sets sail for Cornwall, where he hopes to find peace. On the way, he calms a storm and saves the lives of his fellow voyagers (Beunans Meriasek 587–623).

26 'A vreten sur then povma'/Meriasek and Teudar (1504)
Meriasek asks God to bring forth a holy well in Camborne as he had for Moses in the wilderness (Exodus 17: 1–7). His healing the sick in the name of Jesus displeases Teudar, a tyrant who has set himself up as a ruler in Cornwall. Teudar was a shadowy historical ruler in Kerrier in Cornwall, but it is likely that the author was satirising Henry Tudor, Henry VII of England. The author makes Teudar a Muslim – for his audience the worst kind of villain, the traditional enemy of Christians (Beunans Meriasek 649–955).

27 'Mayl at eua'/The Emperor's Doctors (1504)
The Emperor Constantine (c.274–337) made Christianity the official religion of the Roman Empire. He appears in this text stricken with leprosy and desperate for a cure. Two fast-talking quacks extract a substantial fee for impressive-sounding treatment that leaves him uncured (Beunans Meriasek 1408–74). One of the stage directions here is in English, suggesting that the author could confidently switch between Latin, Cornish and English.

28 'Me yv outlayer'/Outlaws (1504)
Some outlaws set upon two travellers, a merchant and a priest. Untroubled by his warning that they will pay dearly on the Day of Judgement they strip the priest naked, declaring it the only way to treat those with property (Beunans Meriasek 1866–1935).

29 'Me yv duk'/The Duke of Cornwall challenges Teudar (1504)
The idealised Duke of Cornwall sets out to put a stop to Teudar's depredations, asking what rightful possession (using the legal term *kerth* – right) he has in the country. As well as a stronghold as Castle-an-Dinas, the Duke also has a castle at Tintagel, both reputed to be seats of King Arthur (Beunans Meriasek 2205–97).

30 'Ser duk me a wel tevdar'/The Great Battle (1504)
Calling himself emperor and claiming the support of the ancient British kings, Alwar, Tacitus, Mark and Casivellaunus, Teudar is nonetheless put to flight. The Duke turns to the audience,

and invites them to drink and dance at the end of the first day of the play (Beunans Meriasek 2357–2512).

31   'Ellas ow holen yv trogh'/The Two Mothers (1504)
A young man has been imprisoned by a tyrant. His mother prays before the statue of Mary and takes home the image of the infant Jesus when her supplications seem of no avail. Mary, with Jesus' blessing, frees the young man and when he returns home, his mother restores the image of the baby to the statue (Beunans Meriasek 3585–3796). Arthur Quiller Couch retold this story in *Our Lady of Gwithian*.

32   'Dugh why thym'/The Death of Meriasek (1504)
As Meriasek lies dying, he comforts his followers by telling them that anybody who comes to his church at Camborne will receive absolution, and that his feast will be on the first Friday in June (Beunans Meriasek 4252–4309).

33   *From* Homelyes XIII in Cornish/The Tregear Homilies by John Tregear (1555–60)
John Tregear was one of the few Cornish-speaking priests known to have made translations of Christian works for his Cornish-speaking congregation. His translation of these *Homilies* (twelve of which originated with Edward Bonner, the Catholic Bishop of London under Mary Tudor) remains one of the most important texts of Cornish literature, giving us an understanding of the language during this phase. The first extract from *Homily 1* gives praise to God for his creation; the second from *Homily 3* praises God for the redemption of man; the third from *Homily 13* describes the mystery of the sacrament at the altar.

34   Death and Lamech from The Creacion of the World by William Jordan (1611)
Little is known of William Jordan, and there is some doubt as to his authorship of this play. *The Creacion of the World,* or *Gwreans an Bys* was written for performance in Helston. It has some similarities with Origo Mundi and may be part of a lost longer work. It was first translated into English by John Keigwin (1641–1716) at the request of the Bishop of Exeter, Sir Jonathan Trelawny. Lamech, a descendant of Cain, author of moral deterioration and the first polygamist, an apparently poorly-sighted huntsman, meets his infamous forbear and kills him by accident. Lamech in fact is as wicked as the outcast Cain, with his womanising and cruelty to the poor. They both end up in Hell. The story is a reworking of Genesis 4: 23-24. (The Creacion of the World 985–1005, 1431–1511, 1527–1721). *The Creacion of the World* has been somewhat neglected within the corpus of Cornish literature. It has not been performed in its entirety since the seventeenth century.

35   The Flood from The Creacion of the World by William Jordan (1611)
The play's subtitle is 'Noye's Flude' and this extract deals with a subject that, although common to many dramas across Europe, had special significance to Cornish mining communities, where it was believed that their mineral wealth was given to them by the redistribution of the earth's resources in the aftermath of God's cleansing of the world through the Flood (The Creacion of the World 2409– 2548).

36   One Parson's Certificate to Another, to Marry a Couple, whose Banns had been called, from Mr. Drake, Vic. of St. Just, to Mr. Trythal, Cur. of Sennen by William Drake (1636)
This simple certificate records a marriage in Sennen, the banns having been read out in St Just-in-Penwith church by the rector William Drake.

37   John of Chyanhor by Nicholas Boson (as transcribed by Edward Lhuyd) (c.1665)
One of the more famous texts of this period of Cornish literature, this narrative establishes Cornish as a valuable language in the transmission of European folk literature. The story is known throughout Europe as The Servant's Good Counsels, and as the German and Celtic scholar Brian Murdoch has argued, may have links with the eleventh-century Latin poem from Tegersee in Germany, the *Ruodlieb*. An English version was collected by William Bottrell. Boson first heard the story from some of his family's servants.

38   Nebbaz Gerriau Dro Tho Carnoack/A Few Words about Cornish by Nicholas Boson (c.1675)
This is the first example of Cornish language 'revivalism' articulated by a man who had been deprived of the language by those social forces which would eradicate it from social life. Though a member of the gentry and part of that class committed to the 'British project' of national uniformity from the beginning, paradoxically Boson (c. 1624–1703) set about learning Cornish from his neighbours and servants. He anticipates the renaissance of Cornish in the early twentieth century and may be defined as 'proto-revivalist'. He refers to his essay 'The Dutchess of Cornwall's progresse ... ' (see text 94).

39   'Menja Tiz Kernuack buz gasowas'/'If Cornish people would but listen' by John Tonkin (c.1693)
This ballad was composed by John Tonkin, a man of letters who lived in St Just-in-Penwith. He celebrates the re-establishment of constitutional monarchy with the defeat of James II by William of Orange. Henry Jenner, a nostalgic Jacobite, called Tonkin a 'violent Whig'. While Jenner was prepared to promote the linguistic content of such texts he was opposed to their political outlook, which is why they were often rejected by the early twentieth-century 'revivalists'.

40   'Ni Venja pea a munna seer'/A Cornish Song, to the Tune of the Modest Maid of Kent by John Tonkin (c.1695)
This poem advises hard work and trust in God. It celebrates the traditional mainstays of Cornish society: mining, fishing and religion. It is not known who William Mean was.

41   'Ha mî ow môs en gûn lâs'/'As I went on a green plain' by Noel Cater (1698)
Captain Noel Cater wrote this folk song down for Thomas Tonkin, the historian and one of the most important collectors of Cornish material of the period. The song is a riddle; Robert Morton Nance suggested that the answer might be 'octopus'. Tonkin thought it might be a ray, but a ray only has three tails. Tonkin was born in St Agnes in 1678. A member of the lesser gentry, he became the MP for Helston and participated in the Stannary Courts.

42   'Pela era why moaz, moz, fettow teag?'/'Where are you going pretty fair maid?' by Edward Chirgwin (1698)
Chirgwin's innuendo-laden poem is usually thought to be a translation of the English folk-song 'Strawberry Leaves'. The folk-song is common to most languages. The man is trying out stock chat-up lines, while the girl responds to each one by pointing out the immediate practical consequences — pregnancy, and that he will be liable for the child's maintenance.

43   Two Poems of Advice by James Jenkins (c.1700)
Jenkins lived in Alverton, Penzance. Very little of his poetry remains, yet he was regarded by his contemporaries as one of the most learned Cornish writers. The first poem, written with internal rhyme, offers advice about women, relationships and life. The second is written in

rhyming couplets, and the advice is wider, giving suggestions for a successful home and how to survive the sometimes harsh Cornish environment.

44 In Obitum Regis Wilhelmi 3tii Carmen Britannicum, Dialectu Cornubiensis; Ad Normam Poetarum Seculi Sexti/On the Death of King William III a British Song in the Cornish Dialect; according to the pattern of the poets of the sixth century by Edward Lhuyd (1703)

Edward Lhuyd (1660–1709) came from Oswestry, Shropshire, and was a Welsh linguist, chiefly responsible for categorising the Celtic languages. He was Underkeeper of the Ashmolean Museum in Oxford and visited Cornwall in 1700. His great project was the *Archæologia Britannica*, a comparative study of Celtic languages. This rarely anthologised text is a spirited elegy using an *englyn* stanza form in support of the Protestant cause, for which Cornish soldiers fought at the Battle of the Boyne.

45 A Cornish Proverb by William Allen (1704)

Little is known about the life and work of William Allen of St Agnes, although he appears to have been one of Tonkin's informants. The proverb expresses a cynical view of marriage.

46 'Ma Canow vee wor Hern gen Cock ha Rooz'/The Pilchard Curing Rhyme' by John Boson (1710)

John Boson (1665–c.1720) was the son of Nicholas Boson. This remarkable poem demonstrates the importance of pilchard fishing and production in Cornwall in Boson's lifetime. He takes the reader through all the processes of curing, storing and packing the fish, emphasising the social cohesion required to sustain the industry. The last lines show how pilchards were exported to the Catholic countries of the Mediterranean for Lent.

47 'An [Why] poble hui, en pow America'/'You people in the Land of America' by William Gwavas (1710)

William Gwavas (1676–1741) came from Paul in west Cornwall and was a barrister in the Middle Temple. This message was written on the back of the Gwavas manuscript of the Apostles' Creed in the British Museum and was perhaps intended as a specimen of Cornish for people in America, perhaps even Cornish speakers, who no doubt assisted in the colonisation of the continent. The address seems to refer to those undergoing Christian conversion – native Americans perhaps.

48 Letters in Cornish by William Gwavas and Oliver Pender (1711)

The correspondance of those actively trying to prevent the loss of Cornish provides fascinating reading. In this example, Gwavas, to improve his own Cornish, wrote to Pender in Mousehole. Pender wrote back explaining how he has been busy with the pilchard industry. He offers a barbed comment on the Cornish of Lhuyd — which he considered to be not 'genuine' – a position adopted by some of the early twentieth-century revivalists who also doubted the validity of the Welshman's work. Pender was perhaps not aware of the sophistication of Lhuyd's linguistic techniques.

49 'En Lavra coth pa vo Tour Babel gwres'/An Elegy on the Death of James Jenkins by John Boson (1711)

Jenkins was well-respected by other writers of the period for his Cornish scholarship, and here John Boson offers his own tribute, blending the mythological origins of the Cornish and their language with the life of the writer. The Tower of Babel was a biblical symbol of earthly power with the aim of universal uniformity. This was frustrated by God's giving each nation their own tongue. The variety of languages therefore was a divinely ordained foundation of identity. Gomer was the son of Japheth, one of the sons of Noah, and was thought to be the progenitor of the Britons – the Cornish, Welsh and Bretons.

50 'Padn an mean, ma Deskes broaz Dean'/Epitaph for the Death of James Jenkins by William Gwavas (c.1711)

This tribute to the dead poet becomes a symbol of the decline of the Cornish language.

51 Advice to a Friend by John Boson (c.1711)

The worldly-wise Boson gives some survival tips to a friend (Arthur Hitchens) about to plunge into the financial and moral hazards of London. Until recently the poem usually appeared in print without its last word. The date of Hitchens' trip was 1709.

52 On the Death of Mr. John Keigwin by John Boson (1716)

John Keigwin (1641–c.1710)was an important Cornish scholar, translating the *Ordinalia* and other texts. These were of great cultural and linguistic importance and Boson's epitaph demonstrates his significance to the group of writers working at this period.

53 On a Lazy Weaver by William Gwavas (c.1728)

Gwavas was another important scholar and writer of Cornish during this phase. In this poem the weaver's employer makes it plain that he will have to pray and work hard to keep his job. Like most of the short poems which follow, it is uncertain whether Gwavas collected them, or wrote them himself.

54 Verses on the Marazion Bowling-Green and Club by William Gwavas (c.1728)

This short poem is a celebration of good health and conviviality amongst the members of the local bowls club, with the message that leisure and sociability promote the material good of the community.

55 Advice to Drunkards by William Gwavas (c.1728)

Moderation is the message.

56 A Cornish Riddle by William Gwavas (c.1728)

This riddle is the Cornish John Barleycorn. It would appear to that barley made into beer caused the parson of Paul to fall over.

57 'Chee dên krêv'/Advice to all men by William Gwavas (c.1728)

This poem reminds the strong man that not everything is under his control.

58 'Hithow gwrâ gen skîanz da' by William Gwavas (c.1728)

Keep to the truth in your daily life at home or abroad is the message, suggesting the mobility of the Cornish across the globe.

59 'Cara, Gorthya, ha ouna Dêw'/'Today act with good knowledge' by William Gwavas (c.1728)

This epigram advises the reader to be law-abiding and neighbourly.

60 **War an Lavar gwir a'n Dewthack Tiz pêg a'n Pow Middlesex; ha an Brêz a'n padgwar Braneriow enna – Gwavas versus Kelynack/On the verdict of the twelve honest men of the County of Middlesex; and the judgment of the four Barons therein – Gwavas versus Kelynack (1728)**

Gwavas engaged in a great deal of litigation over fishing tithes. This is appears to be idealistic rather than practical advice for anyone thinking of going to law.

61 **Contrevack Nicholas Pentreath/To Neighbour Nicholas Pentreath by William Gwavas (c.1728)**

In a society without a formal bureaucracy the enforcement of rights and obligations depended on the kind of plain-dealing referred to here. The Pentreath in the poem may have been a predecessor of the more famous Dolly.

62 **William Bodinar's Letter (1776)**

Bodinar was a Mousehole fisherman, who died in 1789, and may have been paid to write this letter to Daines Barrington (see text 103). It is widely regarded as the last surviving example of 'native' Cornish prose. William Pryce tells us that Bodinar was 'a very old man' and that in a conversation he had with him the fisherman explained how in Morlaix in Brittany he was able to make himself understood to Breton speakers. Some scholars have undervalued this text, which nonetheless is written in good grammatical Cornish. It is unlikely that there were not other Cornish speakers at this time.

63 **'Coth Doll Pentreath'/Epitaph for Dolly Pentreath by Thomson (c.1777)**

Thomson (or Thompson) was a mining engineer from Truro, who wrote this epitaph for Mousehole's most famous resident.

64 **Cornish proverbs and sayings from Archæalogia Cornu-Britannica by William Pryce (1790)**

These sayings are examples of old Cornish proverbs surviving into the modern era and have been collected from the manuscripts of Tonkin and Gwavas as they appeared in William Pryce's *Archæologia Cornu-Britannica*. According to the Cornish scholar Matthew Spriggs, the compilation was the work not of Pryce but of Tonkin. The advice comes Cornish-style: gritty and to the point. The famous triplet or *englyn* beginning 'An Lavor gôth ewe lavar gwîr/The old saying is a true saying' shows how poetic Cornish could be during this phase. Its simple message is still relevant to a territory that has constantly battled to retain its language and identity. The englyn was originally collected in St Just-in-Penwith in 1700 by Edward Lhuyd, who was told it by the parish clerk.

65 **Padar a'n Arluth/The Lord's Prayer from Archæologia Cornu-Britannica by William Pryce (1790)**

William Pryce (c.1726–1790) was a doctor, Cornish language enthusiast and writer on mining. There are several existing variants of the Lord's Prayer in Cornish. We have selected this late version from Pryce's anthology.

66 **Cornish Family Mottoes (no date)**

These are the mottoes of some of famous Cornish families.

67 Two Poems by Georg Sauerwein (c.1865)
Sauerwein (1831–1903) was born in Gronau in northern Germany. A gifted linguist he spent most of his life working as a biblical translator. He campaigned for the rights of minorities including those under German rule. He later worked as a tutor in the household of Lady Llanover, who codified the Welsh national costume. Through her he came to know Celtic scholars such as Edwin Norris, who had just published an edition of the *Ordinalia* with an English translation. The first poem contains a pun on the name Edwin; 'Edwyn' is the third person singular of the Welsh 'to know'.

68 'A Grankan, a grankan'/The Crankan Rhyme by John Davey (1891)
This satirical poem, compares the fertility of the road between Penzance and Marazion with that of the barren fields at Crankan, near Newmill. The historian J. Hobson Matthews wrote the poem down after hearing it from John Davey (1812–91) of Boswednack, near Zennor. Davey learnt it from his father, who had a good knowledge of Cornish. Matthews had little Cornish himself and it is possible that Davey wrote it down for him. The Crankan Rhyme is perhaps the last piece of poetry from this phase of Cornish literature. The next phase was to preserve and develop the language for the next century, initiating one of the most remarkable linguistic revivals of the modern age.

Complementary Texts

69 *From* The Bodmin Manumissions (c.960)
It was the custom in many countries to record legal transactions on the blank pages of sacred texts. Feudal lords sometimes freed serfs as an act of piety. During the tenth century Saxon landowners in eastern Cornwall recorded these transactions in a manuscript known as the *Bodmin Manumissions,* a manumission being a certificate of freedom from serfdom. In this text, originally written in Anglo-Saxon and Latin, most of the lords have Saxon names while most of the serfs have Cornish names. The Cornishman Cenmennoc, meanwhile, had obviously learnt to work the system.

70 *From* The History of the Kings of Britain by Geoffrey of Monmouth (1136)
Geoffrey of Monmouth died around 1155. This massive Latin compendium is an imaginative blend of historical and mythological material recording the glory of the early Britons from the time of their arrival as refugees from Troy (see text 82). Like many medieval writers, Geoffrey claimed to have translated this from ancient sources. The opening passage of the book suggests that his source material may have been a Brythonic text, possibly Cornish. Geoffrey identifies the four founders of the nations of Britain as Albanactus (Scotland), Locrinus (England), Camber (Wales) and Corineus (Cornwall). The wrestling match between Corineus and Gogmagog is the first wriiten example of the Cornish sport of wrestling, where 'Gwarry wheag yw gwarry teag' (Fair play is good play).

71 The Prophecy of Merlin by John of Cornwall (c.1150)
This Latin text belongs to the medieval tradition of expressing political and religious views in the guise of ancient prophecy, in this case drawing heavily on Cornish and Celtic mythology. Many of the references are now obscure beyond recovery but its finely-crafted delirium is compelling. John of Cornwall was probably born in St Germans in east Cornwall in the early twelfth century. He studied in Paris and died around 1199.

72 *From* The Cornish Glosses of the Prophecy of Merlin by John of Cornwall (c.1150)
This selection from Cornish language glosses to the preceding Latin text, written by the author

himself, reveal something of its geographical and political background. The manuscript of the prophesy and glosses is kept in the Vatican library.

73   *From* **Le Roman de Tristan/The Romance of Tristan by Béroul (c.1150)**
All the evidence suggests there must have been a Cornish provenance for the Tristan and Iseult narratives which subsequently emerged on the continent, confirming the importance of Cornwall in the construction of early European literature. This text was originally written in Norman French. Nothing is known of the author. There are a number of references to Cornwall in Béroul's version and we have included two sequences to illustrate this: Tristran and Isolde in the forest of Moresk and the crossing made at Malpas. Both places are near Truro.

74   *From* **A Letter to certain Cardinals by John de Grandisson, Bishop of Exeter (c.1328)**
De Grandisson was Bishop of Exeter from 1327–1369. In this letter to church leaders abroad he considers it important to point out that Cornwall has its own language.

75   *From* **The Translation of Ranulf Higden's Polychronicon by John Trevisa (c.1385)**
Ranulf Higden (died 1364), chronicler and Benedictine monk, wrote the *Polychronicon* in Latin. John Trevisa (c.1342–1402) was probably born at St Enodor in Mid-Cornwall. He studied at Oxford, and eventually became the vicar at Berkeley. He may have comtributed to Wycliffe's Lollard Bible. The *Polychronicon* was an ambitious history book translated by Trevisa and printed by Caxton. This passage concerns two Cornishmen, ironically probably Cornish speakers, defending the English language against the dominance of French.

76   **Some Accounts for Cornish Drama (1469–1539)**
These accounts relating to performances of medieval Cornish drama in Bodmin and Launceston show that performances existed from the Tamar in the east to St Just-in-Penwith in the far west — where a *plen-an-gwarry,* or arena, still exists. The reference of the King and Queen of Gall suggests that this was a secular drama.

77   *From* **Utopia by Thomas More (1516)**
Thomas More (1477–1535) was Lord Chancellor of England under Henry VIII and author of *Utopia*, the political satire written in Latin and set on an imaginary island. Opposed to Henry VIII's divorce from Catherine of Aragon, More was imprisoned in the Tower of London and executed. In this passage More refers to the Cornish rebellion of 1497 led by Michael Joseph 'An Gof' ('The Smith') from St Keverne, and Thomas Flamank, the lawyer from Bodmin, who were both executed in London for their part in the rebellion. More gives as much weight to the rebellion as to the war with France.

78   *From* **Itinerary by John Leland (c.1540)**
John Leland (c.1503–1552), educated at Christ Church, Oxford, was one of Britain's earliest antiquarians. Apart from observations on the Cornish language Leland notes how polluted the Cornish landscape was, particularly from the tin mining industry. He portrays Athelstan as a public benefactor.

79   *From* **The Fyrst Book of the Introduction of Knowledge: The Apendix in the Fyrst Chapter, Treatinge of Cornewall, and Cornyshe Men by Andrew Boorde (1547)**
Boorde (c.1500–c.1560) studied medicine and was imprisoned for some time in the Tower of London. This extract is from a larger work describing European peoples, their characteristics,

behaviour and failings. In this Cornu-English text Boorde humourously describes a typical Cornishman, his thirst, his love of litigation and prospensity to rebel in London. It also contains one of the earliest references to Tre, Pol and Pen, the celebrated prefixes to Cornish surnames. It contains a short phrase book, one of the few existing secular Cornish language texts from this period.

80   *From* **The Articles of the Rebels (1549)**

The men signing their names to this document were the leaders of the 1549 Prayer Book Rebellion against the imposition of the liturgy in English in Cornwall. One of their arguments was that many Cornish spoke no English.

81   *From* **The Reply to the Rebels by Edward Seymour, Duke of Somerset (1549)**

Seymour (c.1506–1552) was Protector during the reign of the child King Edward VI and introduced religious reforms including the Act of Uniformity in 1549.

82   *From* **The Image of Idleness by Oliver Oldwanton (c.1565–70)**

This comedy, based on the story of Pygmalion, claims to have been translated out of 'the Troyance or Cornysche tounge', Cornwall in popular belief having been populated by refugees from Troy (see text 70). There is an oracular sentence in Cornish in the second paragraph, beginning 'Marsoye thees duan Guisca ....' The play contains two Cornish characters – Maister Jewgur and Syr Ogier Penkeyles.

83   *From* **The Bishops' Consistory Court Depositions at Exeter (1572 and 1595)**

These records show us the ordinary people using Cornish among themselves.

84   **St Ives Accounts for Cornish drama (1573–84)**

These extracts are taken from the St Ives parish accounts and suggest that the end-of-run party in 1575 was well supplied with drink. For the 1584 production, extras appear to have been brought in from nearby Germal (Germoe).

85   *From* **A Topographical and Historical Description of Cornwall by John Norden (c.1584)**

Norden (1548–c.1625) was a topographer, surveyor to the Duchy of Cornwall, and the first to undertake a county history of Britain. In this extract from the history of Cornwall he paints a clear picture of the replacement of Cornish by English, with increasing bilingualism and English spoken east of Truro 'in manner Wholy Englishe'. Cornish is now associated with poverty. The shift to English, however, did not necessarily entail any great fondness for the English people.

86   *From* **The Green Book of St Columb Major (1589–95)**

Dramas concerning Robin Hood were popular throughout Britain during this period and the people of St Columb put on a Cornish variant, although the text of the drama is lost.

87   *From* **Relation of the visit of the Catholic Kings by Don Antonio Ortes (1600)**

Don Antonio Ortes witnessed the visit by the King and Queen of Spain to the English College for training Catholic priests in Valladolid, where they heard an oration given in Cornish. The likely speaker was Richard Pentrey, whose parents were respectable Protestants, but who converted to Catholicism in his early twenties. In Cornwall, as in Wales at the time, there was a high incidence of recusancy. Ortes unfortunately did not write down what the text of Pentrey's oration.

88 *From* **The Survey of Cornwall by Richard Carew (1602)**
Carew (1555–1620), a scholar, poet, historian and soldier, was born at Antony House near Torpoint. In this, his greatest work, *The Survey of Cornwall*, he offers much anecdotal information about the Cornish language, which he did not speak himself. Rather, he regarded Cornish literary culture as grotesque and obsolete and foresaw a rapid and total shift to English – for him, to be welcomed.

89 *From* **The Lives of the Saints by Nicholas Roscarrock (c.1620)**
Roscarrock (c.1548–1634) was born in Roscarrock in the parish of St Endelion in North Cornwall. He was a Catholic, for a time imprisoned in the Tower of London for his beliefs. His greatest work was the lives of the British and Irish saints, of which the lives of Cornish saints was one part. Two are included here – St Columb and St Piran, the latter being the unofficial patron saint of Cornwall. The buried chapel mentioned in the text lies close to the surviving *plen-an-gwary*, Piran Round.

90 *From* **The Probate Documents of Francis John Trevallacke of Wendron by His Testator (1622)**
This short text shows that there were still people in the seventeenth century who were more comfortable in Cornish than English.

91 *From* **The Northern Lasse by Richard Brome (1632)**
Richard Broome (c.1555–1620) was Ben Jonson's secretary and a playwright. *The Northern Lasse* was his first play. Here, Cornwall is presented as being close enough to Spain – or remote enough from England – for a Spaniard to understand Cornish. The comic character Nonsense says in Cornish, 'Big head, will you be hung?' In reality Cornwall was the first line of defence against Spanish naval attack.

92 *From* **Diary of the Marches of the Royal Army during the Civil War by Richard Symonds (1644)**
Symonds was a Royalist officer who recorded his observations during the campaign in Lostwithiel. In general the Cornish favoured the Royalist cause during the Civil War, and with the establishment of the Republic, Cornwall saw its institutions, such as the Duchy and the Stannaries, abolished and vital records and literature destroyed.

93 *From* **Itinerary by John Ray (1662 and 1667)**
John Ray, or Wray (1627–1705) was one of Britain's greatest naturalists with a keen interest in philology. In his travel recollections of West Cornwall in the *Itinerary,* Ray finds only two men still literate in Cornish, one Dickan Gwyn (or Dick Angwin) of Bojewyan; the young people were not learning the language and he believed that it would die out with the older generation.

94 *From* **The Dutchesse of Cornwall's progresse to see the Land's end & to visit the mount by Nicholas Boson (c.1665)**
Nicholas Boson (c.1624–1703) wrote this 'fancy', a mixture of folklore, classical learning, mythology, invention and satire for his children, John, Thomas and Katherine. Boson was a Cornish speaker who learned the language from his neighbours and servants (see text 38). The original manuscript in the Gwavas Collection ends abruptly, and we have added a final

paragraph from William Borlase's copy.

95 Antiquities Cornuontanic: The Causes of Cornish Speech's Decay by William Scawen (1680)

Scawen (died 1686) was a Vice-Warden of the Stannaries – in effect, Chief Justice of Cornwall. With an understanding of the importance of legal status, prestige, literary cultivation and education for the survival of a language he explains in this essay the retreat of Cornish and its replacement by English.

96 *From* The First English Translation of William Camden's Britannia by Edmund Gibson (1695)

William Camden (1551–1623) was an historian and headmaster of Westminster school who undertook an antiquarian tour of Britain, publishing his *Britannia* in 1600. Edmund Gibson (1669–1748) was the Bishop of London (1720–1748) and author of numerous works, including an edition of the *Anglo-Saxon Chronicles* (1692) and this translation from Latin of Camden's *Britannica* (1698). From this text we can see that although Cornish was in decline the recently-learned English still had many features of a second language in Cornwall.

97 *From* Letters written to Thomas Tonkin by Edward Lhuyd (1700–08)

Thomas Tonkin (1678–1742) was educated at Queen's College, Oxford, and Lincoln's Inn. He lived at Trevaunance, St Agnes. These letters between Tonkin and Lhuyd vividly illustrate the practical and financial problems that encumbered every step of Lhuyd's vast intellectual project. His *Archæologia Britannica* was eventually published in 1707. Some letters are additionally dated with the year preceding the year of writing (e.g. 1703–4). Until 1752 the beginning of the year was 25 March and letters were often dated in this way to show that they were written at the beginning rather than the end of the year.

98 *From* The Exmoor Scolding by Andrew Brice (1727)

Andrew Brice (1690–1773) was a printer, apprenticed at Exeter, and playwright. This extract is from the preface to his play *The Exmooor Scolding*.

99 *From* The Compleat History of Cornwall by William Hals (c.1736)

Hals (1655–c.1737) was a scholar and historian of Cornwall. Three parish histories are included here; the first shows that Hals had grasped the doctrinal implications of a Cornish text in his possession. The second has an intriguing reference to an Arthurian work by John Trevisa. The third contains information regarding the usage of Cornish in Falmouth.

100 *From* Archæologia Cornu-Britannica by Thomas Tonkin (c.1736–42)

This text is taken from part eight of Tonkin's unpublished manuscript, *Archæologia Cornu-Britannica,* also the title of the book published by William Pryce in 1790 (see text 106). The Tonkin manuscript of was acquired by the Royal Institution of Cornwall in 1999. Believed lost, but mentioned in other material and correspondance of the period, the manuscript was found in Totnes, Devon, tantalisingly suggesting that there may be more undiscovered Cornish manuscripts . It contains versions of *Origio Mundi, Passio Christi, Resurrexio Domini,* the *Creation of the World* and part of *Pascon Agan Arluth*. Although many pages are missing it is possible to piece it together from copies made by other wiriters, such as Ustick, Borlase and Pryce. In these two selections, Tonkin compares Cornish with Breton and Welsh and explains the Brythonic poetic device – the *englyn*.

101 *From* **Antiquities Historical and Monumental of the County of Cornwall by William Borlase (1754)**

William Borlase was the vicar of Ludgvan, near Penzance, and a Cornish antiquarian with an interest in megalithic monuments, druidry and the Cornish language. He published his *Cornish Antiquities* in 1754. In this approach to the study of Cornish he treats the language as an ancient monument, something to be preserved rather than used. The vocabulary he drew up, however, has proved of great practical use.

102 *From* **The Natural History of Cornwall by William Borlase (1758)**

Borlase is gives us information about Cornish in the form of a conventional grammar.

103 **On the Expiration of the Cornish Language by Daines Barrington (1776)**

Daines Barrington (1727–1800) was a lawyer, antiquary and naturalist, a friend and correspondant of Gilbert White, the author of *The Natural History of Selborne*. He set out to assess the extent of the usage of Cornish at the time it ceased being a community language, and in so doing met its most famous survivor, Dolly Pentreath, who apparently made a little money from speaking it. It seems Barrington had to overcome the scepticism of some of the Cornish scholars who evidently had decided that, as they had no interest in it, the language no longer existed.

104 *From* **An Explanation of Cornu-Technical Terms and Idioms of Tinners in Mineralogia Cornubiensis by William Pryce (1778)**

William Pryce (c.1725–1790) wrote *Mineralogia Cornubiensis* for 'the benefit of gentlemen adventuring in tin', so that they could understand the miners' technical terminology, much of which was derived from the Cornish language.

105 *From* **Universal Magazine by Peter Pindar (1785)**

Peter Pindar was the pseudonym of the satirist John Wolcot (1738–1819). This poem is a response to Barrington's encounter with Dolly Pentreath (see text 103). He disapproved of Dolly Pentreath being treated as a spectacle.

106 *From* **Archæologia Cornu-Britannica by William Pryce (1790)**

This is a recurring theme of Cornish-Breton relations up to the modern era, and refers to William Bodinar (see text 62).

107 *From* **To the Courteous and Noble Inhabitants of Cornwall ... by Edward Lhuyd as found in Archæologia Cornu-Britannica by William Pryce (1790)**

Pryce republished much of Lhuyd and Tonkin's material in his *Archæologia Cornu-Britannica*, giving the impression that the language was more widely used in his day than it was.

108 *From* **Ancient Cathedral of Cornwall and Supplement to Polwhele's First and Second Books of the History of Cornwall by John Whitaker (1804)**

John Whitaker (1735–1808) was rector of Ruan-Lanihorne in Cornwall and author of the *History of Manchester* (1771–5). The first passage is from his *Ancient Cathedral of Cornwall* and refers to the ecclestiastical foundation of St Germans in East Cornwall. He describes the brutality of the imposition of the English language on Cornwall. The second is from his supplement to the *History of Cornwall* by Richard Polwhele (1766–1838) and suggests that a knowledge of Cornish was a good money-maker for the poor of West Cornwall (see text 103), as gentleman antiquarians paid for it to be spoken.

109 *From* The History of Cornwall by Richard Polwhele (1806)
Richard Polwhele (1760–1838) was a clergyman of independent means living in Cornwall, and a prolific writer. His *History* covers every aspect of Cornish life and in this passage he makes one of the rare references to the use of the Cornish language east of the Tamar. Unlike many of his contemporaries, he did not think that the shift to English had been completed.

110 *From* Magna Britannia: Cornwall by Daniel Lysons and Samuel Lysons (1812)
Daniel Lysons (1762–1834) and his brother, Samuel (1763–1819), wrote the *Magna Britannia* as an account of the counties of Britain. This passage is taken from the section on Cornwall and summarises the importance of the language to Cornwall's distinctive identity.

111 Two Cornish Poems by Robert Stephen Hawker (c.1825)
Hawker (1803–1875) was a poet and mystic, born in Plymouth and educated at Pembroke College, Oxford. From 1834, he was vicar of Morwenstow in North Cornwall. A strong critic of Methodism, he converted to Catholicism on his deathbed. The Song of the Western Men, better known as 'Trelawny', is based on the colourful life of Sir John Trelawny, Bishop of Exeter, imprisoned along with six other bishops by James II. The rebellion alluded to in the poem never happened. The title of the second poem refers to Mary, mother of Jesus – 'aunt' being a Cornish word to describe a close relationship. Hawker associated Cornish with pre-modern sensibilities and on occasions used Cornish words and expressions in his work.

112 *From* Mount Calvary, edited by Davies Gilbert (1826)
Davies Gilbert (1767–1839), originally Giddy – he took his wife's name – was the President of the Royal Society, MP for Helston and later Bodmin, and High Sherriff of Cornwall. His publications include *A Parochial History of Cornwall* (1830), *A Collection of Christmas Carols* and an edition of *Pascon agan Arluth*, called *Mount Calvary*. This extract is from its introduction. While rejoicing that Cornish was no longer in daily use, Gilbert studied the language using the emerging scientific methods of philology that had already traced the links between Sanskrit, Greek, Latin and the Germanic and Scandinavian languages, and in another generation would encompass the Celtic tongues.

113 Cornish Cantata by Edward Collins Giddy (1828)
This engaging poem based on Cornish place-names is reminiscent of verses by the twentieth-century Cornish historian and poet A. L. Rowse. Edward Collins Giddy was the pseudonym of Davies Gilbert (see 112 above).

114 *From* Rambles Beyond Railways by Wilkie Collins (1851)
William Wilkie Collins (1824–1889) was a friend of Dickens and author of *The Moonstone*, *The Woman in White* and many other novels. In *Rambles Beyond Railways*, written when Cornwall was considered an isolated place, he gives us an imaginative account of watching a Cornish drama in Renaissance times.

115 *From* Netherton's Cornish Almanac (1854)
Netherton (later Netherton and Worth) were the principal publishers in Cornwall, based in Truro. These lines from their 1854 Almanac show how important knowledge of Cornish language was to the working classes of nineteenth-century Cornwall. Here a selection of

phrases show the place of Cornish within industrial Cornwall. The same almanac also contained an explanation of the months in Cornish, as well as the Lord's Prayer. Much of this was a reprint of William Pryce's work.

116 Two Notes about Cornish Speakers by John Bodinar and Matthias Wallis (1856-59)

These two letters reveal the frantic quest for remnants of the Cornish language and the last speakers in the middle of the nineteenth century, with two writers testifying in writing that their relatives spoke Cornish. Dolly Pentreath may well have been the last fluent speaker to have been recorded, but we may speculate that there were others; and certainly fragmentary knowledge of the language survived.

117 The Memorial to Dolly Pentreath at Paul (1860)

This is the inscription on the memorial to Dolly Pentreath (1692–1777) at Paul. Originally the date read 1778, but was later corrected.

118 *From* On the Cornish Language by John Bellow (1861)

Bellow suggests that Cornish is accessible, and that the people of Cornwall only have to look carefully under their own feet to find it.

119 *From* The Gentleman's Magazine by J. H. Nancekivell (1865)

There are numerous examples of these kinds of rhymes and phrases surviving in west Cornwall. Here Nancekivell writes of two fishermen's chants and the function of the 'myn olla'.

120 *From* Popular Romances of the West of England: The Drolls, Traditions, and Superstitions of Old Cornwall by Robert Hunt (1865)

Robert Hunt (1807–1887) was born in Plymouth and was Keeper of the Mining Record Office in Cornwall. Here he explains the history and function of the Cornish droll-tellers; men and women who perhaps originally told their tales in Cornish. He also defines 'Old Cornwall', an area much larger than present-day Cornwall, and including Devon until the Saxon King Athelstan's expulsion of the Cornish living east of the Tamar.

121 *From* Stories and Folk-Lore of West Cornwall by William Bottrell (1873)

This passage refers to an account of a miracle play being performed at Sancreed, and the subsequent conflict occuring between two people watching the performance. It is of interest since one of the manuscripts of *Pascon Agan Arluth* was found in Sancreed Church.

122 A Letter to Henry Jenner by W. S. Lach-Szyrma (c.1875)

Lach-Szyrma (1841–1915), the son of an ex-patriate Pole, was a poet and vicar at Carnmenellys, near Newlyn. He campaigned for an independent diocese for Cornwall and drew to the attention of Jenner and other scholars the persistence of the oral tradition in Cornwall. Here, he suggests awards for success in Cornish (later championed by Robert Morton Nance in the Cornish Gorseth), criticises Methodism, and offers some observations on different classes of people in Cornwall. Lach-Szyrma proceded with his own language lessons – which were published in *Old Cornwall: A Tale of the Men Scryfa and Essays on Cornish Topics* (c.1907). Henry Jenner was the author of *A Handbook of the Cornish Language* (1904), which would help to initiate the Cornish language revival.

123 A Letter to Henry Jenner by William Copeland Borlase (1878)

This letter from the author of *The Age of the Saints: A Monograph of Early Christianity in Cornwall* urges Jenner to proceed with his future volume on the language. *A Handbook of the Cornish Language* was published twenty years later, in 1904.

124 *From* Last Relics of the Cornish Language by W. Lach-Szyrma (c.1879)

Lach-Szyrma makes interesting comparisons between Cornish and the situation of Luzatian (i.e. Sorb) and other minority Slavonic languages.

125 *From* Stories and Folk-Lore of West Cornwall by William Bottrell (1880)

Bottrell demonstrates his understanding of the development of the Cornish language, arguing that Cornish language and literature were by no means restricted to the peninsula, but that Cornishmen took their language wherever they settled – North America, Australia, South America and South Africa. His collection of Old Cornish words shows the survival and use of Cornish late into the nineteenth century.

126 *From* Bibliotheca Cornubiensis by G. C. Boase and W. P. Courtney (1882)

The lost Sherwood Sermons are a literary grail for scholars. They are mentioned here by the great nineteenth-century authorities on the literature of Cornwall – Boase and Courtney. As a number of Cornish texts have been discovered in the twentieth century, they may still be found.

127 *From* The Introduction to An English-Cornish Dictionary by Frederick W. P. Jago (1887)

In the introduction to his influential English-Cornish dictionary, Jago makes a clumsy attempt to calculate mathematically how much Cornish has survived. The dictionary did, however, stimulate interest in Cornish literature.

128 *From* Guavas the Tinner by Sabine Baring-Gould (c.1897)

Baring-Gould (1834–1924) was a prolific writer and folklorist and author of among other works the hymn 'Onward Christian Soldiers'. He was squire and vicar of Lew Trenchard in Devon. In this short passage from his story of the industrialisation in Cornwall, Baring-Gould repeats the widely-held belief that Cornish tin was deposited by the biblical Flood.

129 *From* Cornish Whiddles for Teenin' Time by Mrs Frank Morris (1898)

Mrs Frank Morris weaves Cornish proverbs into her moral tale for the benefit of her young readership. The Cornish word *pedn* – end, appears as a decorative device at the end of the book.

130 From Mystère de St-Gwénnolé – The Celtic Drama Revived by R. A. H. Bickford-Smith (1899)

The age-old interest in the connection between Cornwall and Brittany is reflected in this article from Arthur Quiller Couch's *Cornish Magazine*, describing Breton scholars and activists reviving the mystery play.

131 *From* **A Book of the West by Sabine Baring-Gould (1899)**
Baring-Gould argues in favour of bilingualism, the study of Cornish and Cornu-English.

132 *From* **The Literature of the Celts by Magnus Maclean (1902)**
Although our selection ends at 1900, these two supplemenary texts are illuminating. Maclean was a professor of literature at the Technical College, Glasgow and his ill-informed observations on the lack of Cornish literature set much of the tone of Celtic Studies towards Cornwall in the twentieth century. One of the few Cornish activists who disputed Maclean's conclusions at the time was L. C. Duncombe Jewell, who after a bitter debate retired from Cornish activism.

133 *From* **From a Cornish Window by Arthur Quiller Couch (1906)**
Arthur Quiller Couch (1863–1944) came from an old Polperro family and was educated at Oxford, where he began to write under the pseudonym 'Q'. He was a professor at the University of Cambridge and editor of the *Oxford Book of English Verse* (1912). He is associated with Fowey in Cornwall, where he lived and set many of his stories. Whilst supportive of the broader efforts of Cornish revivalism in the early twentieth century, he was also sceptical about what could be achieved and how Cornish people would respond.

Sources

Abbreviations:
JRIC – Journal of the Royal Institution of Cornwall
OC – Old Cornwall: Journal of the Old Cornwall Societies
RCPS – Report of the Royal Cornwall Polytechnic Society

Texts in Cornish

1	*Vocabularium Cornicum* (Cottonian or Old Cornish Vocabulary, BL MS Cotton Vespasian A XIB, London).
2	*Charter Fragment* (BL MS Add. Charter 1949, London).
3	*The Glasney Cartulary* (MS Cornwall County Records Office Dd R(S) 59); Richard Carew (1769 [1602]) T*he Survey of Cornwall, and an Epistle concerning the Excellencies of the English Tongue*, Penzance: J.Hewett
4–18	*Ordinalia* (MS Bodl. 791, Oxford). Edwin Norris (ed.) (1859) *The Ancient Cornish Drama*, 2 Vols, Oxford: Oxford University Press.
19–23	*Pascon Agan Arluth* (BL MS Harley 1782, London); Davies Gilbert (ed.) (1826) *Mount Calvary... Interpreted in the English Tongue ... by John Keigwin*, London: Nichols.
24–32	*Beunans Meriasek* (MS Peniarth 105, NLW, Aberystwyth); Whitley Stokes (ed.) (1872) *The Life of Saint Meriasek, Bishop and Confessor*, London: Trübner.
33	*Tregear Homilies* (BL MS Add. 46397, London).
34–35	*Gwreans an bys* (MS Bodley 219, Oxford); Whitley Stokes (ed. and tr.) (1863) *The Creation of the World, A Cornish Mystery*, Berlin: A. Asher and Co.
36	Robert Morton Nance (1925) 'Parson Drake's Cornish Certificate,' in *OC*, October.
37	Edward Lhuyd (1707) *Archeologia Britannica,* Oxford: Oxford University Press.
38	Writings of the Boson Family (BL Add, MS 28 554 Gwavas Papers plus Gatley MS, Truro, RIC and Tonkin MS B, Truro); JRIC VI. 2 (1879)
39	Robert Morton Nance (1930) 'Kanna Kernuak,' in *OC*, October.
40	Robert Morton Nance (1930) ' A Cornish Song to the Tune of the Modest Maid of Kent,' in *OC*, April.
41	Robert Morton Nance (n.d.) 'Folklore recorded in the Cornish Language,' Camborne.
42–44	William Pryce (1790) *Archeologia Cornu-Britannica*, Sherborne.
45	Robert Morton Nance (1938) 'William Allen's Cornish Rhyme,' in *OC*, 4.
46	Robert Morton Nance (1938) 'The Pilchard Rhyme,' in *OC*, Winter.
47	Robert Morton Nance (1925) 'The Cornish Language in America, 1710,' in *OC*, April.
48	Robert Morton Nance (1926) 'A Cornish Letter, 1711,' in *OC*, April.
49	Robert Morton Nance (1934) 'Some Verses by John Boson,' in *OC*, Winter.
50	Gwavas Papers, *op.cit.*
51	Gatley MS, *op.cit.*
52	Gwavas Papers, *op.cit*. Also in Borlase MS.
53–61	Pryce, *op.cit.*
62	Robert Morton Nance (1940) 'William Bodener's Letter,' in *OC*, 3.

63	R. Polwhele (1806) 'The Language, Literature and Literary Characters of Cornwall' in *The History of Cornwall*, London: W. Davies.
64–65	Pryce, *op.cit.*
66	Pryce, *ibid.*; Polwhele, *op.cit.*
67–68	Tim Saunders (ed.) (1999) *The Wheel: An anthology of modern poetry in Cornish 1850–1980*, London: Francis Boutle.

Complementary texts

69	*Bodmin Manumissions* (Bodmin Gospels, St Petroc's Gospel, BL Add. MS 9381, London).
70	J. A. Giles (ed.) (1844) *Galfredi Monumentensis Historia Britonum*, London: Caxton Society.
71–72	John of Cornwall, *Prophetia Merlini* (Cod. Ottobonianus Lat. 1474, Vatican).
73	Ernest Muret (ed.) (1903) *Le Roman de Tristan par Béroul*, Paris: Firmin Didot et Compagnie.
74	F.C. Hingston-Randolph (ed.) (1894–9) *The Register of John de Grandisson, Bishop of Exeter (AD 1327–1369)*, 3 Vols, Exeter: Henry S. Eland.
75	Churchill Babington and Joseph R. Lumby (eds) (1885-6) *Polychronicon Ranulphi Higden... with the English translation of John Trevisa*, London: Longmans.
76	Bodmin Parish Church Accounts 1469–72 in *Camden Society Miscellany*, Vol. 7, (n.d.); R. and O. B. Peter (1885) *The Histories of Launceston and Dunheved*, Plymouth: Brendon; (1882) JRIC, 7.
77	J.H. Lupton (ed.) (1895) *De Optimo Rei Publicae Statu*, Oxford: Clarendon Press.
78	Lucy Tomlin Smith (ed.) (1906–10) *The Itinerary of John Leland*, 5 Vols, London: Bell.
79	F.J. Funivall (1870) *The Fyrst Book of the Introduction of Knowledge made by Andrew Boorde*, Oxford: Oxford University Press.
80–81	'The Articles of the Rebels' and 'The Reply to the Rebels' quoted in Francis Rose-Troup (1913) *The Western Rebellions of 1549*, London: Smith, Elder and Co.
82	Henry Jenner (1929) 'Some Miscellaneous Scraps of Cornish,' in *RCPS*.
83	W. Treffry Hoblyn (1936) 'In English & Not in Cornowok,' in *OC*, Summer.
84	J.H. Matthews (1892) *A History of the Parishes of St Ives, Lelant, Towednack and Zennor*, London: Elliot Stock.
85	John Norden (1728 [c.1584]) *Speculum Magnae Britanniae pars Cornwall – A Topographical and Historical Description of Cornwall*, London: William Pearson.
86	(1912) 'The St. Columb Green Book,' in *JRIC*, XIX.
87	Henry Jenner (1923) 'A Cornish Oration in Spain in the year 1600,' in *RCPS*.
88	Carew, *op.cit.*
89	Nicholas Roscarrock, *Lives of the Saints* (MS Add. 3041, Cambridge).
90	Will and Administration found in County Records Office, Truro, Cornwall.
91	Jenner (1929) *op.cit.*
92	C.E. Long (ed.) (1859) *Diary of the Marches of the Royal Army during the Great Civil War; kept by Richard Symonds*, London: Camden Society LXXIV.
93	Edwin Lankester (ed.) (n.d.) *Memorials of John Ray, consisting of his life by Dr [William] Derham, biographical and critical notices by Sir J. E. Smith and Dupetit Thouers with his itineraries etc*. London: Ray Society.
94	Writings of the Boson Family, *op.cit.* Borlase MS, JRIC xxi (1928).
95	William Scawen [1680] 'Antiquities Cornuontanic: The Causes of Cornish Speech's Decay' in Davies Gilbert (1838) *A Parochial History of Cornwall*, London: J. B. Nichols and Son
96	E. Gibson (ed. and tr.) (1695) *Camden's Britannia, Newly Translated into English, with Large Additions and Improvements*, London: E.Gibson.
97	Pryce (1790) *op.cit.*
98	Andrew Brice (1727) 'The Exmoor Scolding,' in *Brice's Weekly Journal*, No. 52.
99	William Hals (c. 1736) *The Complete History of Cornwall*, Truro, c.1736.
100	*The Maker Manuscript* held in the Royal Institution Cornwall. Purchased 1999.
101	William Borlase (1754) *Antiquities Historical and Monumental of the County of*

        Cornwall, London: W. Bowyer and J. Nicholls.
102   William Borlase (1758) *The Natural History of Cornwall*, Oxford: Clarendon.
103   Daines Barrington (1776) 'On the Expiration of the Cornish Language,' in *Archeologia*, Vol 3.
104   William Pryce (1778) *Mineralogia Cornubiensis*, London: Philips.
105   Peter Pindar (1785) in *Universal Magazine*.
106–107 Pryce (1790) *op.cit.*
108   The first section is from John Whitaker (1804) Ancient Cathedral of Cornwall, London: Stockdale. The second section is from Whitaker's *Supplement to Polwhele's History of Cornwall* — usually bound after Volumes I and II and before Volume III. See John Whitaker (1804) *Supplement to the First and Second Books of the History of Cornwall [by Richard Polwhele]*, London: Cadell and Davies.
109   Polwhele (1806) *op.cit.*
110   Daniel and Samuel Lysons (1812) *Magna Britannia: Cornwall*, London: T. Cadell and W. Davies.
111   C. E. Byles (ed.) (1904) *R. S. Hawker: Cornish Ballads and Other Poems*, London: John Lane –The Bodley Head.
112   Gilbert, *op.cit.*
113   Edward Collins Giddy (1828) 'Cornish Cantata,' in *The Cornish Magazine*.
114   Wilkie Collins (1851) *Rambles Beyond Railways*, London.
115   (1854) *Cornish Almanac*, Truro: Netherton.
116   Notes in Royal Institution of Cornwall Library.
117   See memorial in Paul churchyard, Cornwall.
118   John Bellow (1861) 'On the Cornish Language,' in *RCPS*.
119   R. H. Nanckivel (1865) 'Vestiges of the Celtic and Anglo-Saxon Tongues,' in T*he Gentleman's Magazine*.
120   Robert Hunt (ed.) (1865) *Popular Romances of the West of England: The Drolls, Traditions and Superstitions of Old Cornwall (First Series)*, London: John Camden Hotten.
121   William Bottrell (ed.) (1873) *Stories and Folk-lore of West Cornwall*, Penzance: Beare and Son.
122–123 This correspondence is found in The Jenner Papers, Box Eight, Royal Institution of Cornwall Library.
124   W. Lach-Szyrma (c.1879) 'Last Relics of the Cornish Tongue,' in *Folklore and the Folklore Magazine*.
125   William Bottrell (ed.) (1880) *Stories and Folk-lore of West Cornwall*, Penzance: F. Rodda.
126   G.C. Boase and W.P. Courtney (eds) (1882) *Bibliotheca Cornubiensis*, London: Longman, Green, Reader and Dyer.
127   Frederick W. P. Jago (ed.) (1887) *An English-Cornish Dictionary*, London: Simpkin, Marshall.
128   Sabine Baring-Gould (1897) *Gwavas the Tinner*, London: Methuen.
129   Mrs Frank Morris (1898) *Cornish Whiddles for Teenin' Time*, London: T. Fisher Unwin.
130   R. A. H. Bickford Smith, 'Mystère de St-Gwénnolé – The Celtic Drama Revived' in Arthur Quiller Couch (ed.) (1899) *The Cornish Magazine*, Vol 2.
131   Sabine Baring-Gould (1899) *A Book of the West*, London: Methuen.
132   Magnus Maclean (1902) *The Literature of the Celts*, London: Blackie & Son.
133   Arthur Quiller Couch (1906) *From a Cornish Window*, Cambridge: Cambridge University Press.

Further reading

Angarrack, J. (1999) *Breaking the Chains: Propaganda, Censorship, Deception and the Manipulation of Public Opinion in Cornwall*, Camborne: Cornish Stannary Publications.
Bakere, J. (1980) *The Ordinalia: A Critical Study*, Cardiff: University of Wales Press.
Deane, T. and Shaw T. (1975) *The Folklore of Cornwall*, Totowa, New Jersey: Rowman and Littlefield.
Durkacz, V. E. (1983) *The Decline of the Celtic Languages*, Edinburgh: John Donald.
Ellis, P. B. (1974) *The Cornish Language and its Literature*, London and Boston: Routledge and Kegan Paul. (1993)
Celt and Saxon: The Struggle for Britain AD 410–937, London: Constable.
Fowler, D. (1995) *The Life and Times of John Trevisa, Medieval Scholar*, Seattle and London: University of Washington Press.
Gendall, R. (1994), *1000 Years of Cornish*, Menheniot: Teere ha Tavaz.
George, Ken (1986) *The Pronunciation and Spelling of Revived Cornish*, Cornwall: The Cornish Language Board.
Goodrich, P. (ed.) (1990) T*he Romance of Merlin*, New York and London: Garland.
Hale, A. and Payton, P. (eds.) (2000) *New Directions in Celtic Studies*, Exeter: University of Exeter Press.
Grimbert, J. T. (ed.) (1995) *Tristan and Isolde: A Casebook*, New York and London: Garland.
Halliday, F. E. (ed. and tr.) (1955) *The Legend of the Rood*, London: Gerald Duckworth.
Jenner, H. (1904) *A Handbook of the Cornish Language*, London: David Nutt.
Kent, A.M. (1998) *'Wives, Mothers and Sisters': Feminism, Literature and Women Writers of Cornwall*, Penzance: The Patten Press.
(2000) *The Literature of Cornwall: Continuity, Identity, Difference 1000–2000*, Bristol: Redcliffe.
Longsworth, R. (1967) *The Cornish Ordinalia: Religion and Dramaturgy*, Cambridge, Massachusetts: Harvard University Press.
Murdoch, B. (1993) *Cornish Literature*, Cambridge: D. S. Brewer.
Nic Craith, M. (ed.) (1996), *Watching One's Tongue: Aspects of Romance and Celtic Languages*, Liverpool: Liverpool University Press.
Orme, N. (2000) *The Saints of Cornwall*, Oxford, Oxford University Press.
Padel, O.J. (ed.) (2000) *W. M. M. Picken: A Medieval Cornish Miscellany*, Chichester: Phillimore.
Payton, P. (1992) *The Making of Modern Cornwall: Historical Experience and the Persistence of "Difference"*, Redruth: Dyllansow Truran.
(ed.) (1993–99) *Cornish Studies 1–7*, Exeter: University of Exeter Press.
Pennington, R. R. (1973) *Stannary Law: A History of the Mining Law of Cornwall and Devon*, Newton Abbot: David and Charles.
Phillipps, K. C. (1976) *Westcountry Words and Ways*, Newton Abbot: David and Charles.(ed.) (1993) *A Glossary of Cornish Dialect*, Padstow: Tabb House.
(ed.) (1994) *The Cornish Journal of Charles Lee*, Padstow: Tabb House.
Price, G. (1984) *The Languages of Britain*, London: Edward Arnold.
Rowse, A. L. (1941) *Tudor Cornwall*, London: Jonathan Cape.
Russell, P. (1995) *An Introduction to the Celtic Languages*, London and New York: Longman.
Thomas, C. (ed.) (1973-87) *Cornish Studies/Studhyansow Kernewek 1–15*, Redruth: Institute of Cornish Studies.
(1994) *And Shall These Mute Stones Speak? Post-Roman Inscriptions in Western Britain*, Cardiff: University of Wales Press.

Thomas, D. M. (ed.) (1970) *The Granite Kingdom: Poems of Cornwall*, Truro: Bradford Barton.
Toorians, L. (1991) *The Middle Cornish Charter Endorsement: The Making of a Marriage in Medieval Cornwall*, Innsbruck: Institut für Sprachwissenscharft der Universität Innsbruck.
Wakelin, M. (1974) *Language and History in Cornwall*, Leicester: University of Leicester Press.
Weatherhill, C. (1995) *Cornish Place Names and Language*, Wilmslow: Sigma.
Westland, E. (ed.) (1997) *Cornwall: The Cultural Construction of Place*, Penzance: The Patten Press and Institute of Cornish Studies.
Whetter, J. (1988) *The History of Glasney College*, Padstow: Tabb House.
Wilhelm, J. J. (ed.) (1994) *The Romance of Arthur: An Anthology of Medieval Texts in Translation*, New York and London: Garland.
William, J. E. C. (ed.) (1971) *Literature in Celtic Countries*, Cardiff: University of Wales Press.
Williams, N. J. A. (1995) *Cornish Today: An Examination of the Revived Language*, Sutton Coldfield: Kernewek dre Lytter.